Explorations in Ethics and International Relations

ESSAYS IN HONOUR OF SYDNEY D. BAILEY

EDITED BY NICHOLAS A. SIMS

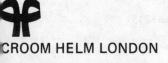

CROOM HELM LONDON

© 1981 Nicholas A. Sims
Croom Helm Ltd, 2-10 St John's Road, London SW11

British Library Cataloguing in Publication Data

Explorations in ethics and international relations.
   1. International relations − Moral and religious aspects.
I. Bailey, Sydney D.
II. Sims, Nicholas A.
172′.4   JX1308

ISBN 0-7099-2300-7

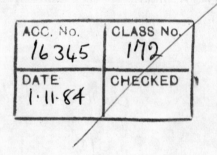
Typesetting by Elephant Productions, London SE15

Printed and bound in Great Britain by
Biddles Ltd, Guildford and King's Lynn

CONTENTS

Frontispiece: (left to right) Brenda and Sydney Bailey, M. Josephine Noble and Marion Glean Outside the Original William Penn House, Opened in the Marylebone Area of London in 1962

Photograph: William Barton

EDITOR'S INTRODUCTION

English possesses no standard term to denote a volume of essays in someone's honour. Instead we are obliged to borrow from other languages: a *Festschrift*, *Mélanges offertes* or *Liber amicorum*. Of these three *Liber amicorum* is peculiarly appropriate, for this is indeed a book written by friends of the person it is intended to honour.

Sydney Bailey inspires friendship, as well as respect, among those who have had the good fortune to enjoy his acquaintance. His contribution to policy and scholarship in the fields which he has made his own would assuredly be recognised, were he the occupant of a university chair, by the publication of essays by academic colleagues and former students, collated in his faculty or department. Sydney Bailey's life, however, has eschewed the conventional *cursus honorum* alike of public office and of the academic career. In the humbler role he has chosen for himself, he has instead bestraddled the too-often mutually uncomprehending worlds of the scholar and the practitioner in international affairs and of the churches and Whitehall too; made connections where they urgently needed to be made, between research and policy, politics and ethics, religion and diplomacy; and brought together for serious discussion and social fellowship people with so little apparently in common that without his determined persuasion they might well never have met. His has been, in the title of one of his more recent addresses (see p. 193), the vocation of reconciliation.

In this volume a group of his friends have sought to honour Sydney Bailey at 65 by means of essays which are broadly located in fields to which he has made a distinguished contribution, and which at the same time have something useful to say on their own account. Inevitably not every area of concern in which he has made his mark could be included within the covers of one book of moderate length. We hope, however, to have demonstrated in these essays some of the most important concerns and interconnections on which Sydney Bailey has laid emphasis; explored a fair range of topics appropriate to our purpose; and conveyed in so doing something of the debt we owe him for his instruction, encouragement and friendship over many years.

The first two essays in this collection each correspond to a major and distinctive interest of Sydney Bailey: the participation of China in international relations, and the protection of human rights through international procedures. Dr Wolf Mendl, Reader in War Studies in the University of London, examines the intriguing interplay of moral principles and power politics in the UN record of the People's Republic of China. Dr Rosalyn Higgins, Professor of International Law in the University of London, contributes an original study of an aspect of international human rights law in rapid evolution: the award of damages for violation of one's rights.

'When Christian duty and national interest coincide, there is no problem; but when they diverge, that is when things become interesting,' remarked Sydney Bailey during one of the many ecumenical committee meetings and drafting exercises to which he has given generously of his time. This compelling interest in the interplay or conflict of ethical demands with the dominant patterns of professional life — whether military, diplomatic, political or scientific — is represented here, first in a pioneering study of the moral and legal duties incumbent upon defence scientists, and second in a fresh exploration of that perennially tantalising problem, the ethics of security. We owe these essays respectively to Barrie Paskins, Lecturer in War Studies at King's College, London, and the Reverend Edward Rogers, for many years secretary of the Christian Citizenship Department of the Methodist Church. Next the ethics of risk are considered, in more than one sphere of public policy where difficult choices have to be made, by the Reverend Canon G.R. Dunstan, Professor of Moral and Social Theology at King's College and Dean of the Faculty of Theology in the University of London. We remain in the realm of moral theology with the reflections on compromise offered by the Right Reverend Dr John Habgood, Bishop of Durham. His fellow bishop, Dr Hermann Kunst, reflects on the peace of God and peace among nations in his Foreword, which is also a tribute to Sydney Bailey from the representative of an older generation and one who has been particularly involved in church-state-army relations in the Federal Republic of Germany. It should come as no surprise to find that among the authors contributing to this book over half are members of the Council on Christian Approaches to Defence and Disarmament (CCADD), an international and ecumenical body which owes much to Sydney Bailey's devoted nurture and skilful chairmanship and whose membership reflects in its diversity his concern to promote mutual understanding across barriers of incomprehension.

Sydney Bailey is best known in academic circles for his many scholarly studies of the principal United Nations organs and their activities. It is therefore only fitting that studies related to the UN should be included in this volume. The problem here has been, as Edward Rogers remarks of the ethics of security (p. 84), the knowledge that Sydney Bailey himself would be the best person to write on many of the most important topics in this field. Conscious of this, and looking forward to the publication by the Clarendon Press at Oxford of his latest book, *How Wars End: the United Nations and the Termination of Armed Conflict,* we have kept clear of the 'central area' of UN institutions and procedures, as likewise UN peacekeeping, truce supervision and the peaceful settlement of disputes. Instead we have chosen cognate but, we trust, sufficiently distinct subjects. Wolf Mendl's contribution has already been noted. Equally appropriate is the essay on patterns of international collaboration among non-governmental organisations (NGOs) including those in consultative status with UN bodies. This is contributed by another colleague of long standing in Quaker international affairs work, J. Duncan Wood, who held many co-ordinating responsibilities in the NGO world while representing Quakers at the UN in Geneva, and is now Chairman of a key Quaker committee on UN affairs in London. Returning to the level of inter-governmental consultation, Nicholas A. Sims explores some similarities and contrasts in patterns of international organisation, in essaying a comparison of UN and Commonwealth experience. The Right Honourable Lord Caradon, PC, GCMG, KCVO, OBE, was Minister of State for Foreign and Commonwealth Affairs and British Ambassador to the UN after a long and distinguished career in public service around the world. Now, as then, a respected spokesman for the international interest, he brings the essay section of this volume to an eloquent conclusion with the plea for a new generation of true internationalists which crowns his Personal Comment on the new international diplomacy.

The essay section is followed by two Appreciations and a Bibliography of Sydney Bailey's work. The purpose of the Appreciations is to convey to those readers who may be unfamiliar with it the substance of Sydney Bailey's work — and, so far as it can be expressed, the special quality which has distinguished it — in two specific perspectives. Professor W. Grigor McClelland, for many years Chairman of the Joseph Rowntree Charitable Trust, and Michael Rose, CMG, Chairman of the British Council of Churches Division of International Affairs, are particularly well placed to appreciate Sydney Bailey's work in Quaker and ecumenical perspectives, although it should be said that in this volume they are writing — as is everyone else — in a purely personal capacity. The first of these Appreciations is the longer of the two because its author was invited additionally to give some idea of the

Trust's thinking in its decision to 'liberate' (in the old Quaker phrase) Sydney Bailey for service 21 years ago. In meeting this request he has drawn on the minutes and other records of the Trust in order to assist in tracing the fruitful relationship which the Trustees have enjoyed with Sydney Bailey in the spirit of the intentions which Joseph Rowntree set out in his memorandum of 1904.

With the variety of subject-matter which is contained within these pages it would have made little sense to insist on uniformity of length or style, beyond our unity in writing these essays and Appreciations especially to honour Sydney Bailey and in locating them within the broad realms of ethics and international relations. It will be seen, for instance, that the conventions for references in law, philosophy and theology have been followed by those writing from within these disciplines and differ slightly from those used within international relations. Some of us, too, have felt the need for more references than have others and must hope that they will not deserve the epithets 'pretentious and distracting' which Sydney Bailey applied to some (unspecified) writers' use of footnotes in his memorable *Note on United Nations Documents* (The General Assembly of the United Nations), 1st edn (London: Stevens; New York: Praeger, 1960), p. xix). This began:

> I once submitted an article to a scholarly quarterly published in a country which it is not necessary to mention here. The editor accepted the article, but asked me to 'insert a few footnotes'. I re-read the article several times, but for the life of me I was unable to see where footnotes were needed. I wrote to the editor asking if he would indicate where footnotes would improve the article. He replied that this was my responsibility, not his. The policy of the journal was to publish articles with footnotes, and he hoped I would co-operate by adapting my article to conform with editorial policy.
>
> On the day I received this letter, I came across a reference in a book to the creation of the world. The author, as if to cite additional evidence that the world did in fact exist, had inserted as a footnote '*Genesis* 1:1'.

Sydney Bailey has been known to remark that disarmament proposals take, on average, seven years to arrive at maturity. The same has been true of the present project, which I set afoot in 1974. I take this opportunity to express my gratitude to those who have helped me bring it to fruition, notably the Right Reverend Bishop Hermann Kunst, DD, and our fellow authors. My thanks go also to Trevor Jepson, who introduced me to the publisher; to the Reverend Brian Duckworth; and to our publisher, Mr David Croom. The photograph of Brenda and Sydney Bailey is reproduced by kind permission of William Barton.

Nicholas A. Sims

ABBREVIATIONS

ASEAN	Association of South-East Asian Nations
BCC	British Council of Churches
CARIFTA	Caribbean Free Trade Area
CB	chemical and biological (warfare/weapons)
CCADD	Council (formerly Conference) on Christian Approaches to Defence and Disarmament
CCIA	Commission of the Churches on International Affairs
CD	Committee on Disarmament
CFTC	Commonwealth Fund for Technical Co-operation
CHOGM	Commonwealth Heads of Goverment Meeting
CHOGRM	Commonwealth Heads of Goverment Regional Meeting
CIIR	Catholic Institute for International Relations
CMEA	Council for Mutual Economic Assistance
CND	Campaign for Nuclear Disarmament
CONGO	Conference of Non-Governmental Organisations in Consultative Status with ECOSOC (q.v.)
COSED	Commission on Social and Economic Development (of ICVA, q.v.)
DIA	Division (formerly Department) of International Affairs (of the BCC, q.v.)
DM	deutschmarks
ECOSOC	Economic and Social Council of the United Nations
EEC	European Economic Community
FAU	Friends Ambulance Unit
FCO	Foreign and Commonwealth Office
FIIG	Fédération des Institutions Internationales semi-officielles et privées établies à Genève
FIPOI	Fondation des Immeubles Pour les Organisations Internationales
FoR	Fellowship of Reconciliation
IBRD	International Bank for Reconstruction and Development
ICVA	International Council of Voluntary Agencies
ICWRY	International Committee for World Refugee Year
IISS	International Institute for Strategic Studies

ILO	International Labour Organisation
IMF	International Monetary Fund
IPPF	International Planned Parenthood Federation
IRO	International Refugee Organisation
ISIO	Institute for the Study of International Organisation
NATO	North Atlantic Treaty Organisation
NEB	New English Bible
NGO	non-governmental organisation
NIEO	New International Economic Order
OAU	Organisation of African Unity
OECD	Organisation for Economic Co-operation and Development
PNG	Papua New Guinea
PPU	Peace Pledge Union
QUNP	Quaker United Nations Programme
RIIA	Royal Institute of International Affairs
SSD	Special Session on Disarmament (of the United Nations General Assembly, 1978)
TUC	Trades Union Congress
UDI	unilateral declaration of independence
UNCLOS III	3rd United Nations Conference on the Law of the Sea
UNCTAD IV	4th United Nations Conference on Trade and Development
UNDP	United Nations Development Programme
UNESCO	United Nations Educational, Scientific and Cultural Organisation
UNFPA	United Nations Fund for Population Activities
UNHCR	Office of the United Nations High Commissioner for Refugees
UNICEF	United Nations Children's Emergency Fund
UNITAR	United Nations Institute for Training and Research
WCC	World Council of Churches
YWCA	Young Women's Christian Association

FOREWORD – THE PEACE OF GOD AND PEACE AMONG NATIONS: TO HONOUR SYDNEY BAILEY

Bishop Hermann Kunst

Following a suggestion by the then Bishop of London, Dr Robert Stopford, a number of Christians from the United Kingdom, the United States of America and the Federal Republic of Germany created, in London in 1961, the Conference on Christian Approaches to Defence and Disarmament (CCADD). We were members of different churches and denominations. It was the period of the cold war, and several times we witnessed an imminent threat to world peace. We shared the conviction that the redemption of the world through Jesus Christ was not determined solely by the salvation of individual human beings. Our faith not only ordained our attitude towards those associated with us: we had to make our contribution in respect of the heavy responsibilities devolving on the present generation to bring about freedom, justice and peace. We sought fellowship in order to listen to each other and in so doing to obtain greater enlightenment on what advice we should give and what action we should take as Christians, in our diverse capacities, faced with the constantly rising level of armaments among nations and the concomitant hazards.

To many, it came as a surprise that within CCADD the relationship between the Quaker Sydney Bailey and a Lutheran, who was moreover still head of the military chaplaincies in his own country, was marked more clearly every year by mutual understanding and shared opinions. One reason for this, of course, was that Sydney Bailey is a personality whose spiritual gifts are as great as his character is strong. His breadth of vision, his lucidity of thought and his winning friendliness make every encounter with him a blessing. But it was something else that caused us to become friends.

We knew the histories and beliefs of the Christian communities in which we each had our spiritual homes. We never discussed the differences, but we did more than merely respect them, we made an effort to practise our beliefs. We were aware that for the preservation and renewal of the world the prayers of Christians are more important than their political opinions. We start from the idea that the Bible's 'God is all in all' does not merely refer in general to God's presence in the world but means also that we can count on the nearness of God and the illumination of His Holy Spirit in all the specific issues and tasks of our lives. At the same time, we did not wish to set out by offering others advice on improving their conduct. We did not want to ask anyone else to do what we were not first willing to perform. We understood each other as friends in truth, called to serve the cause of peace.

So I think the most appropriate way to honour Sydney Bailey on his sixty-fifth birthday is to present him with a contribution to the central question which has occupied us in all our encounters: 'The peace of God and peace among nations'.

Long before the threat to world peace which has loomed ever larger in recent years — that is, long before Vietnam and Afghanistan, before the token wars with their risk of open confrontation of the major powers, before the possibility that industrial nations cut off from sources of raw materials might be driven to take military action — Christianity had examined, unceasingly and with increasing urgency, the question whether it could and should contribute, and if so, in what way, to the solution of current problems and to the preservation of peace. Over the years, from Geneva and Rome, from Canterbury and Moscow, as well as from a large chorus of churches in Germany, there has come a whole library of challenges, statements, memoranda and scholarly studies on the subject. Nor have the churches been content with verbal declarations. Twenty years ago we stated that aid to development was only another word for peace. The churches have acted accordingly and have made available thousands of millions for a multiplicity of activities; they have trained development workers in all kinds of occupations to staff our projects. From the outset, there was clear understanding that peace between North and South could not be achieved solely by charitable measures. The basic problems concerning raw materials, economic co-operation, the population explosion, energy policy, financing and so on, come under the direct responsibility of national governments. I will return to the churches' contribution to these matters in due course.

The more we learn of conditions in the Third and Fourth Worlds and the more experience we gain in the course of our service, the more incomprehensible is a dichotomy which is false through and through, according to which responsibility for temporal well-being seems to be of greater importance for the church's service than concern for the eternal salvation of the individual. The truth is that nobody can have his share in the peace of God unless he takes a stand without hesitation against anything which causes or perpetuates discord, injustice and repression.

This brings us directly to our subject. First of all we ask: what is peace? In Greek, the word *eirene* describes a condition, a state of being. The normal condition was considered to be war. Its ascertainable interruption was called peace. The Latin *pax* is 'firstly, the expression, with regard to both parties, of a reciprocal legal relationship' (H. Fuchs). The term *pax Romana* comprises the two interpretations, the Greek one of a condition in the Mediterranean basin and, simultaneously, the legal security governing all aspects of life. In the Old Testament, *shalom* was understood as temporal well-being, but also as the fruit of the Covenant which God had made with Israel. In either case, *shalom* is a religious concept. In the diversity of man's endowment, it is a gift of God. The New Testament's use of *eirene* has a twofold meaning: God's acceptance of the sacrificial death of Jesus Christ brings about atonement, redemption, peace between God and man. This gift is received by man through faith. He receives the forgiveness that changes his whole life. Peace is being safe in God, no matter what the Christian's plight may be: fear, worry, debts, hardship, sickness or death. Yet despite the importance of this experience in our life on earth, the peace of God has its fulfilment in the new creation in the Kingdom of God. Luther, explaining the Second Article of Faith in Jesus Christ in his Small Catechism, described the glory to which we are going: 'in order that I may be His, live under Him in His Kingdom and serve Him in everlasting righteousness, innocence and blessedness, even as He is risen from the dead and lives and reigns to all eternity'. The peace of God is thus His presence in this our life, our world, and at the same time the goal towards which we and the world are travelling.

What has this peace of God to do with peace among nations? This question is concerned with the establishment of a Christian political ethic. The church is asked, by its young members, by parishioners who have become insecure, and by non-Christians of all kinds, what the position is on the connection between the 'peace of God' and 'peace among nations', indeed, whether the misery which has existed for centuries among the nations does not also make it impossible to believe in the peace of God.

In this matter, I am of Martin Luther's school. As the motivation for his often amazingly practical intervention in worldly affairs, he gave two very different reasons: his duty as a citizen and his duty as a theologian. Of the efforts he made in the disputes of the Count Mansfeld, he said: 'As one born here, it is right that I should serve my native land and my natural ruler with all loyalty,' and that meant making sure the conflict was brought to an end. On the other hand, he said: 'I am also a public preacher, whose duty is to administer rebukes when someone led astray by the devil cannot see the wrong he is doing.'

The determining factors for him, therefore, were the dictates of his conscience and the Gospel. If we consider Luther's conduct from this standpoint, research into the past may provide good counsel for the present.

I will attempt to translate Martin Luther's behaviour into the totally different conditions of today.

In so doing, I have been glad of the instruction obtained from the extensive study carried out by Ulrich Duchroff and Martin Honecker's argument with him.

In Philippians 4, Paul speaks of the peace of God which 'passes all understanding'. That means that the peace of God exceeds everything the human mind is able to attain and accomplish. Is this to devalue human reason? By no means. On the contrary, reason, the *nous*, is an outstanding faculty basically bestowed on all men. Reason stands in our place as representative of all that man at his best is able to do. 'The peace of God goes beyond that.'

For our theme, this provides a vital clue: for Paul, understanding (or reason) is a common basic human faculty for obtaining sensible orientation in this world. It is not, as the philosophy of his time held, an almost divine power. From this it follows that for Paul the Christian in the world and in his dealings with non-Christians must allow himself to be guided by this understanding and — so one might take the argument further — must approach the major problems of the world, among them the utterly insoluble one of peace among nations, with non-Christians under the guiding principle of reason.

What, then, is the effect of the peace of God, which passes all understanding, on work in this world? Paul's letter makes it unmistakably clear that this peace does not relate solely to a strictly 'interior' sphere of Christianity. The Epistle to the Romans, 12.2, says: 'Do not be conformed to this world, but be transformed by the renewal of your mind, that you may prove what is the will of God, what is good and acceptable and perfect.' 'By the renewal of your mind' — does this mean annulling what we have said up to now about reason as the guiding instrument for joint dealings between Christians and non-Christians, or does it mean that Christians are slightly more critical and clever than the children of this world? Certainly not. We Christians are not more critical or more clever or more full of ideas, but vulnerable and perplexed, prone to make mistakes and run risks when we give advice. It is characteristic of the human condition always to be subject to somebody, to be ridden either by sin or by self-seeking and self-will and given over to death, or else to be the 'servant of justice', that is, devoted to God and only then truly alive. Nothing else, in essence, distinguishes the redeemed from the unredeemed.

So Christians are no more clever than non-Christians. Their reason as a guiding instrument for orientation in this world is just as fragile, susceptible and unreliable as that of non-Christians. It may happen, through God's power, that Christians do not seek their own interests but those of others, in other words, in self-sacrifice they allow themselves to be taken into the service of love and in that way try to make a contribution towards peace among nations. This renewal of the mind gives Christians their own outlook on the world. It is expressed classically in Luther's golden rule: 'I should do unto others as I would they should do unto me.'

In the matter of 'renewal of the mind,' we must remember that the Son of God became man. On this subject, the Epistle to the Hebrews says: 'He had to be made like His brethren in every respect, so that He might become . . . merciful . . . For because He Himself has suffered and been tempted, He is able to help those who are tempted.' In concrete terms, this means that the renewal of our minds as Christians makes us able, in talks or negotiations, to creep, as it were, inside the others' skin and see the subject with their eyes. It might be objected that this happens in any kind of discussion. But renewal of the mind through Christ means something specific in this context, that is, to understand one's opponent not only from the rational standpoint, completely intent on one's own advantage, but in a loving way. This does not mean, in politics, being obliged to make concessions in advance, but it certainly means giving proper value to the other person's reasons in his position and above all in the historical context which might be linked with one's own historical guilt.

It may well be that someone, disappointed, asks: Is that all that Christians have to give towards peace among nations? No, not all, but the most decisive part. The church must remain the bird on the roof, singing her song. The church makes God present in the midst of discord by encouraging people to believe. She does not speak in a carping and peevish way from the position of human reason; but against presumption and the self-righteousness of God's gift of the mind she testifies to the renewal of the mind, by means of which the conflict between North and South, as well as that between East and West, is not confined only to the dimension of power politics and economic policies. Attempts to achieve peace among nations may be made under a clear sky or a leaden one.

All this is said with the utmost respect for the intellectual achievements of Christianity, the imagination, dearest child of love, the energy and not least the sacrifices made during these efforts to preserve or prolong peace. These did not begin with the wide-ranging work of the World Council of Churches and the Second Vatican Council, and are far from ending with our churches in the German Democratic Republic publicly making their voices heard to demand cessation of the portrayal of antagonists and the removal of military education from the schools. The churches in this matter must take a stand fundamentally on the words of the apostle Paul, that we must offer our bodies, and so our existence, to the world as a living sacrifice.

At this point I will come back to what I said at the beginning about development policy, so as to give at least one practical example. I stated that the basic problems of raw materials, economic co-operation, the population explosion, energy policy, financing and so on, came under the direct responsibility of national governments.

In Germany, because of the increasingly diverse and difficult nature of the work, the churches, in conjunction with the state, have made efforts to find a sound conception, and have for years negotiated to bring about a dialogue between the state, the parties, the employers, the unions and the agricultural industry. We wanted to discover whether there was basic consensus between us all in this matter and if and how we could then co-operate in our activities. The churches have also put permanent pressure on the Federal Government and the Federal Parliament to ask our people to accept some limitation of their well-being rather than hang back in supplying the means for development policy. We did not make love the first category mentioned, but justice and peace, and also the question if and in what way the social components of the free market economy in our country could be of significance on a world scale. Even more seriously do we take our duty as a national church to create awareness within our parishes. We want to awaken sensitivity and a readiness to acknowledge the requirements of policies, followed by a willingness to agree on restrictions.

My comments are intended as a cool refutation of an optimistic appreciation of the human race and the world, and of the euphoria of feasibility, whether in foreign policy or internal affairs. The church cannot heal all the diseases in the hospital of the world. But she can provide models and in this way orientation and encouragement. Through her witness and her behaviour she can indicate the source of peace. The will towards good, towards the very best, towards renewal of the world as they understood or understand it, has always been present in all

tyrants. The question of course concerns the nature of the source and
thus the content of our will. The source may be in various ways and
different degrees poisonous, but it may also be divine. The sure vision,
the sobriety and the devoted strength of the church in her efforts for
peace among nations and her service for that purpose are dependent on
the fidelity of her prayers and on the purity and force of her belief in
the peace of God.

In the entrance to the Luther Hall in Wittenberg are written Luther's
words: 'Let no-one abandon the belief that God wants to do a great
deed *to him*.' This great deed by God to us is the gift of His peace.
There is no doubt that in receiving this gift Christians are filled with
confidence, composure and energy, so that consequently *through us*
something fruitful is accomplished for peace among nations.

1 MORAL PRINCIPLES AND POWER POLITICS: THE PEOPLE'S REPUBLIC OF CHINA IN THE UNITED NATIONS

Wolf Mendl

Sydney Bailey served with the Friends Ambulance Unit in China during the Second World War and ever since has had a special interest in the country and its people. In the worst days of the Cold War and the Cultural Revolution he did what he could to support Quaker efforts to establish contact with the People's Republic.

In 1970-1 he became actively concerned to rectify the anomaly of its continued exclusion from the UN. This was not a matter of 'admitting' China — it was indeed a founder member and had a permanent seat on the Security Council; it was a matter of deciding who should occupy China's seat: the government in Peking, which was in control of the world's most populous state, or the Chinese government in Taiwan, which ruled about 14 million people. I think that Sydney recognised that the expulsion of the government of Taiwan from the Chinese seat would in effect deprive its population of access to the world body, but this, he rightly saw, was a lesser injustice than excluding the government of one-fifth of the world's population.

Sydney's concern could not by any stretch of the imagination be described as either sentimental or ideologically influenced. His basic interest, as always, was to do everything to strengthen the function of the UN as the only available instrument for steering the world away from the sterile struggles of power politics which have traditionally been settled by war. To make the instrument more effective it had to be universally accepted and for this it was essential to bring China into the fold. I am sure that Sydney had no illusions about China's behaviour in the UN. Given its stridently revolutionary stance at the time, there was every likelihood that it might prove to be an obstructive member. But if one of the largest countries took such a line, then it was all the more necessary to learn how to live with it and perhaps one might hope that the influence of operating within the world organisation would moderate its extremism.

With his characteristic good sense of timing, care and energy, Sydney became a key person in the organisation of several conferences designed to create a climate more favourable to Peking's entry into the UN. I had

21

the privilege of participating in three of these meetings.[1] The timing was excellent. Change was in the air although the dramatic breakthrough in Sino-American relations was not made public until 15 July 1971, three weeks after the last of the conferences I attended. At each of the gatherings, senior officials, academics and journalists, drawn from countries that were partisans of Peking, countries supporting Taiwan and countries sitting on the fence, discussed the problem from its many aspects in the informal and friendly atmosphere which distinguishes conferences sponsored by Quaker organisations.

Peking Takes Over the China Seat: 1971

It is impossible to say precisely what contribution, if any, these consult-ations made to shifting the vote in Peking's favour. On 25 October 1971, the UN General Assembly first rejected by 59 votes to 55, with 15 abstentions, a resolution which would have made the expulsion of Taiwan an 'important question', requiring a two-thirds majority. The resolution which finally seated the Chinese Communists and expelled the Chinese Nationalists was carried by 76 against 35, with 17 abstentions. It may be that the Quaker-sponsored meetings helped to persuade some governments to shift their position from pro-Taiwan to abstention or from abstention to pro-Peking. We shall probably never know, though it might be possible to make some guesses by comparing the final vote with Sydney Bailey's exhaustive analysis of voting behaviour on this issue up to and including 1970.[2]

The China that took its place in the United Nations in 1971 was Janus-faced. For some time there had been signals from Peking that it was interested in establishing relations with Western countries and in playing a more active part in international affairs. The change of direction followed a new appraisal of the global scene: the Soviet Union became the greatest 'threat' and indications that the United States was looking for a way out of the Vietnam War strengthened Peking's perception that its power was declining.

On the other hand, China still posed as an intransigent revolutionary power, even if it did not act as one, determined to lead the revolutionary forces to victory over the forces of imperialism, colonialism and social-imperialism: 'Countries want independence, nations want liberation and people want revolution, this has become an irresistible trend of history.'[3]

The maiden speech delivered by Chiao Kuan-hua as chairman of the delegation from the People's Republic of China to the General Assembly

on 15 November 1971 outlined the principles and policies which were to
inform China's conduct at the United Nations. Welcoming the expulsion
of the 'Chiang Kai-shek clique' from the international organisation, he
called it a defeat of the US government which, in collusion with the
Sato government of Japan, had tried 'to create two Chinas'. The Chinese
were determined 'to liberate Taiwan and no force on earth can stop us
from doing so'. If the Americans were the villains over Taiwan, a reference to the unequal treaties which China had been forced to sign in the
past clearly pointed at Russia as well.

On the specific issues which were agitating the UN at the time, Mr
Chiao expressed full support for the three states of Indochina in their
struggle against the United States; for North Korea against 'all the
illegal resolutions adopted by the United Nations' and for the dis-
solution of the United Nations Commission for the Unification and
Rehabilitation of Korea; for the Palestinians in the struggle against
'Israeli Zionism', which had the 'support and connivance of the superpowers'; for Mozambique, Angola and Guinea Bissau in their struggles
against Portugal; for the people of Southern Africa in their struggle
against racist oppression; for the rights of Latin American countries
over the 200-mile limit of their patrimonial sea.

On the broader issues involving matters of fundamental principle,
Mr Chiao was equally emphatic in outlining China's basic orientation.
China, he declared, 'belongs to the Third World'. He went on:

> We have consistently maintained that all countries, big or small,
> should be equal . . . We are opposed to power politics and hegemony
> . . . At no time, either today or ever in the future, will China be a
> superpower subjecting others to its aggression, subversion, control,
> interference or bullying.

His country would help people struggling for 'socialist construction'
and those fighting against aggression. 'We will never become munition
merchants,' and he explained that because of its own underdevelopment,
China's aid would have to be mainly political and moral. This is what he
had to say on disarmament:

> China will never participate in the so-called nuclear disarmament
> talks between the nuclear powers behind the backs of the non-
> nuclear countries . . . China develops nuclear weapons solely for the
> purpose of defence and for breaking the nuclear monopoly and ulti-
> mately eliminating nuclear weapons and nuclear war.

He promised that 'at no time and under no circumstances will China be the first to use nuclear weapons' and he called on the superpowers to do the same if they really wanted disarmament.

Finally, he linked China's support of the UN Charter to its opposition to the 'hegemonism' of the superpowers, accusing them of having manipulated the UN for their own ends and in contravention of the Charter.

Mr Chiao thus mapped out the guidelines of China's UN policy quite unambiguously. They may be summarised as follows:

1. The equality of all states within the UN, regardless of size, population or resources.
2. Opposition to all forms of hegemonism, especially that exercised by the superpowers. Although the United States and other Western 'imperialists' were named explicitly over specific issues, the Soviet Union was regarded as potentially the more dangerous and aggressive of the two superpowers.
3. China was part of the Third World. It declared its solidarity with the people of the developing countries struggling against hegemonism and oppression. The Chinese distinguished between just and unjust wars and between revolutionary and counter-revolutionary violence.[4] They placed much less emphasis on peace as the absence of war and violence than on peace as the existence of a just social order which could only be achieved and maintained by struggle. As a corollary to this stand, China stressed the need for self-reliance of the poor countries, offering them limited and non-exploitative aid and free military assistance in their just struggles.
4. It follows from the above that the Chinese were less concerned than the liberal pacifists about disarmament. Disarmament, the Chinese said, had to begin with the 'imperialists' and 'oppressors'. Once they had provided substantial evidence that they were disarming, then the rest of the world might join in and achieve universal disarmament. They regarded arms control as a means with which the 'hegemonists' tried to perpetuate their supremacy.
5. On the UN itself, the Chinese took a purist stand, upholding the Charter and disclaiming any responsibility for all that had 'perverted' it during the long period of their absence.

China's Behaviour in the UN

A year after the People's Republic had taken over China's seat, the Western press took stock, expressing great relief and agreeable surprise that the Chinese, far from being wreckers, had played a very modest and becoming role in the UN. They had only been forced to use the veto twice and this was attributed to their inexperience and thus allowing themselves to be outmanoeuvred by the Russians. They had been careful not to get entangled in matters beyond their knowledge and competence. They had allowed Chinese members of the UN Secretariat, who held passports from the Republic of China on Taiwan, to remain at their posts. Altogether, the Chinese were not behaving as great powers tend to do. In the words of an ambassador from a Third World country: 'It is exhilarating when a big power asks a small power what you think. They approach us as equals. Their modesty is so over-whelming that it is embarrassing.'[5] Such a style of behaviour was in contrast to that of diplomats from other great powers who rarely sought out the company of the small fry, except to exercise pressure and elicit a vote on some issue.

As the years passed, the characteristics of Chinese behaviour became clearer so that they could be more easily defined. China's delegates to the UN and its specialised agencies used them as forums to expound the Chinese view of the world with a strong admixture of moralism. To some extent the moralism continues an ancient tradition in Chinese thought; to perceive all human and social relationships in terms of moral principles, the chief difference being that Confucian moralism had now been replaced by revolutionary moralism.[6]

The infrequent Chinese interventions in debates were mainly confined to the tedious and sometimes strident repetition of a few basic themes. One of these was the insistence on an egalitarian view of international society, in contrast to the traditional Chinese view of a strictly ordered world based on hierachical principles. Chinese spokesmen never ceased to attack 'hegemonism', 'big' or 'small' — a dramatic break with the imperial tradition in which the superiority of Chinese civilisation was taken as axiomatic, the 'Son of Heaven' receiving tribute from all 'barbarians'. One could, however, detect a lingering trace of an earlier Chinese view in the frequent references to China's revolutionary experience as a model for the oppressed peoples of the world.

On the other hand, the Chinese took little part in the day-to-day bargaining and diplomacy of the corridors and lounges, nor were they prominent in the formulation of draft resolutions and the detailed debates over texts. In the course of time, this reticent behaviour could no longer be attributed solely to the modesty of the newcomer. The Chinese did not push themselves as candidates for the chairmanship of committees and for other offices. They did, of course, take their turn when chairing was by rota, as in the Security Council or, more recently, in the newly established Committee on Disarmament (CD).[7]

China took no part in caucuses and did not join the so-called Group of 77, even though it championed its cause. It institutionalised non-participation in votes as a way of indicating one's position on a particular issue. Abstention implied a certain indecisiveness about the merits of two sides in an argument; a kind of neutralism. Non-participation, as the Chinese used it, implied a rejection of both sides; a declaration that the formulation of an issue was unimportant, a sham or irrelevant. If the Chinese were not aggressive in their conduct, it was noted that they were equally unwilling to stand alone. In 1971 they had wanted U Thant to be replaced by another non-Westerner as Secretary-General. Thus, in the first two ballots they voted against Waldheim. In the second ballot they had stood alone with the United Kingdom in their opposition and when it became clear that the British would not oppose him in the third ballot, the Chinese immediately withdrew their negative vote.[8]

The contrast between aggressive and revolutionary rhetoric and modest and conciliatory behaviour was not a reflection of China's inconsistency. Both, in fact, have served to promote the national interest. That interest, as pursued within the context of the United Nations, has several dimensions: resisting and weakening superpower domination, especially that of the Soviet Union; winning the support of the Third World by championing its cause; maintaining good relations with the industrialised countries of the West, whose support China needs for its own economic development, without, however, alienating the developing countries.

China's public stance is calculated to undermine the position of the superpowers and to appeal to the Third World majority. Its behind-the-scenes behaviour is calculated to reassure the developing countries that China has no intention of becoming like other major powers, which assume the leadership of blocs, and to win the good will of the Western industrialised states.

The operation is, of course, fraught with difficulties and potential contradictions, and every so often China is caught out in its delicate manoeuvres. Collaboration with the Soviet Union cannot be avoided because of the need to demonstrate support for the anti-colonial movement. An interesting analysis of the pattern of China's voting behaviour in the General Assembly, between 1971 and 1977, has revealed that, in relation to the other four permanent members of the Security Council, China had the highest voting agreement with the Soviet Union on colonial issues and, since 1973, the lowest on arms control and disarmament issues.[9] Taking the three main groupings, the West, the Soviet bloc and the Third World, China was least supportive of the Western powers, with the exception of Japan.

China's attitude to the veto is another example of the difficulty of reconciling different objectives. Until its entry into the UN, China was all in favour of the veto as essential for safeguarding peace, because it required unanimity among the major powers and thus protected the smaller states against the 'superficial' voting majority, which was effectively controlled by the United States in the early years of the organisation.[10] This stand, no doubt, was influenced by the situation at the UN during the Korean War. Since entry into the organisation, Peking no longer supports the institution of the veto in public, especially since it is pledged, in its own constitution, never to be a superpower.[11] China has, indeed, been very sparing in its use of the veto[12] and in practice has relied on other permanent members of the Security Council to resist any move to abolish the veto.[13] Moreover, given its championing of the Third World, it could be argued that it would be against the interest of the Third World should China renounce the veto unilaterally.

On the colonial issue China has been forced to draw a distinction between its ideological posture and the national interest. In principle it is a proponent of revolution and wars of liberation; in practice it has insisted that the colonial issues of Hong Kong and Macao will be solved through negotiations when the time is ripe. Until then, China's policies favour the *status quo* and it has tacitly co-operated with the colonial governments of those territories.[14]

Disarmament and arms control are examples of issues where China has been able to reconcile its ideological professions with the national interest. It listed its proposals 'on the Elements of a Comprehensive Programme of Disarmament' in a formal document submitted to the Chairman of the UN Disarmament Commission on 18 May 1979.[15] China called on the superpowers to reduce their nuclear and conventional armaments first. Only 'when they have . . . closed the huge gap between them and the other nuclear states and militarily significant states', should the others join in making reductions 'according to reasonable ratios'. All chemical and biological (CB) weapons should be destroyed and prohibited. Non-proliferation should not deprive other states of a nuclear industry: 'No disarmament measures may prejudice the right of states to make use of modern scientific and technological achievements to promote their economic development.' Disarmament agreements 'should provide for strict and effective measures of international control to ensure their effective implementation. No control or verification measure may prejudice the sovereignty and security of any state.' Disarmament should also be 'discussed and settled by all States on an equal footing'.

The details of this programme include negative guarantees by all nuclear states to non-nuclear-weapon states and nuclear-free zones; the withdrawal by the superpowers of all troops stationed abroad and the dismantling of all foreign bases; conventional disarmament to start with heavy weapons such as tanks, aircraft, warships and artillery; unequivocal commitments by all states not to use CB weapons, pending their complete prohibition and destruction; South-East Asia to be declared a 'zone of peace, freedom, and neutrality'; the Indian Ocean and Mediterranean to be regarded as zones of peace; the status of Latin America as a nuclear-free zone to be respected by all; and so on.

In a speech introducing the programme, Lai Yali linked disarmament to development and supported the demand that funds released as a result of disarmament by the superpowers should be used for the benefit of the social and economic needs of the developing countries. He also welcomed various structural reforms initiated by the Special Session on Disarmament and forecast China's participation in the Committee on Disarmament.[16]

It is not difficult to see how China has been able to project an image of spokesman for the poor and underprivileged countries in calling for material evidence that first the superpowers, then the remaining nuclear-weapon states and finally all the other 'militarily significant' states have disarmed, before the rest will join the process. It subscribes to popular demands for the prohibition of CB weapons and for a non-discriminatory non-proliferation system. It is on the side of the angels with its insistence that disarmament agreements should be effectively controlled and verified. It does not, however, explain how such measures might be carried out without prejudicing conventional ideas of national sovereignty and security.

In every respect, therefore, its declaratory policy corresponds to the aspirations of the Third World countries and a large segment of world public opinion, in so far as it is represented through international non-governmental organisations. Moreover, the policy is congruent with the requirements of national security. As a state with a limited nuclear capability, China would welcome a scaling down of the superpowers' capabilities to at least its level. Disarmament starting with heavy conventional weapons would remove the threat from the Soviet Union in precisely those areas where Chinese equipment is obsolescent and inadequate. The removal of troops and foreign bases would get rid of the Soviet military presence in the People's Republic of Mongolia and its possible implantation in Vietnam. Nuclear-free zones and 'zones of peace' are useful in blocking the military expansion of the superpowers, especially the Soviet Union. There are, however, some contradictions between China's security interests and the requirements of its ideological position, which we shall discuss later.

The characteristics of China's behaviour and public pronouncements at the United Nations broadly correspond to the perceived requirements of its national interests. The basic objectives of national policy may be consistent over a long period of time, but the evolution of the policy in its detailed application is subject to continual change as a result of pressures from within and outside the country. The cumulative effect of the need for constant adjustments, involving often no more than apparently minor alterations or omissions in the text of a speech or declaration, may, however, lead to significant and lasting changes in the direction of policy. Before looking more closely at the evolution of China's policy in the United Nations, it may be useful to look at the broad development of its national policy over the past decade.

China's National Policy, 1971-1980

When the People's Republic entered the United Nations, China was a declared revolutionary power. Mao was still the great helmsman, though failing in health. Lin Biao's 'plot' had been foiled but the 'Gang of Four' seemed to be in the ascendant. On the other hand, Zhou Enlai was beginning to reassert his authority over the administrative machine and behind the fiery rhetoric the outlines of a much more pragmatic foreign policy became visible. The opening to the West, especially the United States and Japan, was justified as a tactical manoeuvre, with frequent references to the historical precedent of Mao's accommodation with Chiang Kai-shek after the war against Japan.[17]

Until 1976, the domestic scene in China presented a confused pattern dominated by a partly hidden and partly open power struggle. Zhou Enlai had launched the modernisation programme at the 4th National People's Congress held in January 1975, but the radicals still seemed to be in control. There was, however, a basic continuity in foreign policy. Both ideologues and pragmatists agreed that the Soviet

Union was the principal threat to China's national interests. The perception of the United States as a superpower in retreat and decline gained strength after the withdrawal from Vietnam in 1973. Japan and the countries of Western Europe were seen as playing their part in the grand strategy of containing the Soviet Union and as necessary to the modernisation process in China.

But China had not given up its role as spokesman for and model of the world's revolutionary forces. Criticism of the West was muted in the interest of collaboration against the Soviet Union but it did not disappear completely. China still preached the virtue of self-reliance in spite of rapidly expanding trade relations with the West and particularly Japan.

With the deaths of Zhou and Mao in 1976, the power struggle reached its climax and seemed to be resolved with Deng Xiaoping's second resurrection. A hidden struggle continued for some time between those who had been disgraced during the Cultural Revolution and those who had survived and prospered under it. Deng Xiaoping represented the former and Hua Guofeng the latter. More recently, it seems, the Dengist party has consolidated its control over the government, although the legacy of revolutionary turmoil has left very formidable problems for the pragmatists now in power, not only in the economic sphere but also in the morale and structure of party and army.

It may be said that since 1978 China has also become more involved in global power politics. The rhetoric remains the same, with some change in nuance – a noticeably less even-handed approach to 'superpower hegemonism' and more general and less precise attacks on colonialism, with the exceptions of Zionism and racism in Southern Africa. The Treaty of Peace and Friendship with Japan in August 1978 was, no matter how the Japanese choose to look on it, a deliberate attempt to enlist Japanese support in the struggle against the Soviet Union and it has certainly been interpreted as such by the Russians. The normalisation of relations with the United States on 1 January 1979 won the formal recognition by the United States of China's claim to sovereignty over Taiwan at the cost of allowing Taiwan to continue receiving some American military assistance and to enjoy a *de facto* independence for the time being.

The frontier war with Vietnam, described as a 'defensive counter attack', had the balance of power in the South-East Asian region as one of its main objectives, and China's patronage of Democratic Kampuchea has involved it in the kind of lobbying at the United Nations which it had spurned hitherto. Foreign Minister Huang Hua's intense activities during the opening days of the General Assembly in September 1980 had all the flavour of major power diplomacy about it.[18]

Military collaboration with the West is not only confined to the purchase of weapons and weapons-related technology but includes exchanges of personnel. More dramatic still has been the change from the condemnation of Japanese militarism at the beginning of the decade to open encouragement of the Japanese to rearm more substantially. A break with Maoist foreign policy was explicitly indicated by the General Secretary of the Chinese Communist Party in an interview with a party of Yugoslav journalists. Among the mistakes attributed to Mao was his hostility to Western social-democratic parties, which the present leadership intended to correct. He also stressed that there is no conflict of interest with the East European Communist parties and that China enjoys good inter-state relations with the East European countries.[19]

Although revolutionary nonconformism to conventional international relations has always coexisted with a very pragmatic *realpolitik* in the foreign policy of the People's Republic of China – even during the heady days of the Cultural Revolution – the mixture has not always been the same. At the beginning of the 1980s it might be said to include a far greater proportion of *realpolitik*.

The changing perspective reflects domestic changes. The direction of the modernisation programme has been altered in the past year or two. The economic readjustment of 1979 effectively scrapped the ten-year plan launched in 1976. For a variety of reasons, which need not detain us here, there has been a switch in priorities. Agriculture remains, as always, first priority although it has so far attracted a low proportion of the state's investment funds. Light industry, with a bias towards the production of consumer goods, has replaced grandiose projects for heavy industry as coming next in order of priority, and industrial investment is at present directed towards sources of energy (coal, oil, electricity) and the creation of an adequate infrastructure for future industrialisation (transport, communications, management training and so on).

In order to push the country forward along these lines, the government has abandoned rigid adherence to the principles of strict socialism and self-reliance. The emphasis is on encouraging individual initiative, on relaxing centralised state control, on material incentives and on making room for a limited kind of private enterprise along the lines of family businesses. Economic policy includes the acceptance of foreign loans and credit, encouragement of investment by foreign firms and joint ventures with them.

In an important policy speech to some 10,000 cadres in the Great

Hall of the People on 16 January 1980, Deng Xiaoping outlined the objectives of the modernisation programme. The goal is to raise the *per capita* income from the present figure of about $200 to $1000 by the end of the century — a figure equal to the present *per capita* income of Taiwan and less than that of Singapore and Hong Kong. More significantly, Deng is reported to have said that China did not intend to

> carry out modernization in the manner of Taiwan, where the economy is actually under the control of the United States . . . Our politics and economic system are superior to Taiwan's and we must also achieve a certain degree of superiority over Taiwan in economic development. We cannot succeed without this.[20]

He added that China must catch up with Taiwan economically before it could recapture the island. He also stressed the need for peace so that China could achieve its objectives. This last remark was particularly noteworthy and in the past year one has heard far less about the inevitability of war from Chinese leaders than previously, though the idea may not have disappeared completely.[21]

China's picture of the world is, therefore, not a simple map of inevitable confrontation leading to war between two alliances. While it encourages the United States, Western Europe and Japan to meet the Soviet challenge head on, China does not entirely neglect its relations with the Russians. The outlook is not very promising but there have been a number of small indications that both sides are waiting for opportunities to relax tensions. There is continued contact on a variety of issues between the two countries. Some progress was reported on border talks which ended in March 1980. The Soviet Union is still regarded as a socialist state, though it has erred grievously in several respects. A trade agreement was signed in June 1980, and the Chinese have always insisted that they are not against negotiations with the Soviet Union.[22]

Chinese policies thus assume a complex character. At the global level, the 'objective' assessment points towards the dangers of an inevitable confrontation between the two superpowers, struggling for mastery of the world. The Soviet Union is seen as the more determined and advantageously placed in the next few years. China's interests require that the world be alerted to the danger from the Soviet Union without, however, drawing China into a war. Containment of the Soviet Union must, therefore, be accomplished without involving China in the risks of alliance politics. Indeed, the Chinese have no interest in a war between the superpowers and would probably welcome a certain degree of détente between them, in spite of their public condemnation of super-power connivance.

There is in addition an element of isolationism in Chinese policy which has roots in China's history and in the lack of contact with and knowledge of the world outside, characteristic of most of China's Communist leaders with one or two notable exceptions. The isolation-ism is balanced by the consciousness that China is part of the wave of the future in world politics, which is seen to belong to the Third World. China identifies with the Third World and balances uneasily, on the one hand, between the aim to become a new model world power, dis-tinguished in its conduct from the old-style imperialist powers, and, on the other hand, the inclination to assume a leadership role in world politics. Anyone who doubts the reality of this last temptation should see the giant new Chinese Embassy in Tokyo.

These conflicting and contradictory elements in Chinese policy are duly reflected in its policy in the United Nations.

Continuities and Discontinuities in China's Policy

A re-reading of Chiao's first speech nine years later suggests at first sight that there has been remarkably little change in China's position over the issues which exercise the world organisation. The same topics which featured in Chinese statements then feature in the statements of China's representatives now, including such specific problems as Korea, Indo-china, Palestine and Southern Africa. Only Taiwan seems to have disappeared from the agenda. The main themes are also the same: 'superpower hegemonism'; disarmament; and the rights and needs of the developing countries, now commonly referred to under the require-ments of a New International Economic Order (NIEO).

A closer comparison of what was said nine years ago with what is being said now reveals a somewhat different picture: a subtle movement in Chinese perceptions and policies behind the façade, but not necessarily in only one direction. To take each of the topics in turn:

Taiwan: This may have ceased to be an 'international' problem, especially after January 1979 and *pace* Mr Reagan's indiscretions during the presidential campaign. Yet even here there has been a quiet shift. Deng's speech in January 1980 indicates a lower priority for the 'liber-ation' of Taiwan on the national agenda. The objective has certainly not been given up and it would be foolish for the new American administration to think that the Chinese would react with anything but the utmost vigour to any move which departs from the agreement of December 1978. But the proverbial Chinese patience and sense of time will come to the aid of the government in Peking, as it reluctantly settles down to wait for a more favourable opportunity to bring back the island to the motherland.

Korea: Whenever the Korean issue comes up for consideration in the United Nations, China must appear to support North Korea and attack the United States. The withdrawal of American troops and bases is given as a necessary precondition of peaceful reunification.

Privately, the Chinese speak and behave rather differently. In 1973 they co-operated with the Americans in creating a consensus in the General Assembly for postponing the issue until the following General Assembly.[23] In 1979 the Chinese gave assurances that the North would not intervene in the political crisis in South Korea, following the assassination of President Park, and their demands for American withdrawal have appeared to be *pro forma* rather than a matter of urgency. The Americans are encouraged to 'think over the problem carefully' and the emphasis is on the peaceful reunification of the peninsula through a dialogue between the Korean states. In the meanwhile, they argue that their guarantee of the good conduct of North Korea could be balanced by the guarantee of South Korea from American bases in Japan, which are now perfectly acceptable to the Chinese.[24]

Indochina: Here the change has been more marked and open. The Chinese point with perhaps some justification to the consistency of their stand, which does not violate the basic principles on which their policies are based. Until 1973, at least, the 'imperialist threat' in the region came from the United States. Since 1975 it has been posed by the 'little hegemonism' of Vietnam as a proxy for the 'big hegemonism' of the Soviet Union. So it seems as if only the hegemonists have changed. But China is caught in a dilemma. Opposition to the United States in the past could be justified not only on the principle of anti-imperialism but also in the name of the struggles of the poor countries against the rich. Opposition to Vietnam cannot be justified so easily. Many of the Third World see Vietnam as part of their fraternity; they are not convinced that the Vietnamese are stooges of the Soviet Union. Moreover, they entertain a suspicion that China may be trying to play the role of regional hegemonist — a fear that is strong among some members of the Association of South-East Asian Nations (ASEAN).

Palestine, Southern Africa, and colonialism: On all these issues there appears to be very little change in Chinese rhetoric and behaviour. That is, China is long on principle and short on action, taking no diplomatic initiatives.

'Superpower hegemonism': The basic thesis continues to hold, but the attacks on the Soviet Union have become more specific and those on the United States less so. Russia is no longer referred to as 'a super-power' or 'one of the superpowers', but singled out by name.[25] Occasionally, the United States will also be the target of criticism, but on limited and less serious grounds.[26]

Disarmament: The Chinese programme and proposals for disarmament have not changed substantially over the years. The same themes continue to dominate speeches and declarations. The approach to the subject has, however, become more specific. In 1973 Peking signed Protocol II of the Tlatelolco Treaty and ratified it in the following year. This was the first arms control agreement to which the People's Republic of China has adhered. The fact that the Soviet Union had not subscribed to it no doubt had something to do with the action.[27]

China took its place as a full member of the Committee on Dis-armament at the beginning of 1980. When I asked in Peking why China should have chosen this particular time to join the Committee, I was told that there was no special reason other than that it had been pressured to do so by some 'friendly nations'. A few months later it took a rare initiative and submitted a proposal to the CD, calling for a ban on chemical weapons, which it linked to their alleged use in Afghanistan and Kampuchea. Though not perhaps original, it had provisions for verification and control and was announced as its first substantive proposal in this field.[28]

In other respects, however, the Chinese position has accorded ill with its professions, particularly as a spokesman for the have-not countries. Some observers noted the alignment of the French and Chinese positions over disarmament and security issues.[29] But the contrast in the style of the two countries was striking: the French almost priding themselves on their cynical approach to these matters and the Chinese always starting from the standpoint of high moral principle. Whatever their philosophical approach, both countries shared interests over nuclear questions.

There were also more obvious contradictions in the Chinese position. Peking was a great champion of the establishment of nuclear-free zones, but it also championed the right of a country to have nuclear weapons for its defence. It can no doubt be argued that these are not necessarily contradictory positions and that both serve the purpose of resisting the 'expansionism' of the superpowers. Nevertheless, the issue of 'defensive' nuclear armament is such a complex and subjective concept that no one could seriously imagine Peking accepting it if Vietnam, for instance, decided to acquire nuclear weapons to protect itself against threats from China.

The solemn declaration that the Chinese would 'never become munition merchants' must also be called into question. China's arms exports have indeed been modest compared with those of the other four permanent members of the Security Council[30] and perhaps they can be justified in terms of aiding the weaker states to defend themselves against the stronger. But here, too, national interest rather than abstract principle dictates the definition. In 1979 Bangladesh was deemed worthy of an arms deal; seven years earlier, China had vetoed its admission to membership of the UN.

The Third World: The official line has not changed in the least over the past decade, but in one very important respect there has been a change in policy. As far as its own development is concerned, China no longer practises self-reliance. Students of Chinese behaviour in the UN were quick to note that, in contrast to the rhetoric, China did not act like a revolutionary or even 'progressive' power.[31] But the statement that 'Chinese pride, embodied in the principle of self-reliance, is too strong to admit the possibility of China becoming the recipient of any UN assistance program in the foreseeable future'[32] has been overtaken by events.

Since 1973, China has contributed to the United Nations Development Programme (UNDP) and given technical assistance to developing countries. In September 1979, a UNDP office was opened in Peking and at the end of November a UN mission went there in response to Chinese interest in receiving assistance.[33] On 17 April 1980, China joined the handful of Communist countries (Romania, Yugoslavia and the three states of Indochina) who are members of the International Monetary Fund (IMF). This was a necessary precondition for admission to the World Bank (IBRD), which lends money for development projects. A month later it was admitted to the IBRD and in the autumn of 1980 China's quota of Special Drawing Rights in the IMF was increased to make it the eighth largest among the members, thereby increasing both its voting strength and borrowing rights.[34]

Another example of China's willingness to enter into reciprocal relationships and accept assistance from international organisations is the Programme Agreement signed with the United Nations Fund for Population Activities (UNFPA) on 9 September 1980.[35] In terms of the funds involved it is a modest agreement; $50 million spread over four years; but it is symbolic of China's growing involvement in international functional arrangements.

China's Place in the World Community

China entered the United Nations after 20 years of quasi-isolation; an isolation marked by Chinese ignorance of the outside world and the outside world's ignorance of China. China did, of course, have contacts with many countries and there were periods during those years, as in the mid-1950s, when Chinese diplomacy was active in world affairs. But it had seemed to outsiders that China retained an element of the traditional views of its place in the world.

Ancient China had seen itself as the centre of a civilisation governed by moral values; the New China projected itself as the centre of a new civilisation governed by a new set of moral values. Both ancient and modern China regarded their societies as models for the world, but neither exhibited the crusading form of imperialism that has been characteristic of great Western states from Rome to the United States and the Soviet Union, although the Chinese have displayed the same tendency as the Russians to expand into the land areas on their borders and bring the people who inhabit them under their control.

In the first two decades of its existence, the People's Republic pursued a modest and pragmatic foreign policy under cover of a fiery message to the world. Its relationship with the disciples of the new orthodoxy in other lands was free from the attempt to dominate them that marked the relationship between the Russian Communists and the world Communist movement. There was no Peking-based Comintern or Cominform to serve as an instrument of Chinese imperialism. The nearest that China came to such ambitions was the talk of establishing a rival 'revolutionary UN', presumably under Chinese leadership, at the time of Indonesia's short-lived withdrawal from the world organisation in 1965. The few aid programmes that China undertook were conducted not only under very generous terms but with a scrupulous regard for the recipients' sovereignty and national sensitivities, in striking contrast to the aid programmes of other powers.

Against this view it is often argued that China's modest policies have only been a realistic reflection of China's very limited ability to project its power abroad. The occupation of Tibet is cited as an example of what China would do once it had the means to do it. Indeed, considering the very small material resources at its disposal, China has made a remarkable impact on the world and it is logical to assume that once it has succeeded in modernising itself, it will in its turn make a bid for world power.

Many who supported China's entry into the United Nations did so with these reservations in their minds. It seemed a sensible and realistic thing to do but there was considerable apprehension that Peking might prove to be an awkward and disruptive member of the organisation.

Its first decade in the UN has been characterised by modest and self-effacing behaviour and loyal co-operation in managing the institutions and procedures of the UN and its agencies. There has been no attempt to disrupt the system, though China has exercised the right of every member to call for changes and reform. It has tried, very successfully on the whole, not to abuse its privileged position as a permanent member of the Security Council. Whenever it was at odds with the majority, or with the consensus, it has established the practice of non-participation in votes. It has declined to contribute to activities on the grounds of principle, as in the case of some peacekeeping operations, and has become a kind of conscientious objector on such occasions. The modesty of the Chinese delegates in their encounters with other diplomats and their eagerness to listen and to learn has been a most welcome surprise after expectations of arrogant and doctrinaire attitudes.

Much of this may be explained in terms of China's overall international policy. That policy is governed by a firm intention to make China an industrially and technologically powerful state in the twenty-first century. The task is enormous and fraught with difficulties and uncertainties. The methods and means may not be the right ones but that is beside the point. The present leadership is determined in the pursuit of 'modernisation', which has overriding priority in national policy. Therefore, all else is designed to support it.

The greatest fear is that other powers, and particularly the Soviet Union, have an interest in preventing China's emergence as a powerful state because it threatens their own status and ambitions. China's obsession with 'hegemonism', it has been pointed out, is a legacy of China's historic experience as a victim of imperialism during the century preceding Liberation.[36]

The main objective in foreign policy, therefore, is to prevent any one state from acquiring sufficient power in the world to threaten China with impunity. At first the principal source of danger was the United States but since the late 1960s that threat has been superseded by the Soviet threat. On the classic principle that 'my enemy's enemy is my friend',[37] the Chinese have readjusted their policy so as to strengthen the resistance of the United States and its allies against Soviet expansionism. They will do so in every way short of entering a formal alliance, for the Chinese are realist enough to recognise that they must somehow coexist with a state with which they share a 4,600 mile border (7,000 miles if one includes the border with the Mongolian People's Republic, where the Soviet Union has stationed three divisions).

Belief in the inevitability of world war between the superpowers may have been based on a particular conception of the dynamics of international politics but it was also a means with which to alert the opponents of the Soviet Union, and to encourage them to strengthen their armaments, which would have the effect of restraining Russian policies or, if it came to the worst, provoke a clash of arms in a region far removed from China: Europe or the Middle East, for instance. Since the end of 1979 the inevitability of war thesis has been allowed to drop out of sight, until the secretary of the Chinese Communist Party, Hu Yaobang, declared that it might be possible to prevent the outbreak of such a war altogether.[38] Whatever their private thoughts on the subject might be, the Chinese leaders have gradually adjusted their publicly expressed views of the trend of world politics to reassure their friends in Europe and elsewhere that they too are for détente and peace. It also indicates their acceptance of the prevailing Western orthodoxy about the nature of the central strategic balance. Moreover, in spite of bitter public denunciations, China has continued to foster relations with the Soviet Union, albeit in a minor key. When the Chinese gave notice of terminating the Sino-Soviet Treaty of 1950, they took the initiative in proposing talks with the Russians and since then there have been a number of hints that the door to improving relations with the Soviet Union is not shut completely.

Apart from providing a useful platform for expounding the Chinese view of the world, the United Nations is also the best instrument for demonstrating the credibility of its solidarity with the Third World. It satisfies the moral imperatives of Chinese policy and also serves a strategic function, especially if the countries of southern Asia, the Middle East and northern Africa are to become the battlefield for world supremacy.

The problem for China is whether it can sustain a role in the UN which has won it so much respect and admiration in the early years of its participation in the organisation's work.

There have been signs recently that the discrepancy between the profession of principle and the requirements of national interest is becoming more obvious and more difficult to defend. The clash between

Angola and Zaire brought the Chinese, judged by their own principles, into some very unsavoury company. In nuclear testing, abhorrent to the Third World as a symbol of the nuclear arms race and as a cause of pollution, China ranked fourth in the league table with 15 tests between 1970 and 1979.[39] During the general debate in the General Assembly in the autumn of 1978, Albania's foreign minister accused China of stopping aid and credits because his country would not do as China demanded.[40] Nearer home, in the conflict areas of South-East Asia, China has acted in the way great powers are expected to behave: lobbying on behalf of the disreputable Pol Pot regime, allying itself with Thailand, whose regime is, if anything, the antithesis of its own. Its general policy has raised the fear in some countries of the region that China is working to replace the hegemonism of others with its own.

In practice, China has abandoned the principle of self-sufficiency, has entered into bilateral and multilateral economic arrangements with Western capitalist enterprises and accepts aid from individual countries and UN agencies. China also displays greater interest in the detailed working of international organisation and by accepting full membership of the Committee on Disarmament is likely to get its hands dirty working on the intricate details of arms control agreements. It is a member of the IMF and IBRD, institutions generally shunned by Communist countries as instruments of capitalist exploitation.

Alongside these developments, China has lost its innocence in United Nations affairs. It is no longer valid to plead non-participation on the grounds that it had no responsibility for certain matters which were decided before it occupied the China seat. Nor is it possible to argue that the Chinese must get to know the world after having been cut off from it during the turbulent years of the Cultural Revolution. Huang Hua, its first Permanent Representative at the UN, is now Foreign Minister. A large number of officials and leaders in all walks of life have been abroad for shorter or longer periods in the past ten years. The People's Republic of China enters its second decade in the United Nations as an experienced, respected and increasingly active member. Will its behaviour, then, conform more to the pattern of other major powers?

One can only speculate on the basis of past experience. It is probably reasonably safe to predict that three characteristics will continue to distinguish China's participation in international organisations. The emphasis on doctrine and morality is likely to persist. Both China's tradition and revolution support it. Secondly, China will continue to identify with the poor and developing countries. Though not poor in human and material resources, China is economically and technically far behind the Western industrialised societies and the Soviet Union. In some respects, particularly in military technology, it is faced with a growing rather than a diminishing gap. China's solidarity with the under-privileged also stems from the philosophical foundations of the present regime. But it is more doubtful whether this identification can be maintained for very much longer. The time may come when China's protestations to this effect will appear to the rest of the world to be unconvincing and no longer ring true.

It is not only the fast diminishing authority of Mao and Mao's doctrines which is weakening China's claim to be the champion of the revolutionary wave of the future. The methods which are being intro-duced to effect the country's modernisation may, if pursued to their logical conclusion, eventually undermine the foundations of a socialist society. On the other hand, the deep-rooted Confucian social ethic, which was such a powerful factor in Japan's rapid modernisation, may also enable the Chinese to succeed where other countries with different cultural traditions are failing, thus creating another kind of gap between China and the developing world. This is to take a long-term view. For the next decade, at least, China should be able to maintain its claim to belong to the Third World with some credibility.

The third characteristic, and the most difficult to define, is the uniqueness of China's contribution in the United Nations. In a sense each state has its own style of conduct and the Chinese are certainly not unique in being unique. Americans, British, French or Germans approach issues and try to deal with them in different ways, even though they have similar political and social structures. The Chinese 'style' has been noteworthy for the great importance attached to moral principle as a guide to conduct — to be distinguished from ideology as a guide to understanding the world. As far as their ideology is concerned, the Chinese have had no great difficulty in combining it with a pragmatic, flexible and sometimes contradictory stand over particular issues. The contradictions may be explained as necessary tactical manoeuvres in pursuit of the grand strategic objective dictated by the ideology. On moral principle they have been rather more consistent. When they have said that they will not behave like a superpower or a great power, they have usually behaved as if they meant it. When other great powers profess their concern for the smaller and weaker countries few believe them and their public and private behaviour often gives it the lie.

It remains to be seen whether the Chinese will continue on this course. Their behaviour is likely to be greatly influenced by their success or failure in avoiding the temptations of great power politics. It is possible that they will fail. Already they are playing the game of balancing power, though they may not wish to be part of the confrontation of global alliances. It is not clear whether they will succeed in staying out of the big league and in the East Asian region there are indications that they will not.

China's participation in the United Nations has enriched the organisation. It has introduced a new perspective to the debates, even though it may suffer from tedious repetition. It has developed a new form of participation through its non-participation in votes, which has been aptly described as signifying 'at one and the same time both passive opposition and passive co-operation'.[41] In turn, the UN experience is broadening China's understanding of the world and in the last year or two it has begun to emerge from its self-imposed isolation within the organisation to play a more active part. This emergence may have been prompted by the imperatives of China's global strategy and not by a particular concern for the international organisation. Indeed, all the evidence points to the UN occupying a rather low place in China's foreign policy objectives. But the United Nations has a habit of forcing itself on the attention of the big powers, which sometimes pretend that it is of no importance to them. In the end they find that they really cannot do without it. This must surely have been Sydney Bailey's hope when he promoted the participation of the People's Republic of China in its work.

Notes

1. They were sponsored by three Quaker Service bodies: the American Friends Service Committee, Friends Service Council (now known as Quaker Peace and Service), London, and Canadian Friends Service Committee. The three I attended were at Rastenfeld, Austria, 15-21 April 1970, on the theme 'China in the Family of Nations'; Geneva, 29-31 January 1971, which was called 'UN/China Consultation'; London, 25 June 1971, titled 'China and the United Nations'. The meeting at Rastenfeld was attended by 40 participants from 21 countries. Sixty per cent were diplomats, including four ambassadors, and the remainder academics and journalists. The Geneva and London Consultations were much smaller affairs, attended mainly by senior officials of ambassador or minister-counsellor rank and a few politicians. There were other meetings in New York and various capitals.

2. See also Sydney Bailey, 'China and the United Nations', *The World Today*, vol. 27, no. 9 (September 1971), pp. 365-72, especially pp. 366-8.

3. Speech delivered by Chiao Kuan-hua to the UN General Assembly on 15 November 1971 (*Xinhua News Agency*, 17 November 1971). All subsequent references to Mr Chiao's speech come from this source.

4. Samuel S. Kim, *China, the United Nations, and World Order* (Princeton,

New Jersey: Princeton University Press, 1979), p. 66. For a discussion of the Chinese theories of the 'intermediate zone' and the 'three worlds', see ibid., pp. 75-82.

5. The *Christian Science Monitor*, 21 September 1972. See also the *Guardian*, 19 September 1972; the *Daily Telegraph*, 9 November 1972.

6. Kim, *China, The United Nations, and World Order*, pp. 90-3.

7. China gave official notification on 11 December 1979 of its intention to take its seat in the Committee on Disarmament, of which it had been an absent member throughout the first year. Its turn to assume the chairmanship came in March 1980.

8. Dominique David, 'Deux ans d'activités chinoises à l'ONU', *Problèmes politiques et sociaux, La Documentation Française*, 25 January 1974; Samuel S. Kim, 'Behavioural Dimensions of Chinese Multilateral Diplomacy', the *China Quarterly*, no. 72 (December 1977), pp. 730-1.

9. Trong R. Chai, 'Chinese Policy towards the Third World and the Superpowers in the UN General Assembly 1971-1977: a Voting Analysis', *International Organization*, vol. 33, no. 3 (Summer 1979), p. 403.

10. Suzanne Ogden, 'China's Position on UN Charter Review', *Pacific Affairs*, vol. 52, no. 2 (Summer 1979), pp. 221-3.

11. Constitution of the Chinese Communist Party, 28 August 1973, ch. I; Preamble of the Constitution of the People's Congress of the People's Republic of China, January 1975. Kim, *China, the United Nations, and World Order*, p. 90, note 142.

12. Between November 1971 and December 1976, the five powers cast the veto as follows: US 17, UK 9, USSR 5, France 4, China 2. Kim, 'Behavioural Dimensions of Chinese Multilateral Diplomacy', pp. 725-6.

13. Ogden, 'China's Position on UN Charter Review', p. 211.

14. Kim, *China, the United Nations, and World Order*, pp. 71-2. See also Gordon Laurie, 'Hong Kong and the People's Republic of China: Past and Future', *International Affairs*, vol. 56, no. 2 (Spring 1980), pp. 280-95.

15. Letter from Acting Permanent Representative Lai Yali, UN General Assembly, Disarmament Commission (UN Doc. A/CN. 10/5: 18 May 1979).

16. UN General Assembly, Disarmament Commission, Verbatim Record of the Eleventh Meeting (UN Doc. A/CN. 10/PV. 11: 15 May 1979).

17. The so-called Chungking Agreement of 10 October 1945. Stuart Schram, *Mao Tse-tung* (Harmondsworth, Middlesex: Penguin Books, 1970), pp. 235-40. The negotiations leading to the agreement had become a subject of compulsory study after the Ninth National People's Congress in April 1969. Michio Royama, 'Again on the China Problem', *Chuo Koron* (November 1971), US Embassy Translation (Tokyo, November 1971).

18. *Xinhua News Agency*, 23, 24, 25, 26 and 27 September 1980. In four days, between 22 and 26 September, he had meetings with the Foreign Ministers of ten Western states, of eight pro-Western members of the Group of 77, of seven non-aligned members of that Group, and of three Communist members of the Group: Democratic Kampuchea (two encounters), Romania and Yugoslavia.

19. *Süddeutsche Zeitung*, 25 June 1980.

20. *The Times*, 7 February 1980; the *Guardian*, 11 March 1980.

21. See the report of an interview with Deng Xiaoping, the *Guardian*, 2 September 1980.

22. Ibid., 22 March and 8 April 1980. This is also borne out by what I was told in Peking in January 1980.

23. Kim, *China, the United Nations, and World Order*, pp. 135-6.

24. The *Guardian*, 31 May 1980. Some of these points were made to me by officials during my visit to Peking in January 1980.

25. Huang Hua's keynote speech at the UN General Assembly, 24 September 1980. *Xinhua News Agency*, 25 September 1980. The preamble of the Constitution of March 1978 put Soviet hegemonism first and declared China's opposition to oppression, bullying and so on, 'by the social-imperialist and imperialist super-powers' and expressed its determination 'to form the broadest possible international united front against the hegemonism of the superpowers and against a new world war'. Bogdan Szajkowski, *Documents in Communist Affairs 1979* (Cardiff: University College Cardiff Press, 1979), p. 100.

26. For example, when the Chinese representative on the Security Council regretted the American decision to grant Mr Ian Smith a visa. *United Nations London Weekly Summary*, WS/78/42 (17 October 1978).

27. William R. Feeney, 'Sino-Soviet Competition in the United Nations', *Asia Survey*, vol. 17, no. 9 (September 1977), pp. 813-15.

28. *Xinhua News Agency*, 20 June 1980. Committee on Disarmament document CD/102, 19 June 1980: 'The Chinese Delegation's proposals on the main contents of a convention on the prohibition of chemical weapons'.

29. The *Financial Times*, 25 August 1972; Chai, 'Chinese Policy', p. 403; the *Guardian*, 6 February 1980.

30. Kim, *China, the United Nations, and World Order*, p. 481, fig. 9.1. In the year from July 1979 to June 1980, China signed at least three major arms agree-ments, with Bangladesh, Egypt and Sudan. *The Military Balance 1980-1981* (London: International Institute for Strategic Studies, 1980), pp. 102, 104-5. Indian sources have reported that China is supplying three squadrons of its latest FANTAN jet fighters to Pakistan. The Chinese were also said to be supplying SAM-2 missiles to Pakistan. The *Guardian*, 10 November 1980.

31. Kim, *China, the United Nations, and World Order*, p. 404.

32. Ibid., p. 495.

33. *United Nations London Weekly Summary*, WS/78/47 (24 November 1978), p. 5.

34. The *New York Times*, 18 April 1980; the *Financial Times*, 18 April, 11 September and 2 October 1980; *The Times*, 12 and 16 May 1980.

35. *Xinhua News Agency*, 10 September 1980.

36. Kim, *China, the United Nations, and World Order*, pp. 92-3.

37. J.K. Fairbank (ed.), *The Chinese World Order: Traditional China's Foreign Relations* (Cambridge, Massachusetts: Harvard University Press, 1968), pp. 11-13.

38. The statement followed the visit of the leader of the Spanish Communist Party. The *Guardian*, 27 November 1980.

39. During this period, the Soviet Union conducted 191 tests, the US 154, France 55, Britain 5 and India 1. *The Times*, 18 January 1980.

40. *United Nations London Weekly Summary*, WS/78/40 (13 October 1978), p. 5.

41. Kim, *China, the United Nations, and World Order*, p. 229.

2 DAMAGES FOR VIOLATION OF ONE'S HUMAN RIGHTS

Rosalyn Higgins

Sydney Bailey is a person of enormous knowledge in the fields of international institutions, disarmament, ethics and religion. He is also extraordinarily meticulous, fair and open minded. His good judgement is matched only by his kindness, and I have valued him as colleague and friend alike. The underlying concern of all his interests is about how we treat each other. And he has shown great interest in the contribution that international law can make. It is for that reason that I have thought it appropriate to offer an essay on a legal aspect of human rights.

Traditional international law provides little guidance on damages that might be appropriate for violation of an individual's human rights. Individuals have not been able to bring claims directly before the International Court of Justice and have had to rely, through the nationality of claims rule, upon their national states to bring action on their behalf. The theory has been that a wrong to the individual is a wrong to his state: damages therefore relate not only to the individual's loss or damage but also to the wrong done to his national state. Harm done to an individual can very readily be perceived as harm done to his national state when the individual concerned is in the diplomatic service. In the matter of the American hostages held in Iran the International Court held that the Iranian government 'is under an obligation to make reparation to the Government of the United States of America for the injury caused to the latter by the events of 4 November 1979 and what followed from these events'.[1] In many inter-state claims, the individual's involvement arose out of the expropriation of his property or his personal maltreatment by the defendant state. Where compensation has been awarded in expropriation cases, the question of compensation has largely turned upon whether the expropriation itself was lawful (in which case compensation for the market value of the assets would be due) or whether the expropriation was contrary to a treaty or an international concession or contract. In the latter case, there has often been in addition to the compensation a figure representing damages for the loss of expected profits.[2] But where the injury has been a personal one (not involving the loss of property) penal damages have sometimes been awarded.[3]

At the same time, international tribunals have not always felt that financial awards — whether compensatory or penal — were appropriate. In one case concerning a concession the Permanent Court of International Justice, though finding that a concession did indeed retain its validity, declined to award damages as there had been no financial loss attributable to the governmental assertion that the concession was invalid.[4] And in the *Corfu Channel* case the International Court of Justice thought that its declaration that the United Kingdom had violated Albanian sovereignty by virtue of its minesweeping activities was 'in itself appropriate satisfaction'.[5]

A note of warning had been struck in the 1961 Harvard Draft Convention on State Responsibility. The Explanatory Comment on the article dealing with failure of a state to exercise due diligence to apprehend persons committing an unlawful act against an alien read:

> Unless the alien has, through failure of the State to apprehend or detain the criminal, been denied the means of bringing a civil action against him for damages and has thereby suffered a financial detriment, he suffers no injury if the criminal is not brought to justice. All that the alien has lost is the opportunity to see the criminal punished, and this is not recognised by any mature legal system as a legally protected right.[6]

While this is not the occasion for a detailed examination of the question of damages in international litigation, it may safely be said that the practice is variable, both as to the circumstances in which damages are appropriate, and as to the valuation of any loss.[7] It is therefore perhaps not surprising that these underlying questions seem to remain unclear and uncertain in the leading international instruments on the protection of human rights. The Universal Declaration[8] did not address the subject (save that Article 8 provided that 'everyone has the right to an effective remedy by the competent national tribunals for acts violating the fundamental rights granted him by the constitution or by law'). The same is true of the Covenant on Civil and Political Rights.[9] The awarding of damages is not within the remit of the Human Rights Committee set up under Article 28 of the instrument, notwithstanding important powers to report on violations that may come into operation under the optional procedure of Article 41. The International Convention on the Elimination of all forms of Racial Discrimination[10] has fairly effective scrutinising machinery, but also does not itself make any provision for compensation to individuals whose rights have been violated.

By contrast, the European Convention on Human Rights[11] does make reference to the question of compensation for a breach of the Convention, though it does so in somewhat unclear terminology. Article 50 provides:

> If the Court finds that a decision or measure taken by a legal authority of a High Contracting Party is completely or partially in conflict with the obligations arising from the present Convention, and if the internal law of the said Party allows only partial reparation to be made for the consquences of this decision or measure, the decision of the Court shall, if necessary, afford just satisfaction to the injured party.

The phrase 'the decision of the Court shall if necessary afford just satisfaction to the party' does *not* refer to the Court's decision (judgment) as to whether there has been a breach of the Convention. In other words, the intention is not that a party has to rest content, in the last analysis, with the judgment as his satisfaction. In spite of the unclear terminology, the intention is exactly the opposite — that the Court shall itself be able to assist by providing, if necessary, for 'just satisfaction'. The wording of the entire clause leaves a lot to be desired. On the face of it, the Court's own ability to act to afford just satisfaction only comes into operation when the law of the party in breach allows *partial* reparation. It might therefore be argued that the Court has no role to play in this matter where the internal law of the country allows for *no* reparation. Notwithstanding the poor drafting of Article 50, this absurd result clearly cannot have been intended. The wording equally leaves uncertain the position where internal law does allow reparations but a Minister then exercises his discretion not to award such compensation. The European Court of Human Rights, setting its sights firmly on the broad purposes of the Convention and its overriding purpose to protect the rights of individuals, has refused to rely on the strict letter of the somewhat unfortunate drafting of Article 50. To prevent the possibility that a state could avoid Article 50 simply by noting that its law *did* allow reparation but that it had decided against allowing this remedy, the Court has interpreted Article 50 as covering the failure to receive entitled compensation, for whatever reason.

The Court in its jurisprudence has held that the purpose of Article 50 is to enable the Court to avoid further delay in providing just satisfaction to a victim of a violation of the Convention. But this does not answer the question of whether every violation of a right protected under the Convention necessarily entitles the victim to compensation. In English law a finding of a wrong (whether in contract or tort) entitles the plaintiff to judgment. That entitlement is based on *injuria* rather than damage.[12] Proof of loss or damage will entitle a successful plaintiff to an award in that amount. But where a wrong entitles a plaintiff to a judgment in his favour, even where there is no loss or damage shown, nominal damages will be awarded.[13]

How far these practices are to be imputed into the law of compensation as it relates to violation of an individual's rights under a treaty is uncertain. Some violations of the European Convention may involve an applicant in direct financial loss — for example, a taking of property contrary to the provisions of Article 1 or the Fourth Protocol. In respect of other violations he may be able to show indirect (but causally linked) loss — for example, an applicant claiming that his pre-trial detention was so lengthy as in all the circumstances to be in violation of Article 5, contended that his business suffered badly because of his absence. Again, our familiarity with concepts of loss and damage in domestic law makes it easy to accept that certain types of breach of the Convention do entail compensation — for example, improper detention by the authorities. Physical maltreatment by government authorities would also readily be seen as entitling compensation. At the same time, the domestic law analogy does not take us very far, because in certain areas (relevant to the European Convention) the authorities will normally have immunity. So if a plaintiff fails initially to get a fair trial and a new trial is ordered, the judge is immune from suit and counsel are in these circumstances protected.

In interpreting the notion of 'just satisfaction' under the European Convention one is therefore very much thrown back on the practice under that instrument itself. The starting point — after the text of Article 50 of the Convention — is the Rules of Procedure of the Court, amended in 1972 to include Rule 47 bis. This is headed '(Question of the application of Article 50 of the Convention)' and provides:

1. If proposals or observations on the question of the application of Article 50 of the Convention have not been presented to the Court in the document instituting proceedings, they may be presented by a Party or by the Commission at any stage of the written or oral procedure.
2. The Chamber may at any time invite any Party and the Commission to present observations on the issue.

Certain introductory and explanatory comments are here called for. Under the European Convention the respondent will always be a state. This is because it is states who are the signatories of the Convention and who have undertaken its obligations. If a state's officials violate the guaranteed human rights of others, liability will be imputed to the state. If persons for whom the state has no responsibility violate human rights, the victim will normally have an action in domestic law. It is only if the domestic law fails to provide a remedy for such violation that the liability of the violator's national state under the Convention will be incurred. The applicant, however, may be either a state or an individual. State-to-state applications are provided for in article 24 of the Convention.[14] Article 25[15] allows for applications by individuals, providing that the state against whom the complaint is made has accepted the optional procedures for individual petition. It therefore follows that 'the injured party' referred to in Article 50 may in principle be an individual or a state, and that 'just satisfaction' under that article is available to either. In fact, however, in the one inter-state case that has reached the Court,[16] no claims under Article 50 were made. This was because the application was not on behalf of nationals and therefore there could have been no question of any damage to them being treated as damage to Ireland.[17] The practice has centred on claims by individuals against governments.

The reference in Rule 47 bis of the Court's Rules of Procedure refers to 'any Party' (whether a state or not) and the Commission. Technically, once the Commission finds an application admissible, and when that application proceeds to the Court,[18] the Commission presents the case on behalf of the applicant. In actual practice, there are flexible arrangements for allowing the applicant's own legal advisor to 'assist' the Commission. The Commission is thus well placed to comment on the issue of just satisfaction at this juncture, though it will not have had to deal with the issue itself at the admissibility stage or when preparing its own report on the merits of the case.

Rule 47 bis, paragraph 1, makes it clear that arguments on the appropriateness of applying Article 50 may be advanced when proceedings are commenced before the Court; but equally it may be introduced at any stage during written or oral argument or proceedings. Paragraph 2 of Rule 47 bis is to be read as allowing the Court the discretion to call for submissions on the point even after it has given judgement, notwithstanding that the matter was not raised by the parties or by the Commission at an earlier stage. This was in fact done in the *Engel* case.[19] The Commission presented a memorial to the Court on matters relating to compensation one month after the Court's judgment on the merits of the case.

If the question of compensation is raised either when proceedings are instituted or during written or oral proceedings, must the Court make its findings on this question as a component part of its findings on the merits? The Convention itself provides no answer, but it is clear from the Rules of Procedure that the answer is 'no'. Rule 50(3) stipulates:

> Where the Court finds that there is a breach of the Convention, it shall give in the same judgment a decision on the applicability of Article 50 of the Convention if that question, after being raised under Rule 47 bis is ready for decision; if the question is not ready for decision, the Court shall reserve it in whole or in part and shall fix the further procedure. If, on the other hand, this question has not been raised under Rule 47 bis, the Court shall fix the time within which it may be raised by any party or by the Commission.

The drafting of the last sentence is less than clear. Presumably it is to be read in a way compatible with Rule 47 bis (paragraph 2), and simply means that if the initiative has come not from the parties or Commission under paragraph 1 of Rule 47 bis, but rather from the Court under paragraph 2 thereof, the Court shall then fix time limits. To read it in a different sense would appear to give an extra opportunity, outside of Rule 47 bis, paragraph 1, to a party or the Commission to raise the issue belatedly. If Article 50 of the Convention leaves unanswered the question of when compensation is deemed applicable at all, Rule 50(3) raises the further problem of when the issue is 'ready for decision'. The former issue we may term 'substantive' and the latter 'procedural'. On both issues one can only turn to the case law.

Obviously, if the Court in its judgment finds that there has been no violation of the Convention, issues under Article 50 simply do not arise. And if the matter has been broached, the Court will say in its judgment that it therefore finds Article 50 inapplicable. But where the Court finds a violation of the Convention, its handling of 'just satisfaction' is often hard to predict. There are both procedural aspects and substantive aspects of the question to deal with and we now look at each in turn.

Procedural Matters

So far as procedure is concerned, the Court will sometimes ask that the parties and the Commission make submissions, during the hearings on the merits, about the applicability of Article 50. But at other times the Court will simply add to its findings on the law a paragraph indicating that it reserves to the applicant the right to come back to the Court about just satisfaction under Article 50 should that be necessary. It is not always apparent when the Court will follow one course rather than another.

In June 1972 the Court dealt with the application of Article 50 to the earlier judgment it had given in the *Ringeisen* case in July 1971. The case centred on the compatibility of two periods that the applicant spent in detention on remand with Austria's duties under Article 5 of the Convention.[20] In particular, the Court found that the detention was not a 'reasonable time' within the meaning of Article 5(3).[21] In the judgment the Court reserved for Ringeisen the right, 'should the occasion arise', to apply for just satisfaction. Ringeisen's lawyer wrote to the Austrian Federal Minister of Justice, urging that his client be paid damages to reflect the unjustified detention, and the results that it claimed followed from it – loss of health, of future prospects, medical costs. It was suggested that at least 50,000 DM should be paid on account. When no reply had been received Ringeisen's lawyer instituted Article 50 proceedings under the European Convention. The Federal Ministry of Justice replied in September – after these proceedings were instituted – stating that it did not have the competence under the constitution to handle the matter. There is no suggestion in the Court's judgment on the application of Article 50 that it thought the commencement of these proceedings premature. It would seem that it expects a certain promptness on the part of governments in dealing with claims for damages for violation of the Convention.

Is an application for assistance from the Court in the matter of 'just satisfaction' a new application? Must it proceed through the Commission, being scrutinised for admissibility – and, importantly, needing to show that all local remedies have been exhausted in this matter?[22] This was the view taken by the Austrian government, which urged that the original proceedings had been terminated with the Court's judgment of July 1971 and that it was now necessary for Ringeisen to begin afresh. The (somewhat curious) wording of Article 50 itself lends a certain weight to the Austrian view. A literal reading of that article might lead one to believe that the Court's task is to assess, when making its judgment, whether the internal law of the respondent state allows only partial reparation, and if so, to order just satisfaction when making its finding on the merits. Any application for just satisfaction made subsequently must necessarily represent a new proceeding. The Austrian government pointed for further support to Article 52, which provides: 'The judgement of the Court shall be final.'

These arguments were rejected. Ringeisen was not required to make a new application (which could have failed the test of Articles 26 and 27 on admissibility) to the Commission.[23] The Court noted that if a fresh petition was really required under Article 25 of the Convention it would make getting redress under Article 50 more lengthy, problematic and hazardous. This was clearly not the underlying intention of Article 50 and the Court declared:

> It would be a formalistic attitude alien to international law to main-
> tain that the Court may not apply Article 50 save on condition that
> it either rules on the matter by the same judgment which found a
> violation or that this judgment has expressly kept the case open.[24]

The Court thus staked out a position of maximum flexibility, going further than it needed to on the particular facts of the case, as in the judgment of 16 July 1971 it had expressly reserved 'for the applicant the right, should the occasion arise, to apply for just satisfaction as regards these violations'. The clear implication is that expressed reservations of this sort serve to draw the applicant's attention to assistance that the Court may be able to offer; but it is not a procedural *sine qua non*.

The Court also rejected Austria's argument on Article 52, saying that the purpose of that article, with its reference to the finality of judgments, was solely to make the Court's judgment not subject to any appeal to another authority. The Court also added a further reason for not requiring a successful applicant to treat an application under Article 50 as an application *de novo* under the Convention. Each new case requires, by virtue of Article 43 of the Convention, the setting up of a new chamber.[25] But it was 'in the interests of the proper administration of justice' that the consideration of the reparation of damage flowing from a violation of the Convention should be entrusted to the judicial body which has found the violation in question.[26]

Although an application under Article 50 does not represent a new application, and will not fail at the level of admissibility before the Commission, it is nevertheless to the Commission that the request must be addressed. This is because the applicant has no *locus standi* before the Court and will need the Commission to act on his behalf. Arguably, counsel for the applicant should also notify the Committee of Ministers — which is the organ responsible for execution of the Court's judgments —

when the applicant has been unable to secure reparation under the relevant domestic law. This was in fact done in the *Vagrancy* case,[27] before asking the Commission (as was done in the *Ringeisen* case) to bring the matter before the Court under Article 50. Finally, the Court affirmed that applicants proceeding under Article 50 are indeed not required to exhaust local remedies in the same way as they are required to in their original applications. Here the Court's position in the *Vagrancy* case was being affirmed. In that case the Belgian government had taken the position that if local remedies were not exhausted, then there was no way that an applicant could meet the test of showing under Article 50 that the internal law allows 'only partial reparation to be made for the consequences of the violation'. But the Court — without ever robustly addressing that argument — preferred the view that Article 50 is one phase in the case as a whole and that if the draftsman of the Convention had meant to make just satisfaction applications subject to the exhaustion of local remedies, this would have been specified in Article 50.

There are a variety of procedures which the Court can follow in dealing with this question of reparation; as indicated by Rule 50(3) of the Rules of Procedure. If the matter of just satisfaction has been raised under Rule 47 bis (i.e. if they are included in the documents instituting proceedings, or if the parties or Commission present arguments during written or oral proceedings (Rule 47 bis (1)) or if the Court invites observations (Rule 47 bis (2)), then the Court can decide on the applicability of Article 50 *when giving its judgment on the merits* if the matter 'is ready for decision' (Rule 50 (3)). This has been done in several cases.

Thus in the *Golder* case the applicant claimed certain breaches of the Convention by the United Kingdom. He was detained in prison and was later accused by a prison officer of having assaulted him during certain disturbances there. Anxious of the impact of such an accusation on his prospects of parole, Golder wanted to correspond with a solicitor in order to bring a civil action against the prison officer for damages for defamation and thereby to have his name cleared. The Court found that, by virtue of the prison authorities' refusal to allow such communication with a solicitor, the United Kingdom was in breach of Articles 6(1) and 8 of the Convention.[28] During the hearing on the merits the Court was at its own request addressed on the subject of compensation by the government, the Commission and the applicant's lawyer who was assisting the Commission. The President of the Court asked whether the Commission was going to present a request for just satisfaction or make a reservation in respect of this. A negative reply led the Court to express the view that the matter was 'ready for decision'. The Court on 21 February 1975 found that there had been a violation of articles 6(1) and 8 and at the same time stated that these findings were sufficient satisfaction.

The same procedure was followed in the *Marckx* case.[29] This case concerned the inheritance rights under Belgian law of illegitimacy. The Court found various violations of Article 8, Article 8 taken with Article 14, and Article 1 of Protocol number 1 taken with Article 14. During the oral hearings the applicant's counsel, assisting the Commission, asked the Court to award one Belgian franc as 'compensation for moral damage'. No comment was entered by the Belgian government. The Court made a finding that the question was 'ready for decision' — though in the event it found that the findings of violations were adequate satisfaction.

In the *Tyrer* case the Court also disposed of the Article 50 issue in its judgment on the merits, but for rather different reasons. The application concerned a claim that judicial birching was contrary to Article 3[30] of the Convention. The applicant was a minor when the proceedings were commenced, but upon attaining his majority he sought to withdraw his application. He was not permitted to do so for various public interest reasons. Judgment was eventually given in favour of Tyrer, and the question arose as to whether he could still be afforded just satisfaction under Article 50. The Court stated that it shared the Commission's view that it was 'not necessary to apply Article 50 to the present case'.[31] In the *Guzzardi* case the Court found by ten votes to eight that the applicant was the victim of a breach of Article (5)1 while subject to an order for compulsory residence on the island of Sardinia under an Act directed against the mafia. During the judgment on the merits (6 November 1980) the Court by twelve votes to six awarded him a sum of one million Italian lire under article 50.

The *Golder* and *Tyrer* cases seem clearly to show that the Court, even if it avails itself of Article 47 bis, paragraph (2), will not be inclined *proprio motu* to order compensation under Article 50. Unless some action on the point is taken by the applicant (technically by the Commission acting on his behalf), then the Court will find it 'unnecessary' to go beyond providing satisfaction in the form of the finding on the merits itself. A dissent from this approach was expressed by an important grouping of judges in the *Marckx* case, however; Judges Balladore Palieri, Pedersen, Ganshof van der Meersch, Evrigenis, Pinheiro Farinha and Garcia de Enterria, on the specific question of Article 50, observed that in the *Golder* case the applicant had submitted no request for just satisfaction and that the Court had raised the issue itself. But that fact of itself should not lead automatically to the view that a finding of violation constitutes just satisfaction. The Court must look at the facts and circumstances of each case.

Rule 50(3) of the Rules of Procedure provides an alternative way of proceeding when the question has been raised under Rule 47 bis, i.e. either by the parties or by the Court: 'if the question is not ready for decision, the Court shall reserve it in whole or in part and shall fix the further procedure'. What does the phrase 'not ready for decision' mean? It certainly does not mean that the parties, when the Court itself takes the initiative under Rule 47 bis, paragraph (2), have not had enough time to prepare. In the *Golder* case the parties and the Commission were requested to deal with the issue on the day following the Court's request to them, and the matter was found 'ready for decision'. In the case of *Engel et al. v. the Netherlands*, five applicants, who were conscripted NCOs in the Netherlands armed forces, were punished on separate occasions for breaches of military discipline. They claimed that the punishments entailed a deprivation of liberty contrary to Article 5 of the Convention, and that the proceedings before the various military authorities did not satisfy the requirements of Article 6 for a fair and public hearing by an independent and impartial tribunal established by law. Certain other claims under other articles of the Convention were also made. However, no claim had been made for compensation as such. Counsel for the applicants indicated that they did expect to be granted just satisfaction but did not at the present time (i.e. during proceedings on the merits) have views as to whether the just satisfaction should take the form of financial compensation, and if so, how much. In these circumstances the Court thought it inappropriate to extend proceedings to have hearings on the Article 50 point. The Court here effectively found that 'the question' was 'not ready for decision' in the broadest sense of the term – i.e. that it was not even appropriate to follow the *Ringeisen* procedure of reserving the applicant's right to come back on Article 50, the entire issue was reserved. The Commission and Dutch government were invited to submit written memorials. This was done within two months of the judgment on the merits. And in November 1976 the Court made its findings on Article 50 (on the substance of which see below, p. 62). 'Not ready for decision' appeared here to mean nothing more or less than that the parties had not yet adequately turned their minds to the issue.

Substantive Matters

Are Costs and Fees Recoverable as 'Just Satisfaction'?

To what extent is Article 50 an appropriate vehicle for the recovery of expenses and costs? Or is it intended solely to provide reparation in the sense of non-cost-related damages (whether these damages be nominal or related to loss suffered)? The practice of the Court indicates that it is prepared, within certain operational principles, to allow the notion of 'just satisfaction' to include costs and expenses. The early case of *Neumeister* laid the groundwork for this, and the underlying principles have been elaborated in the more recent case law. Once one goes down this path it is of course impossible to deal with the matter in isolation from the question of legal aid.

In the case of *Luedicke, Belkacem and Koc* the requirement by the Federal Republic of Germany that the applicants, foreigners facing criminal charges, be required after the trial and conviction to pay for Court interpretation was found to be a violation of Article 6(3) of the Convention.[32] The Court decided in its judgement on the merits[33] that the Federal Republic must reimburse Mr Luedicke for the interpretation costs that he had already paid. These costs were the essence of the violation and the matter was clear on that basis. However, the Court reserved the question of the application of Article 50 as regards the applicant's other claims.

Agreement was eventually reached as to the amount of fees to be paid to Mr Koc's lawyer and procedures for the repayment to Mr Koc of amounts that he had advanced. As for Mr Belkacem, he had never actually paid interpretation costs: the demand for him to do so had been suspended pending clarification by the Court of the meaning of Article 6(3)(e) of the Convention. Only the fees of his lawyer remained a live issue under Article 50. But Mr Belkacem received free legal aid. He thus bore no costs himself and suffered no loss that could be compensated under Article 50. The Court added that it was not open to an applicant's lawyer to seek just satisfaction on his own account: 'he accepted of his own free will the conditions, including the scale of fees, applicable to the legal aid granted to his client'.[34] If it was felt that this view would discourage lawyers from offering their services under legal aid, it should be dealt with by the Council of Europe and not by a misreading of Article 50.

The question of reimbursement of costs arose also in the *Konig* case, where the Court found[35] that certain proceedings instituted against the applicant before the Frankfurt Administrative Court exceeded the 'reasonable time' provided for in Article 6(1) of the Convention. Having reserved the question of the application of Article 50, the Court gave its judgment on that aspect on 10 March 1980. The Court found that the applicant could recover, *inter alia,* for the costs disbursed in litigation before the German courts and before the Convention institutions. But Article 50 would only cover such costs as related to attempts to accelerate the progress of the actions (because this claim was about dilatoriness, and not about the rightfulness or otherwise of the German judgements). Dr Konig could recover such expenditures if they were reasonable in the circumstances of the case. Although in the *Neumeister* case the Court had proceeded on the basis of scales in force under the legal aid scheme operated for proceedings before Convention organs, it was not bound by this when, as in Dr Konig's case, the applicant produced detailed fee notes. Dr Konig did not receive legal aid and in principle could recover on the full amount paid if it was necessary and reasonable. In that context the Court accepted certain fees as recoverable under Article 50, while rejecting others. Interestingly, they also reimbursed Dr Konig for his own expenses in making various journeys to Strasbourg, finding that even though he was not a party to proceedings before the Court his presence in the Court room was 'of great value', as it assisted the Court in immediately ascertaining his views.[36]

The *Sunday Times* case has been particularly interesting in the matter of costs, fees and Article 50. The applicants claimed some £15,800 for the litigation in the English courts and some £24,760 for proceedings before the Commission and Court (with an additional amount for the article 50 proceedings). In addition, interest at 10 per cent was claimed. In the English proceedings the House of Lords ordered, by consent, that each party was to bear its own legal costs. The Attorney General now pointed out to the European Court that in the usual way he would have asked for costs before the House of Lords, but by consent refrained from doing so. The Government now felt that for the *Sunday Times* to be awarded costs under Article 50 would be contrary to the express agreement reached between the applicants and the Attorney General – an agreement at the request of and for the benefit of the *Sunday Times.*

The applicants interpreted the agreement differently, saying it related not to their own costs (which they had to bear as losing party in the English Courts) but to the Attorney General's costs. Its only effect was to reduce their Article 50 claim, in the sense that they were not now also seeking to recover under that article the Attorney General's costs also. On this point the Court preferred the Government's view and found that it was 'not appropriate to include the English costs in any "satisfaction" under Article 50, the issue of costs having been settled once and for all by each party paying his own'.[37]

The United Kingdom government further noted that such costs were not incurred for the purpose of establishing a breach of the Convention. The Court was less impressed with this argument, observing (as it had done previously in the *Vagrancy* case judgment of 18 June 1971) that the domestic proceedings, even if not directly for the purpose of showing a breach under the Convention, were a necessary precondition to the matter coming before the Commission and Court. It urged that compensation should be considered only for those costs which were necessarily incurred in establishing a breach of Article 10. As a gloss on this point, the Government asked that the Court deny costs incurred in advancing submissions which were rejected by the Commission and Court. Finally, the Government thought that any costs awarded should be calculated by reference to the current rates payable under the free legal aid scheme operated by the Commission.

The Court noted that 'just satisfaction' is to be afforded 'if necessary'. It distinguished[38] between damage caused by a violation of the Convention and costs necessarily incurred by the applicant. The Court observed that it was difficult to envisage circumstances in which a finding of a violation could ever constitute just satisfaction so far as costs were concerned. The fact that the English proceedings were perhaps welcomed by the applicants as a 'test case' would not cause the European Court to depart from its usual considerations in respect of Article 50.

Most interesting, perhaps, was the Court's detailed elaboration of the principle that it had enunciated in earlier case law,[39] namely, that costs and expenses will not be awarded under Article 50 unless it is shown that they were actually incurred, necessarily incurred and were also reasonable as to quantum. The Court was prepared to accept that the expenses were actually incurred, though the sum of £7,500 expended by the legal manager of Times Newspapers Ltd did raise problems which it had to address. It was the Commission (acting on behalf, but not as the mouthpiece, of the applicant) that thought that this work was covered by the normal duties of a company's legal manager and therefore was perhaps not 'actually incurred' for purposes of Article 50. But the Court thought that what was relevant was that otherwise these activities would have to be provided by independent lawyers paid by Times Newspapers Ltd. The £7,500 was therefore to be regarded as 'actually incurred'. Three judges dissented on this point.[40]

The Court then turned to whether the costs were 'necessarily incurred'. It found — surely correctly — that it was unacceptable to make a distinction between costs referable to successful pleas and costs referable to submissions that had been rejected.[41] A lawyer had to present all possible arguments for his client, and evaluation by hindsight was not the right approach.

Were expenditures on applicants' counsel 'necessary', given the role that the Commission plays in presenting arguments to the Court? The Court found that the retention of separate counsel by the applicant was necessary in principle, as the Commission does not represent the applicants as such but rather assists the Court in representing the public interest as guardian of the Convention. But the Court did not accept all the claimed expenditures as being 'necessary' even if they were understandable.[42]

As to reasonableness of the costs, the Court was satisfied that these expenditures (including counsel fees) were not disproportionate: and that that, rather than the English system of assessment of costs, was the relevant test. Nor would it limit the costs to a sum calculated by reference to the free legal aid scheme operated by the Commission.

As for interest on the sums allowed, the Court observed that it was only now that financial awards were being made and that therefore no interest ran from the judgment on the merits of April 1979. This claim was disallowed.

The impact of this developing case law on costs and fees is becoming clear. Thus in the most recent case on Article 50 — the *Airey* case — the Irish government, between judgment on the merits (9 October 1979) and judgment on Article 50 (6 February 1981), agreed to indemnify Mrs Airey against legal costs and expenditures (not yet assessed or paid) reasonably incurred in pursuing before the Irish Courts the remedy of judicial separation. (It was the lack of an effective right of access to the Irish High Court in respect of this that had been found to be in violation of the Convention.) But as Mrs Airey had legal aid in the Strasbourg proceedings, no recovery in respect of these under Article 50 was permitted.

When is an Applicant Entitled to Damages or Reparation?

The earliest European Convention case dealing directly with the subject of reparation for human rights violation was the so-called *Vagrancy* case (*de Wilde, Ooms and Versyp v. Government of Belgium*). The applicants had been detained under Belgian vagrancy laws and although claims under Article 5 were rejected by the Court, it did, in June 1971, affirm that there had been a breach of Article 5(4) in that the applicants 'had no remedy open to them before a court against the decisions ordering their detention'. The Court had followed the technique of ordering for the applicants the right, should the occasion arise, to apply for just satisfaction on this issue. At the end of July 1971 the applicants' counsel asked the Commission to request the Court to award damages for unlawful detention; and this was transmitted to the Court on 27 September 1971. The Belgian government asked the Court to rule that the conditions for the application of Article 50 had not been fulfilled, as the applicants had not sought reparation through the national courts. This aspect we have dealt with above (p. 52), and the contention was rejected by the Court. The claims were neither inadmissible nor ill-founded. There were, as Article 50 requires, 'decisions or measures taken' which violated the Convention; this phrase included deficiencies in legislation and case law; and the applicants were 'injured parties' within the meaning of Article 50. None of this could be denied by the Government.

What the Government could do, however, was to question what loss the applicants had suffered and therefore whether damages were necessary. The applicants claimed 300 Belgian francs per day of their detention. The Court indicated:

> For this claim to be successful, it would be necessary that their deprivation of liberty had been caused by the absence — found by the Court to be contrary to Article 5(4) of the Convention — of any right to take proceedings before a court by which the lawfulness of their detention might be decided. But this is not the case here.[43]

Further, they had received free legal aid. Importantly, the Court then added: 'Finally, the Court does not find that in the present cases any moral damage could have been caused by the lack of a remedy which met the requirements of Article 5(4).' Thus although the claims under Article 50 were admissible, they did not succeed.

The shape of the Court's thinking (and the lines along which it has developed over the ensuing ten years) was thus clearly outlined. Costs may be recoverable, but they are unlikely to be where there is legal aid and/or no claim about them is made. Reparation will only be given if damages can be shown and the damage is directly attributable to the violation that the Court has found. The notion of 'moral damage' (i.e. non-quantifiable damage) is not ruled out, but it must meet the same test of attributability.

In the *Ringeisen* case the Court had found a violation of Article 5(3) (detention exceeding a 'reasonable time') and had in its judgment of Article 5(3) reserved the right for the applicant, should the occasion arise, to apply for just satisfaction. The procedural aspects of this case have been looked at above. The Government had in fact deducted the time spent in pre-trial detention from the custodial sentence passed on Ringeisen, and claimed that this amounted to full reparation. Moreover, pre-trial detention was a less strict regime. The Court thought that this was a factor to be

> taken into consideration in assessing the extent of the damage flowing from the excessive duration of that detention; but it does not in any way thus acquire the character of *restitutio in integrum*, for no freedom is given in place of the freedom unlawfully taken away.[44]

We here see the introduction of the yardstick of *restitutio in integrum* in the context of damages. The Court also noted that the detention made it more difficult for Ringeisen to terminate his bankruptcy. Ringeisen had requested reparation for 'material and non-material damage' and indicated financial loss. But the Court thought that he had neither submitted acceptable proof as to the loss nor shown its causal link with the excessive detention. Nor, as a matter of evidence, was it convinced that a significant deterioration in his health had occurred. Assessing all these factors, the Court awarded 20,000 DM to be paid in compensation.

In the *Neumeister* case the Court held on 27 June 1968 that Austria was in breach of Article 5(3) (detention for a period longer than a 'reasonable time'), and similar issues under Article 50 arose.[45] In this case not only was the time that had been spent in detention reckoned as part of his sentence, but he was granted remission as to the remainder of his sentence. The Court observed: 'While remission of sentence, like the reckoning of detention as part of a sentence, does not constitute real *restitutio in integrum*, it comes as close to it as is possible in the nature of things.'[46] The Court was therefore not prepared to award compensation for 'material damage'. The 'moral damage' of the unlawfully long detention continued, but the Court appeared to assess *this* by reference back to other factors it looked at in connection with material damage — namely, the full remission and the fact that that was 'far more advantageous to him than payment of a sum of money'.[47] The present writer finds this non-reference in reasoning difficult to appreciate. The only just satisfaction that the Court was prepared to give was in respect of lawyer's fees, as for most of the relevant proceedings Neumeister had not received free legal aid.

The case of *Engel and others* had concerned disciplinary measures against Dutch conscripts and had resulted in a finding that Engel's provisional strict arrest violated Article 5(1) and that the hearings *in camera* of charges against de Wit, Dona and Schul violated Article 6(1).[48] In the hearing on Article 50, the applicants did not allege any material damage, loss of income or legal expenses, but each of them claimed a 'symbolic sum' of 1,000 French francs for moral damage. The Commission itself followed the trend implied in the earlier cases of giving Article 5 violations some special status, by urging that financial compensation was due to Engel for breach of Article 5 'as such'. By contrast, the Commission thought that the Article 6(1) violation caused no special damage, and that in respect of that the judgment of itself should be regarded as just satisfaction. The Court affirmed this view. It found that Engel, during his deprivation of liberty in a manner contrary to Article 5(1), suffered moral damage through the 'disagreeable effects of a regime of strict arrest'. But in evaluating that moral damage, the Court could not overlook the brevity of the detention. Further, his provisional arrest was set off against the penalty imposed, and although – following *Neumeister* – this was not to be regarded as *restitutio in integrum*, it was relevant in assessing compensation.[49] A token award of 100 Dutch guilders was ordered. No suffering at all could be shown in respect of the unlawful *in camera* hearings, and no award was made in respect of that violation. A separate opinion was appended by Judges Ganshof van der Meersch and Evrigenis (which this writer must admit she does not understand) which indicated that they agreed that the *in camera* hearings gave rise to no just satisfaction, but for different reasons, namely:

> According to Article 50 of the Convention, the Court shall afford, on the conditions laid down in that provision, 'just satisfaction' to the injured party if it finds a breach of the Convention. It seems difficult to accept the proposition that the finding by the Court of a breach of the substantive provisions of the Convention, whilst constituting a condition for the application of Article 50, can at the same time be the consequence in law following from that same provision.[50]

The extent to which the Court will be prepared to do more than admit the principle of compensation for non-material damage was explored further in the *Marckx* case. In this case Belgian law concerning rights to property of an illegitimate child was found to violate the Convention.[51] The Court deemed the finding itself just satisfaction. But in a powerful joint dissent several judges rejected this finding. They observed that the claim for compensation by Paula Marckx and her daughter had been kept to a minimum due to their dignity and reticence.

> Their claim is for token satisfaction but such a satisfaction, due as compensation for moral damage, must retain a personal character adapted to the effects of law in their particular case; it is based . . . on the damage they have suffered and on the interest they have in being recognized individually as victims of the legal situation brought about by the State. What is more, neither in the Convention nor in the principles of international law are there to be found any rules preventing the grant, on such facts, of a token satisfaction appropriate to the individual concerned.[52]

In the *Konig* case[53] to which we have referred above, and in which the whole question of Article 50 was reserved, proceedings before the Frankfurt Administrative Court had been sufficiently dilatory to constitute a violation of the 'reasonable time' requirement in Article 6(1). The Court invited written pleadings and oral hearings on the Article 50 issue. The government had in the meantime offered 20,000 DM which the applicant had rejected as insufficient. He sought compensation in two regards — for what he termed the probably permanent ruin of his financial and professional situation, and the indirect lowering of his personal and professional reputation. He left the assessment of the sum to the Court's discretion. The Commission found it impossible to attribute specific material losses but thought that:

> account should be taken of the fact that the applicant was left in a prolonged state of uncertainty as to his professional future, and this at a time of life — between the ages of forty-nine (in 1967) and sixty (in 1978) — when a man is normally at the peak of his career.[54]

The Commission also thought that a breach of Article 6(1), of itself, should incur some award of damages. The Court noted that the various delays (concerning a withdrawal of Dr Konig's authorisation to practise) were overlapping and interconnected[55] and not susceptible to simple addition. Equally, it was extremely difficult to identify with precision the prejudice suffered as a result of these delays. Although an applicant should normally quantify his claim, the Court was prepared to forgo this requirement in the present case. The Court endeavoured to assess damage 'on an adjustable basis' and ordered payment of 30,000 DM. This did not appear to include any element for violation of article 6(1) 'of itself'.

The most recent case on Article 50 — the *Airey* case — was based on findings of violations of Articles 6(1) and 8 (family life) due to lack of effective access to the Irish High Court for purposes of petitioning for judicial separation.[56] Having reserved the position, the Court has now allowed £3,140 for 'miscellaneous expenses and mental anxiety'. A claim of unquantifiable non-financial damage has here succeeded in benefiting from Article 50, even outside of Articles 5 and 6.

In summary, it may be said that we now have an emerging international law of compensation for denials of human rights. The procedural aspects are becoming clearer and the substantive law is developing in an intellectually coherent fashion. Notions of restitution, of material loss and direct attributability, of compensation for personally expended costs and fees, are playing an important part. Questions of compensation for violation *per se,* and the circumstances in which awards will be made for the acknowledged head of moral damage, still remain to be further elaborated.

Notes

1. *United States Diplomatic and Consular Staff in Tehran (United States of America v. Iran),* ICJ Reports 1980, Judgment, para. 95(5). Losses to corporations and private persons were not a matter before the Court. Initially the President of the United States sought to use the freezing of Iranian assets as a vehicle for making provision for such damages. Later the matter fell to be resolved as part of the agreement reached between the two countries.

2. See D.P. O'Connell, *International Law,* 2nd edn (London: Stevens, 1970) vol. 2, p. 1116; and *Delgoa Bay Railway Co.,* Moore Int. Arb. (1893), 1865; *Shufeldt* case, UN Rep. Int. Arb. Awards, vol. 2, p. 1079 at 1099; *Robert H. May* case, UN Rep. Int. Arb. Awards, vol. 15, p. 47 at 71.

3. See the *I'm Alone* case, UN Rep. Int. Arb. Awards, vol. 3, p. 1609.

4. *Mavrommatis Concessions* case, PCIJ, series A, no. 5, p. 44.

5. ICJ Reports 1949, p. 35.

6. Article 13 and Explanatory Note to the Draft Convention on the International Responsibility of States for Injuries to Aliens, 55 *AJIL* (1961) 545 at 575.

7. But see M. M. Whiteman, *Digest of International Law* (Washington: USGPO for Department of State, 1967), vol. 8, pp. 1186ff.; and for an earlier and more detailed assessment, Whiteman, *Damages in International Law,* 2 vols. (Washington: USGPO for Department of State, 1937).

8. Text in Ian Brownlie, *Basic Documents on Human Rights*, 2nd edn (Oxford: Clarendon Press, 1980) p. 21.

9. Brownlie, *Basic Documents*, p. 128.

10. Ibid., p. 150; and see the admirable study by N. Lerner, *The UN Convention on the Elimination of all Forms of Racial Discrimination*, 2nd edn (Leyden: Sijthoft 1980).

11. Brownlie, *Basic Documents*, p. 242.

12. 'The proper approach is to regard an *injuria* or wrong as entitling the plaintiff to a judgment for damages in his favour without loss or damage, but where there is no loss or damage such judgment will be for nominal damages only.' H. McGregor on *Damages* (London: Sweet and Maxwell, 1972), para. 294.

13. 'It is sometimes said that the law presumes or implies damage in every breach of contract or in every tortious invasion of legal right, and that this, therefore, would justify an award of nominal damages in such cases without proof of actual loss . . . This approach is only confusing.' Ibid., para. 294.

14. Article 24 provides, 'Any High Contracting Party may refer to the Commission, through the Secretary-General of the Council of Europe, any alleged breach of the provisions of the Convention by another High Contracting Party.'

15. Article 25(1) provides, 'The Commission may receive petitions . . . from any person, non-governmental organization or group of individuals claiming to be the victim of a violation by one of the High Contracting Parties of the rights set forth in this Convention, providing that the High Contracting Party against which the complaint has been lodged has declared that it recognises the competence of the Commission to receive such petitions . . .'

16. *Ireland v. United Kingdom*, Judgment of 18 January 1978. Other interstate applications have been commenced but have been handled by the Commission and Committee of Ministers, who have no powers comparable to those given to the Court under Article 50.

17. And, incidentally, claims procedures for such categories of persons – regardless of any findings of breach under the Convention – had already been set up by the United Kingdom.

18. After an unsuccessful attempt at friendly settlement by the Commission, and in the alternative circumstances laid down in Article 48 of the Convention.

19. *Engel et al. v. the Netherlands*, Judgment of 8 June 1976.

20. Article 5 concerns the right to liberty and security of person.

21. Article 5(3) provides, 'Everyone arrested or detained in accordance with the provisions of paragraph 1(c) of this Article shall be brought promptly before a judge or officer authorised by law to exercise judicial power and shall be entitled to trial within a reasonable time or to release pending trial . . .'

22. For the Commission's functions in testing admissibility, see Articles 26 and 27 of the Convention.

23. In fact, his Article 50 application had been notified to the Commission and not directly to the Court. But the critical point was that it was not a 'new' application, which could still fail for various technical reasons to reach the Court.

24. Judgment, 22 June 1972, para. 18.

25. The European Court of Human Rights consists of the same number of judges as there are members of the Council of Europe. But for each case the Court consists of a chamber of seven judges. The Court's Rules of Procedure determine the selection of those seven.

26. Judgment, 22 June 1972, para. 15.

27. Judgment on the merits, 18 June 1971; and on Article 50, 10 March 1972.

28. Article 6(1) provides, 'In the determination of his civil rights and obligations or of any criminal charge against him, everyone is entitled to a fair and public hearing within a reasonable time by a independent and impartial tribunal

established by law . . . ' Article 8 provides, 'Everyone has the right to respect for his private and family life, his house and his correspondence.'

29. Judgment, 13 June 1979.

30. Article 3 provides, 'No one shall be subjected to torture or to inhuman or degrading treatment or punishment.'

31. Judgment, 25 April 1978, s.V.

32. Article 6(3)(c) provides that everyone charged with a criminal offence is entitled to 'the free assistance of an interpreter if he cannot understand or speak the language used in Court'.

33. 28 November 1978.

34. Judgment, 10 March 1980, para. 15.

35. Judgment, 28 June 1978.

36. Either directly or through those members of the Commission appearing before the Court: Rules 38 and 29 of the Rules of the Court. See further Rule 26(3) of the Commission's Rules of Procedure.

37. Judgment, 6 November 1980, para. 22.

38. As it had done in the *Neumeister* case, Judgment, 7 May 1974, para. 43.

39. *Neumeister* case, Judgment, 7 May 1974, para. 43; *Konig* case, Judgment, 10 March 1980, paras. 24-6.

40. Judges Sir Gerald Fitzmaurice, Liesch and Farinha. Judge Fitzmaurice dissented on the underlying basis of the judgment. He thought that, in view of the character of the case, the complex issues and the narrow majority in favour of a finding of a breach, the Court should exercise the full discretion which it had under Article 50 and award no costs (whether English or Strasbourg costs) to the applicants.

41. The Court had not made any such distinction in the *Neumeister* judgment, 7 May 1974, para. 42.

42. Thus the attendance of the editor of the *Sunday Times* and two of his staff at the reading of the judgment was not a 'necessary' expense: para. 35. Cf. the presence of the applicant during the hearings of the case, in respect of which the Court in the *Konig* case allowed costs.

43. *Vagrancy* cases, Judgment, 10 March 1972, para. 24.

44. Judgment, 22 June 1972, para. 21.

45. An interesting argument was advanced by the Government, which pointed to the provision in Article 5(5) that 'everyone who has been the victim of arrest or detention in contravention of the provisions of this Article shall have an enforceable right to compensation'. The Austrian government contended that this was a special rule for compensation which displaced the general rule in Article 50. The Court refrained that Article 5(5) lays down a rule of substance while Article 50 lays down a rule of competence, indicating the Court's role. Further, the Austrian view would lead to consequences incompatible with the aim and object of the Convention, in that a victim of violation of liberty of person would have to lodge successive petitions to be heard *de novo* over an extended period. Judgment, 7 May 1974, para. 31.

46. Ibid., para. 40.

47. Ibid., para. 41.

48. Judgment, 8 June 1976.

49. Judgment, 23 November 1976, para. 10.

50. Ibid., separate opinion.

51. Judgment, 13 June 1979.

52. Ibid., para. 33.

53. Judgment, 28 June 1978.

54. Judgment, 10 March 1980, para. 12.

55. At the time of the Judgment on the merits of 28 June 1978, one set of

proceedings (the running of a clinic) had been pending for over ten years; and the second (the practice of medicine) for more than seven.

    56.   Judgment, 9 October 1979.

3 PROHIBITIONS, RESTRAINTS AND SCIENTISTS

Barrie Paskins

This essay is about the moral and legal duties of defence scientists. I begin with some personal remarks which may serve to indicate the background to my argument. In 1971 I was a trained Cambridge philosopher looking for work. To my great surprise I found myself lecturing on the ethical aspects of war to students of military history, strategic studies and civil-military relations in a department of war studies. The post had been created through an approach by King's College to the Ministry of Defence at the suggestion of Sydney Bailey. Without the Ministry's funding and extraordinary forbearance and generosity I could never have embarked on the work of which the present essay is a part (and which is now supported by ordinary university funding). Sydney's combination of unwavering Quaker witness, meticulous scholarship, constructive criticism and patient respect for the plurality of opinions that are inescapable in the defence field is a challenge to many officials, activists and scholars. In the Council on Christian Approaches to Defence and Disarmament, of which Sydney has always been a leading member and through which I came to know him, it has been possible to pursue discussions that disclose areas of agreement underlying disagreement which tend to get concealed in the harsh polemics of much that passes for defence debate.[1] Sydney has also been a seminal examiner of the just war tradition,[2] insisting that it constitutes prohibitions and restraints upon the initiation and continuation of war rather than a formula for blessing the guns or a way of identifying cases in which war is a duty.[3] He has done much to make it clear that the law of war as developed and debated among modern lawyers and statesmen is a kind of continuation of the just war tradition in changed circumstances that include the sovereignty claimed by a plurality of states and the need, already at work in the classic just war texts, to make the principles increasingly definite in their meaning and institutionalised in their application. These notions have guided my argument in this essay. I have sought to take account both of the law's precise demands and of the intrinsically controversial questions of its larger meaning which need to be faced by a variety of people including, I shall argue, defence scientists. There is a widely shared feeling that science has somehow changed the nature of military affairs but ideas about how to respond to this change are hard to find. In this essay, I seek to show that the just war tradition and its modern offspring, the law of war, viewed in the precise but broad way characteristic of Sydney Bailey, can help us to think and act constructively to control 'the military-industrial complex'.

The ascendancy of defence science was, of course, demonstrated above all by the invention of nuclear weapons. The original initiative was by private individuals, refugees from Hitler's Europe who understood the theoretical possibility of a nuclear explosion and persuaded the British and American authorities of the grave implications that would result if Hitler were the first to develop an atom bomb. The theoretical and engineering work involved in making the bomb proved to be immense, drawing large numbers of highly gifted individuals into the Manhattan Project. The professional ethics and political involvements of the scientist[4] were altered drastically and irrevocably by the Manhattan Project. Before 1939 the researcher in, say, basic physics expected to publish his work for the attention of a world-wide scientific community set somewhat apart from the rush of ordinary affairs and, by its detached pursuit of knowledge, improving mankind by a route somewhat independent of the vicissitudes of politics. In the Manhattan Project even fundamental work was done in the deepest of secrecy and with a military objective. After Nagasaki, many of those involved had lost the optimistic faith that science can be counted on to advance the interests of humanity. Furthermore, at least some of the scientists had found themselves drawn into political decision-making about their work in an inferior capacity. For example, those invited to suggest how the atom bomb might be used best in the struggle against Japan were *allowed to express a view* without being furnished all of the available information (e.g. about Japanese peace feelers as early as 1944) and without being given any authority to decide how their invention should be used.

The deep involvement of scientists in the defence field has increased since 1945 in interaction with the quickening pace of technological innovation. Any scientist, from the purest researcher to the most product-oriented engineer, is likely to be doing work of military significance. He may not be in the position of those eminent scientists who amid fierce controversy drove through the invention of the hydrogen bomb, but so much of our technology is now military in its point or implication that his work can be expected at some time during his career to draw him into the great web of military affairs. What attitude if any should the scientist have to this likely involvement? What view should we, who are not scientists, take of the special responsibilities of our numerate brethren?

I have discussed these questions with a number of scientists very various in their expertise, age and rank, military involvement, politics and religion or philosophy. I have the impression from these conversations[5] that opinions divide broadly into two types which I shall call the private conscience view and the social responsibility view. The private conscience view is that questions about the scientist's involvement with military affairs are moral questions which must be left to the conscience of the individual scientist. It is for him to raise questions or not, and for him to answer for himself as seems right to him any questions he may see fit to raise. The social responsibility view is that science is part of a larger socio-economic-political whole about which the scientist needs a certain social scientific understanding if he is to avoid being irresponsible. The deep questions about his involvement with military affairs are inescapably political. Believers in the private conscience view seem to be scattered across the political spectrum; adherents to the social responsibility view tend to cluster towards the left. The suggestion I want to make in this essay is that there is a third possibility which promises to steer a kind of middle course between the private conscience and social responsibility views, and which can in logic be embraced by adherents of both of those views without contradiction. This third way offers a framework for the articulation of the defence scientist's responsibilities which respects the dignity of conscience and leaves open for further discussion the broad-brush political analyses and commitments which seem to be inseparable from the social responsibility view.

The private conscience view tends to minimise the extent to which defence scientists think about their moral responsibilities. There are at least four reasons for this. Left to oneself, one does not tend to brood on matters which might, on reflection, prove to be subversive of what one is doing, or painful to oneself: it is only human to refrain from moralising about one's own activity in critical spirit unless prodded to do so from without. Nor is it obvious how one should think about military affairs in moral terms. The intellectual climate which has shaped us all is imbued with pessimistic fatalism about the nature if not the outbreak of war. We now take it for granted that war will normally be total. That modern war is total war was an idea already gaining ground in World War I. That war came to be conceived as a struggle between whole nations to organise their entire human and material resources for victory; every man expected to be conscripted into the fight; great bitterness was felt against 'the home front' as though people not under fire had something to be ashamed of; and blockade constituted a massive and lethal if slow-working direct attack upon whole populations. The Nazi onslaught advanced the conviction that war is bound to be total by exposing peoples in 'peace' and war to genocide. Nazi aggression elicited from the Allies implementation of a strategy of indiscriminate bombing that had been in making from 1916 if not earlier, thus involving the defenders of humanity against Nazism in direct assaults upon noncombatants. Nuclear war would be still more indiscriminate and devastating, working genetic damage through future human generations and destroying in hours anything worth calling civilisation. 'Small wars' regularly involve military attacks upon, and violent intimidation of, civilians who are claimed as being part of a political struggle entitled to conscript everyone. If war is thus total, what is there for private conscience to think about?

A third reason why the private conscience view inhibits reflection upon the defence scientist's responsibilities is to be found in a shift of meaning that the word 'conscience' has undergone.[6] In the medieval period, conscience was thought of as consciousness of moral truth. The appropriate authorities instructed people in this truth, requiring them to deploy it as the framework of their moral reasoning. The Reformation spread a conviction that in religion and (later) in morality matters of conscience were for the individual, alone with his Bible, to judge. Conscience has come to mean something very like conviction. The more 'conscience' is thought to be a private, ultimately unarguable conviction of right and wrong as contrasted with a consciousness of correct principles the same for all rational beings, the more the individual who relies on his conscience is apt to have no structured thinking to do about moral matters in which the relevant principles are unobvious. The principles of just war are unobvious especially in an age that believes in total war, so the individual is apt to find himself with very little principled guidance about how to reflect upon what responsibilities he may have as one involved with military affairs.

Finally, a certain kind of understanding of democracy tends to minimise the extent to which private conscience prompts substantial moral thinking about politically sensitive issues. This has been made explicit to me by scientists who hold the private conscience view. Who am I, they say, to usurp political authority? Morals must be distinguished from politics; political action is subject to domocratic political control in the West; it is for the authorities, not me, to decide about the (political, not moral) rights and wrongs of the military significance that my work

may possess. It is for the authorities in the light of intelligence information, much of which is quite properly secret, to judge what defensive
and deterrent military programmes are needed, not for a private individual to decide that his country should not engage in research into
chemical and biological warfare. No individual in our country is forced
to work on research that is against his conscience. If he undertakes
defence work, he thereby acquires a commitment to secrecy as laid
down by the competent, democratic authorities. If he subsequently
develops scruples of conscience, he is permitted to resign but continues
to be bound by his freely given undertaking of confidentiality. His
conscience is respected at all stages, and he in turn must respect the
discretion democratically accorded to the political authorities.

Whatever the merits of our belief in total war, of the post-Reformation
understanding of conscience and of the democracy argument, these
factors interact with one another and with inclination to inhibit the
defence scientist's thinking about his responsibilities. What of the social
responsibility view? It pictures military affairs as part of a larger pattern.
The primary importance of this pattern is far from self-evident, as
debate about the significance of the military-industrial complex in US
foreign and military policy attests. No one doubts that commercial
considerations, bureaucratic politics, interservice rivalry and so on are
factors in decision-making, but to establish their primacy involves the
adopting of highly controversial analytic assumptions, usually involving
some type of Marxist perspective. Furthermore, there is a plurality of
such analyses available, perhaps inevitably. Those who would instruct
or prick the defence scientist's conscience from within the social
responsibility view are therefore faced with formidable obstacles. Some
consciences are closed to such goadings by the questionable assumptions
whereby military affairs are made to depend on underlying structures;
others will be confused, repelled or drawn into conflicts among differing
social responsibility analyses by the plurality of counsels on offer. Nor
are these counsels to be depended on to guide the defence scientist
about *what to do*: the very depth of the supposed structure makes one
doubt the possibility of worthwhile remedial action, and some analyses
though not all attribute to the substructure a determinism which makes
it pointless to kick against the drift of history. The result of this impasse
between the private conscience and social responsibility views is a
depressing babel which lacks agreed assumptions and the possibility of
moving towards agreed assumptions from which the argument may proceed with the mutual respect that should flow from common principle.

Is this inevitable? It might be. We are all too accustomed in the late twentieth century to thinking of ourselves as inhabiting a time of vanished consensus in which we expect on a huge variety of topics to be talking past one another out of different, incommensurable thought-worlds. Nevertheless, I shall argue that in the matter of the scientist's responsibilities for the military point or implications of his work we can make surprisingly common cause. The unifying factor is what I shall call, in broad terms, the law of war.

The Nuremberg Trial and a huge complexity of law, institution and thought which has flowed from it is most instructive about the defence scientist's responsibilities.[7] Those who drew up the Charter of the International Military Tribunal which conducted the trial[8] knew that they were going to be faced with pleas by the defendants of act of state and superior orders. The act of state plea was going to be that the accused could not be held responsible for actions he performed as a state official. The plea of superior orders was going to be that defendants could not be held accountable when acting on orders. In the Charter, act of state is rejected completely, as constituting neither defence nor grounds for mitigation of punishment. Superior orders is rejected as a defence but might constitute a ground for mitigation of punishment, the latter presumably in recognition of the pressure to obey in a military or quasi-military organisation. Outright rejection of act of state and qualified rejection of superior orders remains the law today. It is one focus of a great shift in the nature of international law. Before Nuremberg, international law was pictured as being a system regulating relations among states. Nuremberg brought the individual into the international legal arena. It insisted that every individual is answerable for his actions to international criminal law. Subsequent development of this thought, e.g. in the UN, has concentrated largely though not exclusively on the rights of individuals. The controversial preoccupation with human rights illustrates this. But what we need to ponder for present purposes is the Nuremberg and post-Nuremberg law concerning individual *duties*. The duties of the soldier relative to the law of war have been clarified since Nuremberg and furnish a useful model for thinking about the duties of the defence scientist.

The law now establishes a clear division of responsibilities, requiring the state to instruct its soldiery in the laws and customs of war and the soldier to disobey manifestly illegal orders.[9] The demand that states teach the law of war to their soldiers is eminently reasonable, since this law is not something one could be expected to think of for oneself: it is something one needs to be taught. The obligation to instruct can be met to the letter in ways that show contempt for its spirit. It is alleged, for example, that conscripts destined for Vietnam were taught the law of war before leaving the US on wet days by instructors whose style spoke contempt for the rules.[10] This is contrary to the point of the law, which (it is plain) needs the state to put its authority behind the rules if they are to carry conviction with sceptical soldiers.

The requirement that a soldier disobey manifestly illegal orders presumably refers to orders whose illegality would be manifest to one properly instructed in the laws of war. It would obviously be unreasonable to require soldiers to disobey all illegal orders, for this would involve the subordinate in evaluating the often inescapably secret purposes of his military and political superiors. The law could perhaps be somewhat more demanding: rejection of orders that it would be reasonable to think illegal might be enjoined. But even this would set the soldier in judgement over his superiors and it is not surprising that his legal duty is minimal.

It is on reflection astounding that the law is more demanding of soldiers than of scientists. In the great cycle from research and development through deployment to combat use, the soldier occupies a peculiarly difficult position, subject as he is to the rigours of military discipline, the emphasis upon obedience and loyalty in the military ethos and not least the urgent dangers of combat. The defence scientist is not liable to be shot at in battle. He works far from the field of combat in an environment in which there is or should be room if anywhere for sustained deliberation about the legitimacy of actions that may have military significance. If the soldier is required only to disobey manifestly illegal orders, some higher expectation seems in order with respect to the scientist in view of his greater freedom of manoeuvre. But this is not what we find. Instead, the law imposes no specific obligation upon the defence scientist corresponding to that laid down for the soldier. Here, surely, is a loophole which needs to be closed if the law is to continue to develop towards clear articulation of the international duties of the individual.

Does it matter whether the soldier has, or the scientist lacks, clear duties laid down for him relative to the law of war? What is it about this law that is worth the effort given the absence of an international law enforcement agency and the widespread disillusion with the way in which the UN has discharged its Charter obligations to provide a new context for international relations? Two functions of law need to be distinguished if we are to answer these questions.[11] First, the law of war like domestic criminal law has the usual function of regulating conduct and providing for the punishment of offenders. All armies have military codes of law. These codes are evidence of what the law of war is at a given time and normally incorporate explicit international law as it evolves. Armies have this law not out of nebulous internationalist sentiment but because an army without law would lack discipline and amount to no more than a lethally dangerous armed mob. Not the least important reason for proceeding with prosecutions for massacres, however invidiously selective such prosecutions may be in leaving the high command untouched, has been in order for the rule of law in the affected army to be (re-)asserted. The controversial prosecutions of Lieutenant Calley and Major Medina for the My Lai massacre illustrate this.[12]

A second function of the law of war is to provide a framework for the examination of foreign and military policy. An example may serve to make this plain. The political campaigns against US involvement in Vietnam drew heavily upon concepts hammered out for and at the Nuremberg Trial. These concepts were peculiarly appropriate in that the US, having applied them to Nazi Germany (and Japan), could hardly complain if its conduct in turn was measured by them. Within the Nuremberg precedent, two distinct bases were found for objection to American policy.[13] One line of argument, pursued for example by the Sartre-Russell tribunal, concentrated on the types of action classified at Nuremberg as crimes against peace and crimes against humanity. These correspond roughly to post-Nuremberg discussions of aggression and genocide respectively. Applying them involves large-scale judgement on the nature and intent of a state's military activity. Thus the leaders in Nazi Germany were charged with conspiring to wage aggressive war; critics of US involvement on this count sought to establish that the US was and North Vietnam was not an aggressor. Nazi leaders were charged with planning and carrying through the mass murders, slaveries, crushing deportations and so on which have made them the very image of evil in the postwar world: critics of US policy drew analogies between such genocide and, for example, the strategic hamlets policy by which South Vietnamese villagers were removed from their homes for military purposes.

A different line of argument concentrated upon war crimes. War crimes, such as wanton destruction beyond the necessities of combat, have long been prohibited in manuals of military law. If there was any innovation with respect to them at Nuremberg it was merely that high-ranking officials were brought to book. The category of war crime constituted a basis for protesting against the US involvement

in Vietnam without standing in judgement over the causes espoused
by the belligerents or the aims pursued relative to populations. The
argument was that atrocities had been committed and in the type
of war that had proved inescapable were unavoidable. The war must
be abandoned on principle because of the impossibility of avoiding
such atrocities.

Both of these types of criticism of the US intervention elicited
counter-argument couched in the same basic legal terms. Thus, the
Nuremberg concepts furnished a common vocabulary of moral discourse. Within this vocabulary there were conceptual choices to be
made, for example concerning the relative importance of aggression,
genocide and war crimes, as well as the possibility of disagreement
about how the particular case, America's record in Vietnam, stood
relative to the legal categories. The law thus fulfilled a function other
than, over and above, that of regulating conduct and providing for the
punishment of offenders. It provided for well-ordered, mutually intel-
ligible argument about policy. I am of course not suggesting that this
tidiness characterised all of the acrimonious polemic about the Vietnam
war. The availability of the common language is what concerns me, not
the undoubted capacity of human beings to refrain from availing
themselves of what is available.

The lawyer on a case and the soldier anxious not to be had up
for war crimes want to know what 'the law' is. But in so far as what
interests one is the law's ability to provide a framework for the discussion
of policy, one need not be too dismayed if one is confronted with
diversity and conflict among legal principles rather than with the
unambiguous ruling which, ideally, settles any question of law in a
particular case. An example of such tension is to be found in the
Nuremberg concepts. The tribunal had to choose between two possible
understandings of 'crime against humanity'. On one interpretation, such
crime might be committed in 'peace' without any relation to war, for
example in the atrocities of the Nazi regime within Germany before the
first of Hitler's international aggressions. But the tribunal decided
instead to confine its attention to crimes against humanity committed
in connection with the criminal conspiracy to wage aggressive war. No
doubt one reason for this narrowing of the court's terms of reference
lay with Stalin, who could hardly have welcomed an enquiry that
would involve *tu quoque* reference to the Great Terror and whom the
Allies were ardent to keep a party to the trial. Another reason is more
interesting, however, for it illustrates a dilemma of international order.
If one determines to count as criminal state acts wholly unconnected

with the prosecution of war then one has moved a long way towards recognising a legitimate cause of war other than the one which both the League of Nations and the UN have insisted is the sole legitimate cause of international war, namely defence against aggression. The point is readily illustrated by Vietnam's intervention in Kampuchea. The Pol Pot regime appears to have perpetrated in time of 'peace' precisely the kinds of abomination condemned at Nuremberg as crimes against humanity. An intervention which has put a stop to these actions and removed their perpetrators from political authority is hard to condemn; yet the UN has seen fit to make such condemnation. The Nuremberg precedent has served the UN well in this regard.

There is thus a tension between the ideas of aggression and genocide. A large part of the point of the idea of aggression is to remove war as a legitimate instrument of foreign policy by prohibiting aggression and making defence against it the sole just cause of war. Genocide seems equally abominable whenever it occurs but if thought criminal in every case threatens to undermine the basic norms whose aim is to prevent war by removing its pretexts.

One should not in reason be unduly perturbed about such conflicts among even rather basic principles. Aristotle made plain that one mark of rationality is to look for no greater precision than one's subject-matter permits, and that unambiguous conclusions beyond rational dispute in particular cases are not to be expected in ethics and politics.[14]

The uncertainty and indeterminacy of particular cases did not prevent Aristotle from contributing mightily to the development of a substantive philosophy of morals and politics, nor need it prevent the law of war from providing a significant framework for the analysis of foreign and military policy. The law matters in different ways to persons with different responsibilities and opportunities. For the soldier who must act under the urgencies of danger and military discipline, clear-cut instructions are what is needed. For those with a place in military affairs less urgent and permitting more latitude for reasoning and controversy, the law as framework is what counts. This, I think, is the key to our problem concerning the responsibilities of the defence scientist.

Let us proceed by analogy with the soldier. What division of responsibilities would be reasonable if one wanted to close the loophole whereby the defence scientist, unlike the soldier, has no specific duties relative to the law of war? In what should he be instructed, by whom and with what consequent obligations and accountability?

The scientist needs to know both some of the fine-print complexities of the law and also something of its broad history, purposes, dilemmas and relation to technology. Clear-cut rules of action of the sort a soldier requires to control combat are less important for the defence scientist than the informed conviction that there are questions to be asked about the lawfulness of his work, answers to which are to be sought within relatively definite limits and fairly well defined areas of legitimate controversy. This is the knowledge appropriate to his position. With it, he should be able to contribute towards making the law applicable to the early stages of the research-development-deployment-use cycle.

Education in these matters needs to be by persons competent in law in the rather broad sense that we have been considering and at the same time possessing enough acquaintance with the nature of scientific work to command the respect of defence scientists. And if the soldier analogy is any guide, the appropriate educators require some form of backing which lends political authority to their work. In the case of the soldier the task of finding appropriate educators and backing them devolves upon the state. In the scientist's case, two possible authorities seem to be worth considering: the state and the profession. Regulation of the conduct of medical personnel is to a large extent by professional bodies backed by the force of domestic law. Such co-operation provides a useful model for thinking about the education of defence scientists. In this essay I shall not make precise suggestions for institutional action, leaving this for further discussion once the broad argument has been made plain. One does need some picture of how instruction in the law of war might be effected, however. Perhaps the most prudent route would be for the UN to require states to encourage and report progress among the scientists' professional bodies towards seeing to it that knowledge of the law of war becomes an integral part of every defence scientist's education.

The obligation of a soldier consequent upon his instruction in the law of war is that he disobey manifestly illegal orders. The obligation that should devolve upon the defence scientist cannot be pinned down so precisely. One is worried about the scientist because the growing research and development efforts of which he is a part are peculiarly difficult to control even given the will. Suppose the title of his research project is published: this is utterly uninformative to the innumerate citizen such as myself and almost equally unilluminating, I am told, even for the scientifically literate worker in a closely kindred field. Furthermore, very many scientists are innocents about strategy and proceed in almost entire ignorance of the basic characteristics of the strategic ideas by which the societies in which they live conduct military affairs. As things stand now, external regulation of 'the military-industrial complex' is simply unfeasible even given the political will: any watchdog would have insuperable technical difficulties invigilating defence-related work, and a grave political problem of balancing defence secrecy and the need to be at a distance from the state. As for self-regulation by the scientists, so long as the scientist's responsibilities are seen exclusively in terms of the private conscience and social responsibility views there seems to be no way in which the scientists, who occupy many different points on the moral and political spectra, can make common cause to move towards self-regulation. This is the problem from which to determine the responsibilities of the defence scientist who has been educated in the law of war. It is of course imperative for him to use his freedom of enquiry to ensure that his work is not contributing to definite breaching of the law of war (for example, by contributing to the development of illegal weapons). Equally if not more important is that he accept a modicum of responsibility to contribute to extending the capacity of the law of war to regulate all aspects of the weapons cycle and not solely the intrinsically difficult stage of the cycle at which soldiers in danger have the new weapons in their hands. To formulate the defence scientist's responsibility in this way is to recognise the enormous discretion that lies with him. Our dependence on him in this regard, however, is not a weakness in my argument but a stark fact. What I am attempting to do is not to curtail this freedom of his by some external fiat but to draw attention to that body of thought which may enable him to exercise his freedom in the knowledge that he has it and that it brings with it a responsibility which forms part of the international duties of the individual.

The law's demands upon the soldier are backed by stern sanctions. He may be imprisoned or executed for war crimes. The professional demands upon a doctor are also backed by sanctions which, together with the law, carry serious implications for the individual (e.g. the implications of being struck off). What sanctions if any should be part of the defence scientist's duties? The sanction I would propose is a modest one: that the individual be answerable to his professional body for the discharge in good faith of his obligation to avoid work on projects which are prohibited by the law of war and to join in extending that law to regulate the entire weapons cycle. This may rarely or never mean a penalty such as striking off but one would be mistaken if one supposed that accountability without such sanctions is toothless: many will be concerned to be good professionals for the sake of professionalism; some of those, not least the ambitious, who lack such high standards, will nevertheless have an anxiety about reputation which will give professional expectations a hold over them. Above all, perhaps, the body of argument which professional seriousness about this matter would inevitably call forth would surely make *recherché* work more available to and regulable by a wider public.

I am, then, suggesting the following division of responsibility:

for the UN, to prod states towards encouraging initiatives by professional bodies;

for states, to strengthen (not least by supportive legislation) such moves as may be forthcoming from professional bodies to incorporate education in the law of war among the requirements for professional competence of members who are likely to engage in scientific activity with military significance;

for professional bodies, to find educators capable of developing in the scientist serious practical reflectiveness about the relation between the detailed provisions of the law of war, the purposes of that law and the legality and morality of his own work;

for the individual scientist, to make reasonably extensive enquiries to ensure that a project does not threaten to contribute towards breach of the law of war, and to join in extending that law's power to regulate and contain the destructive potential of military affairs.

I shall call this proposal the authority of law view of the defence scientist's responsibilities. It represents a genuine alternative to the private conscience and social responsibility views, but is not incompatible with them in the way that they are with one another.

About the private conscience view, I should say that on some matters if not all there is a distinction to be drawn between a well-informed conscience and the conscience which is not well-informed of a person however worthy. The informing in question is not a matter of being up to date with the latest information so much as of practical familiarity with the relevant principles: in the case of defence, with the principles of the law of war. A defence scientist could be a wholly admirable individual and yet lack a well-informed conscience on defence questions through ignorance (not by any means wholly his own fault) of the relevant principles.

This argument is neither dogmatic nor anti-democratic. It is undogmatic in that I am calling for a balanced, rounded education in the law of war that makes plain divergences of view where these exist and aims to bring it about that the well-informed defence scientist can think for himself within the widely agreed outlines of long-running world-wide debate. The argument avoids being anti-democratic in that the law of war is something to which all the world's democracies have, in the wisdom of separate sovereignties, committed themselves. The law has been and continues to be made by states. The most determined adherent of the view that democracy is the final arbiter of right in political and military affairs cannot dismiss the law of war as an alien imposition: it was made by that to which he looks as the final authority. Believers in the private conscience view should in reason modify their opinion to support something like the authority of law view which I have been outlining.

Adherents of the social responsibility view differ one from another in their understanding of law in general and/or international law specifically. Some see it as so much a mere reflection of underlying structures or events, a mere instrument of political struggle, that the authority of law view can have little to commend it unless as tactics. But there seems to be a broad band of believers in social responsibility that recognises law and international law as constituting something of an independent variable in our history, capable of working changes in our predicament in terms at least partly independent of the vicissitudes of partisan politics. For this group, the authority of law view should have its attractions. It does not require them to view law as an entirely independent reality, nor to accept the finality of states' actions in determining what to do politically. If law is interpreted in the broad way I have been suggesting, the tensions between members of this group, and between them and their opponents, can be contained, reformulated and somewhat transformed within the authority of law view.

A group of engineering students with whom I was discussing the problem of social responsibility in science volunteered a terse summary of the moral-professional guidance that they as trainee engineers had been given: if your bridge falls down, you might go to prison. Yet the scientist's responsibilities, at least in respect of military affairs, excite eager interest among students. It is not that the subject is rebarbatively dry. Given the will and a sound conception of the aim, education in this field can count on seizing the imagination of those who are to be educated. Such education cannot usefully be a merely factual presentation, for this would swamp the students with information to no useful purpose. Nor would it be appropriate in a secular society such as ours to structure the education according to the just war principles. Any intelligent interest in the law of war is bound to consider those principles as representing a way in which the law might be developed, but to make them the central focus would be to presuppose a jurisprudence (natural law) which is highly controversial. The law of war, to which states have bound themselves, is an altogether more promising framework, confronting the student with fascinating factual material in a way that emphasises practical and moral issues.

I am aware that the terms in which I have developed the argument of this essay need refining. For example, I have spoken of 'the law of war' in a loose and question-begging way which might make a lawyer weep. Such imprecision need not be damaging. It is not for a philosopher specialising in war studies to tell the defence scientists exactly how to conceive of their responsibilities. I have sought only to draw attention to inadequacies of the current conceptions of these responsibilities, to highlight an anomaly whereby more is demanded of the hard-pressed soldier than of the scientist, and to outline a programme which may permit the profession to initiate effective self-examination. It would be impertinent for me to be too categorical or prematurely concrete. The next step, if my argument is sound, should presumably be for a group of sympathetic scientists, lawyers, defence experts and enthusiasts to frame a more concrete, agreed proposal for UN initiative.

There is an incongruity between the modest proposal which I have been outlining and the stark dangers with which military developments are confronting the world, dangers both urgent and seeming to require the most drastic and radical of changes in our political environment. Ultimately, I believe, such incongruities have to be accepted as a brute fact of human life, but a general remark about them seems in order. One is strongly tempted to feel that as a political problem becomes deeper and darker, the appropriate response needs to deepen and darken. The moderate strikes one as becoming increasingly irrelevant as our circumstances worsen. The temptation to think thus is misleading and dangerous. Man is so passionate that he is apt to become reasonable only when he has to, only when experience has removed all other options. This applies above all to military problems. Proposals to mend matters by remedies that can be counted on to constitute further causes (just or unjust) for military deployments or political violence are contrary to reason. What we need is not the deep analysis which, however true, can be given effect only by the sword. We need to be driven to the point where the only option is moderation. The forces of technology and political disintegration are driving us that way hard. Extension of the law of war through the self-regulation of scientists out of professional conviction seems to me the kind of moderation that is *timely* as the world darkens. If we are to use the nuclear weapons we have invented to wipe ourselves out, I should rather that Armageddon find me arguing such proposals than pointing a gun at my neighbour to keep him out of my fall-out shelter, or dancing around the maypole of my nation's sovereignty to celebrate driving allied forces from my soil.

Notes

1. This useful organisation seeks to accommodate all of whatever conviction, or of none, who believe that Christian perspectives on defence and disarmament need to be taken seriously. It can be contacted through its director at St Katharine Cree, 86 Leadenhall Street, London EC3A 3DH.

2. *Prohibitions and Restraints in War* (London: Oxford University Press for the Royal Institute of International Affairs, 1972).

3. Michael Walzer, *Just and Unjust Wars* (London: Allen Lane, 1978) seeks a doctrine of just war that makes some operations mandatory, but his premisses and preoccupations are not those of the classic just war writers.

4. Cf. Robert Jungk, *Brighter than a Thousand Suns* (London: Gollancz & Hart-Davis, 1958; Harmondsworth: Penguin, 1964).

5. It would be very interesting to see whether systematic investigation confirms my impression. I suspect that such investigation would need to supplement questionnaire by interview since the issues are not readily susceptible to cut-and-dried questionnaire formulation.

6. For a good discussion see Michael Walzer, *Obligations* (Cambridge, Massachusetts: Harvard University Press, 1970).

7. General introductions to Nuremberg are Peter Calvocoressi, *Nuremberg: the Facts, the Law, and the Consequences* (London: Chatto & Windus, 1947); Robert K. Woetzel, *The Nuremberg Trials in International Law* (London: Stevens, 1962); and (parts of) Barrie Paskins and Michael Dockrill, *The Ethics of War* (London: Duckworth, 1979).

8. Reprinted by Calvocoressi, *Nuremberg.*

9. Morris Greenspan, *The Modern Law of Land Warfare* (Berkeley, California: University of California Press, 1959), p. 495.

10. Robert Jay Lifton, *Home from the War* (London: Wildwood House, 1974).

11. I have found Roger Fisher, *Points of Choice* (London: Oxford University Press, 1978) helpful in envisaging the variety of functions that law can have.

12. Mary McCarthy, *Medina* (London: Wildwood House, 1973) is a perceptive discussion of the massacre.

13. This part of my argument derives from Telford Taylor, *Nuremberg and Vietnam* (New York: Bantam, 1971).

14. *Ethics,* book 1, ch. 3.

4 THE ETHICS OF SECURITY
Edward Rogers

It is a privilege to offer a tribute to Sydney Bailey. When he writes or speaks on some complex aspect of defence or disarmament he is read or listened to always with well-deserved respect; often with admiring wonder. He never evades awkward questions or makes facile judgements. Others in this volume will no doubt refer to such books of his as *Prohibitions and Restraints in War* and his writings on the peaceful settlement of international disputes. I have been his colleague on committees and working parties, borrowing largely from the riches of his mind and deferring to his wisdom. Frequently I have heard his masterly expositions on behalf of the Division of International Affairs to Assemblies of the British Council of Churches. His expertise is acknowledged. But it is always obvious that for him the mastering of technical detail or political analysis has never been an end in itself. It is the necessary means to the end of making a personal contribution, and of helping others to contribute intelligently, to the establishment of a more peaceful and more just world. He is a committed Christian. Though the problems he tackles with such meticulous care are strategic, diplomatic or legal, he is sure that when they are analysed they are fundamentally moral. It is therefore altogether fitting that in this offering from his friends and admirers there should be an essay on the ethics of security. My own immediate personal problem is that he would certainly be the best person to write it.

Plunging in at the deep end, preparatory to temporary strategic withdrawal, I assert that two of the major contemporary security debates are inescapably moral. One is related to the Christian doctrine of stewardship, the right use of the large but finite resources of the planet. It is an incontrovertible, distressing fact that vastly more skill, wealth and material is devoted to 'defence' than to 'welfare'. The development of developing countries is crippled, the economies of the developed distorted, by the burden of the defence expenditure that they feel compelled to bear. It may be argued that the imbalance is deplorable but necessary. It may be argued that it is stupid and wrong. Each is an ethical judgement.

The second major debate relates to the concept of 'deterrence', which is greatly exercising the minds of the theologians. The simple theory is that the assurance of powerful retaliation helps to deter a would-be aggressor. The production of nuclear weapons, and their possession by a limited number of nations, has disturbed the simplicity by infusing into it the sophisticated concept of a balance of nuclear terror. We have grown used to thinking of deterrence as meaning that the United States and the Soviet Union have been deterred from open war because their nuclear armouries are more or less evenly matched. It is considered that global war will best be averted if the armouries of these two major powers remain at rough parity. One objective of the Strategic Arms Limitation Talks between the USA and the USSR has been to give to each side confidence that the balance will be maintained. One reason for the protracted hassles in negotiation and hesitation over ratification is suspicion that the other side might prove to have the decisive edge if the showdown came. But when one considers calmly the probable consequences of a nuclear war it is reasonable to ask if the use of, or even the declared intention to use, such weapons can ever be morally justified. The question is plain enough, but the answer is not; as two brief comments in a 1962 report to the British Council of Churches will testify.

No Christian can rest easy in his conscience while his nation is prepared to annihilate vast populations in another country.

While the Churches are bound to bear witness to this fundamental situation . . . such witness does not of itself reveal the way of escape.[1]

We must return later to these debates, hoping to come to some conclusions about them, but it would be wise to lead to them by way of preliminary reconnaissance of the ground. 'Security' is a Protean word, meaning different things in different contexts, ranging from keeping confidential information secret to stationing cruise missiles. Some clarification and classification is essential if we are not to be baffled by the various shades of meaning. As a later British Council of Churches report, *The Search for Security*, helpfully observed on its second page:

The word has become a *mélange* of concepts; it has become elusive because there are in it so many shades of meaning. It conjures up the preservation of national identity, the display of military strength, fear of aggression, or the preservation of an existing political or social system. It is beginning to acquire the additional overtone of near-pathological obsession with secrecy. If our problem is considered to be essentially a security problem, there is real danger that discussion will go no further than proximate ends, and that it will be imprisoned in confusing and misleading categories. This does not necessarily mean that the word security must be rejected. It does mean that it must be much more precisely interpreted and defined.[2]

(I venture to quote this at length as I wrote it myself.)

One thing at least is clear. Security most certainly cannot be what the military strategists would dearly love it to be, an impregnable defence against any possible form of attack from every conceivable source. The force screens of the science fiction spaceships manage it, but they have not been invented yet. On that understanding security is something relative, not absolute; a complex, maybe, of diplomatic activity and military preparedness designed to preserve the nation in reasonable safety; not a 100 per cent guarantee but the best that can be obtained with the available national skill and resources in a fluctuating international situation. So defined it may be held that the objective is ethically justifiable; provided, that is, that that which is to be defended is national safety and not national ossification.

All human societies are continually changing, for change — and adaptation to change — is essential to survival. But change is disturbing. It challenges a deep-rooted desire to keep things as they are, to stay with the familiar, for 'life was so much richer and happier in the good old days': untrue but psychologically congenial. So it is that tucked within the *mélange* of concepts associated with security is the idea of stability; fair enough if it corresponds to the stability of a journeying ship, delusive if it means social rigidity. If it were ever possible to prevent any movement, which is highly improbable, the deadly result would be social paralysis. There have been many periods in human history when change has come very slowly. There have been others, like our own, when all seems to be in the melting pot. But so long as it is evident that no form of economic relationship, political regime or international order is perfect — and that has been the case throughout recorded history, is so now and will be so in the foreseeable future — change is desirable, provided that it is in the right direction.

As always, a nice, neat conclusion — with a proviso that blurs all the edges. Who is to decide, and how, what is the right direction? Tactfully stepping aside from all the implications of that deceptively simple question, it may be said that though there is room for lively debate about specific next steps there should at least be general agreement that the direction desired is towards the establishment of institutions and implementation of actions that will further promote human welfare.

It follows therefore that the 'reasonable safety' which can be commended preserves the liberty to develop such institutions and to encourage such actions. Choice and approval depend upon ethical appraisal. Quoting again from *The Search for Security* I select a passage which Sydney Bailey believed to be of central importance:

> We are looking to the furtherance of a human society that can liber-ate and encourage the development of human potentiality; a society which proclaims and defends positive values discovered and revealed, but which is responsive to the changes necessary to promote such liberation and encouragement. The Christian firmly believes that such a goal is in accordance with the will of God, but that it can be attained only with the guiding power of the Holy Spirit.

I have deliberately omitted one brief phrase from that quotation. The text actually begins: 'We are looking beyond security to the furtherance . . .'[3] On further reflection I am moving to the view that an ethically valid concept of security must include within itself the defence and extension of right values.

The incorporation of a specifically ethical dimension underlines the necessity of maintaining a clear distinction between absolute and relative security. Coming at once to the crucial point, it is an axiom of theology that the slaughter and destructive energies of war are evil and contrary to the will of God. It is an axiom of applied ethics that in a world of sinful and disobedient humans the Divine purpose will be frustrated and delayed. The two consequent conclusions are: (a) that total security demands total obedience to the will of God expressed in the Dominical commands of love to God and love to one's neighbour; and (b) that, failing this, we must strive for a better ordering of society, national and international, moving as close to the ideal as we can get but always acknowledging that we shall fall short of the goal.

The distinction between the absolute and the relative is clearly seen in the doctrine of the just war, as also is the tension between them. The doctrine in its classical form is by no means a bald assertion that war is justified. On the contrary, it is a carefully reasoned argument that war is indeed evil but that, provided that there are due restraints on and in its waging, it may in certain precisely defined circumstances be the lesser of two evils. Resort to war must be undertaken only when every peaceful means of righting an evident wrong has been tried and has failed. The force employed must be enough, and no more, to secure the victory that is sought. There must be sufficient reason to believe that the good intended will be greater than the evil inevitably wrought in fighting for a good cause. There must also be good reason to believe that the victory will be won. Finally, the means employed must be in accordance with man's nature as a rational being, with moral principles and with such international obligations as the nation going to war has previously accepted.

Because so much of my active ministry was spent, at the command of my Church, in dealing with current problems, I am using the scanty spare time of my so-called retirement to delve more deeply into history. I have just finished a fascinating course on Britain in the period between the departure of the Romans and the arrival of the Normans. I am now working my way through the Napoleonic Wars and, at the time of writing this, have reached the eve of Waterloo. With all the gory detail fresh in mind, the admirably lucid restrictions of the just war look like paper chains, casually snapped by the pressures of international disagreement and shrivelling in the flames of conflict. Judged by the doctrinal criteria there have been singularly few just wars; few that have been preceded by earnest and vigorous exploration of peaceful resolutions of a dispute; many that have been cynically stage-managed; few in which the force used has been willingly reduced to the minimum necessary. In general, it must be regretfully concluded, wars have been fought in accordance with man's nature as an irrational being.

This is not to say, of course, that there have been no efforts to limit the savagery of battle. There are codes of conduct, more or less widely observed, on the treatment of prisoners and the rights of non-combatants. Treaties and international conventions ban the use of particularly inhumane weapons. The motives behind the codes are mixed. In all of them there is a considerable element of enlightened self-interest, a sensible desire to avoid the worst retribution if by some mischance one's own side is defeated. There is a residue of the camaraderie and mutual prudence that developed when wars were fought by comparatively small, professional mercenary armies. Both these motives are rooted in past history, and their influence appears to be declining in the massive totalitarianism of modern warfare. There is, however, an approach which has gained some impetus in the twentieth century. Within a civilised nation it is an acknowledged responsibility of government to devise and approve procedures for the peaceful resolution of group conflicts and to restrain wrongdoers by the rule of law. Human perversity can, and often does, shape a legal system as a weapon of oppression, but this is an aberration. Law should be the impartial administration of justice. There is a measure of hope in the increasingly articulated desire that an effective corpus of international law should be established. One has only to study the resolutions of the General Assembly of the United Nations to discover that the aim is more praised than practised, hindered as it is at every turn by the insistence of every nation on its own undisputed sovereignty; but the efforts continue.

The moralist who would consider himself to be a realist — that is, one who does not confine himself to glowing descriptions of a world order in which all individuals and nations are activated by perfect love — hopes that on this foundation there may steadily be built an architecture of agreements that will diminish the occasions of war and will moderate its cruelty so long as war is considered to be the ultimate assurance of security. He can compile a quite impressive list: the Geneva Protocol, the Partial Test Ban Treaty, the Non-Proliferation Treaty, the Latin American Nuclear Free Zone Treaty, the Seabed Arms Control Treaty, for example. He presses on but, being a realist, has at the back of his mind an uneasy fear that the weapons of modern war, the clash of ideologies and the erosion of moral standards will not only shatter the architecture but could also destroy the still flimsy foundation.

Many Christians, a minority but a substantial minority, regard such an approach as too faithless in its hopes and too timorous in its fears. The dominant purpose of Christian ethics, they insist, is to declare plainly that which is right according to the revealed Divine will. If, as they believe, it is true that the security men and nations seek is impossible in an imperfect world, let that be unambiguously proclaimed — but as the solid ground for confident advocacy of the way that surely leads to life, not as a despairing acquiescence in paralysing impotence. A revealed will? Certainly. We have been told, and all history confirms the truth of the teaching, that they who would live by the sword will perish by the sword, that the strong man armed keeps his goods in peace only until another stronger than he comes and wrests them from him, that by its very nature evil inevitably breeds more evil. If the waging of war is evil — as it is — then to seek security with bow and arrow, with bullet and shell, with bomb and laser beam, is a pathetic delusion. The logical, theological conclusion is that casuistical half-satisfaction with 'security' expressed in the attempt to give to war a humane face is a rationalisation of sin and an ethical distortion.

One can acknowledge without condescension the convinced sincerity of those who hold this view. More than that, one can acknowledge that it is essential to be reminded continuously and unambiguously of the ideal lest we become content with something less. But there is a valid distinction between being content and seeking to make better, if not perfect, that which is admittedly less; a distinction which the great majority of moral theologians have always recognised. Applied ethics is concerned with moral choices in actual situations. When the choice lies between undoubted right and undoubted wrong the guidance is straightforward. But when, as sometimes happens, decision has to be made between two courses of action each of which is good or, as happens much more often, when each course is bad, ethical judgement is a nice balancing of greater good against lesser good, of lesser evil against greater evil — which brings us back to the heart of the doctrine of the just war and of its so far more vaguely defined corollary, the doctrine of the just rebellion.

The central thesis of the doctrine is that there are situations, from which there is no escape, in which war can be conscientiously judged to be the lesser of the evils presented. By implication, therefore, realistic preparation for defence against aggression can be morally justified. The thoughtful pacifist, aware of the probable consequences of submission to aggression, nevertheless holds that the waging of war is still a greater evil. Though the ultimate judgements differ, the holder of each conviction has sought to assess the options and to estimate how the balance tilts. It should be noted that this assumes a strict adherence to the discipline of ethical scrutiny which is not always evident in practice. It is the duty of the moral theologian to insist that balanced judgement demands accurate knowledge of facts and, after that, thorough and honest appraisal of the deducible consequences of the alternative options for action.

It may be protested that to lay so much continual stress on likely consequences is subtly to pervert the positive message of the gospel which is essentially and primarily 'good news', transforming it into a selection of gloomy forecasts. This is not necessarily so. Though the phrase one prefers may indicate a frame of mind, the 'greater good' and the 'lesser evil' amount to the same thing. Is it, for example, less agonising to sink beneath a sea of troubles than to suffer the slings and arrows of outrageous fortune? Or is it better to suffer the slings and arrows? *Au fond,* the meaning would be identical in either phrasing.

Furthermore, it ought not to be too readily assumed that the gospel is wholly good news, as though it consisted entirely of attractive promises of salvation and redemption. The actual pattern of light and shade is dramatically portrayed in Deuteronomy; the context suggested being the last words of Moses to the children of Israel at the end of the desert wandering and before they cross the Jordan into an unknown future — a future that will be shaped by the strength or frailty of their faith. The choice they must make is starkly announced as being between life and death, good and evil. The stirring prospect of prosperity in the land of milk and honey, of springs of water and fertile fields, is accompanied by stern warning of the tragedies that will inevitably follow ethical disobedience. This is the message of all the prophets; promise and warning indissolubly joined. It infuses the teaching of Jesus. There is not one way before us but two; a narrow way that leads to life and the broad way that leads to destruction. If a fool builds his house on the sand he must endure the consequences of his folly. The blessings shine the more brightly against the dark backcloth of the woes, and both belong together. To warn of the probably grim consequences of contemplated decisions is therefore a wholly valid ethical argument. It is also a powerful one. If we stubbornly resist loving the highest when we see it, we may yet be saved by fear.

Where has our apparently zigzag progress brought us? We began by looking at the mixture of concepts bundled together in the word 'security'. We can now, I suggest, push to one side those that refer to secrecy, security checks or MI-5. We can by a little narrow the field of enquiry by concentrating on the still complicated network of ideas associated with defence. In that field the first argument has been that absolute security is unattainable, with a very strong hint that that should give us no cause for distress. We have considered the case for and against the claim that the justified ethical quest is for that which, after all the available evidence has been weighed and all the possible options judged, seems to be reasonably hopeful and practicable in a wicked and turbulent world. It could, however, be fair comment that this brief summary reveals that one factor has been inadequately discussed. The point has been made that one of the adduced reasons for a security system is that there are civilised values, and hopes of progress in human welfare, that ought to be defended; a reasonable argument provided that the security system does actually defend them. But time and again in the history of nations — Sparta, Prussia, Napoleonic France, for instance — the mounting demands of a military regime have eroded the values and hindered or reversed progress to welfare. The stirring music of patriotism and liberty has too often been orchestrated by a tyrant. Possibly more often, and more subtly, values have been tarnished by the apparent necessities of security. Evil is evident in the destruction each side inflicts upon the other in the carnage of conflict. It can be more insidious, but no less real, in the life of a nation at peace and prepared for war, which adds yet one more complicating factor to the equation which the ethical theologian must try to resolve.

Though many of my illustrations and examples in the argument so far have been contemporary or fairly recent, the general line could have been (and has been) followed for centuries. More than one eminent theologian has declared, perhaps for our comfort, perhaps for our chastening, that there are no new moral problems, only old problems in new guises. Empires rise and fall. Power centres shift. New weapons are invented. New causes arouse the loyalty of new generations. But, they say, human hearts and human motives do not change. When the local and temporary trappings have been stripped away, the ethical questions raised (and the unethical answers given) when Greeks were in conflict with Trojans, Mercians with men of Wessex, Americans with Russians, are fundamentally the same.

The assertion has a long and distinguished pedigree but it may, however tentatively, be queried. There comes a time when difference of degree becomes so marked that it looks suspiciously like difference in kind. We may have slid into that phase now in world affairs. For most of history the human population has been sparse. It was always undoubtedly true that the whole population lived on one planet, even when the village agricultural labourer never travelled more than ten miles from his own home in his lifetime, or when it took four months for the news of Nelson's Caribbean triumphs to reach London, or ten years for news from mysterious China to trickle to the West, or a thousand years for agricultural innovation in the valleys of the Tigris and Euphrates to affect primitive farming in Britain. Now that we are pressing on to the 5,000 million mark in population and expecting within a generation to pass 6,000 million; now that news of wars, earthquakes, murders, stock exchange prices and football results is flashed instantaneously around the globe; now that cryptic information· released on a Thursday morning about changes in the pecking order of the Chinese hierarchy sets the world chancelleries anxiously or hopefully speculating by Thursday afternoon; it is a different world. 'One world' has a new meaning.

We are cerebrally aware of interdependence. For a generation, and not for very much longer than that, we have been grudgingly learning the obvious lesson that pollution of air, water and soil damages the whole of the planet, wherever it originates. But there has not been much time so far to overlay the reactions and attitudes ingrained by those many centuries of comparative isolation. The root problem today of international conflict or co-operation is that it is international, between nations. The issues to be faced are global: the solving mechanisms to hand are national. If slight exaggeration to make a point may be permitted: just as the English TUC is better at rotund generalisations than at guiding effectively the trade union movement because each member union insists on its own inviolable independence, so the United Nations, the meeting ground of sovereign nations, distributes a plethora of platitudes and little action. The converging crises that are sweeping on humanity — poverty, overpopulation, pollution, nuclear war — are global in a way that has never been known before. Contemporary ethics is compelled to take seriously into its thinking the one-world dimension.

So we return to those two major concerns with which we began: the use of world resources and the ethics of nuclear war. Poverty, toil and hardship, except for the favoured few, have until now been universally accepted as the inevitable human lot. Only within living memory has the stage been reached when the majority of the citizens of some nations could no longer be classed as poor. Even when poverty (as slippery a word as security) is defined, as in the USA, as an annual income less than $4,000, or, as in Britain, inability to buy a washing machine and refrigerator and television set, the majority in the wealthier nations are not poor. But over the whole world the great majority are poor, as they have always been. The difference now is that through the network of world communication they are aware of their poverty and are beginning to believe that it is not inevitable. Behind the confused, turbulent revolutionary ferment of the twentieth century lies 'the revolution of rising expectations', as H.J.P. Arnold put it in his book *Aid for Developing Countries.*[4]

The thrust of the report of the Brandt Commission[5] is that the greatest danger to world peace is not to be found in the ideological confrontation between East and West, but in the rich-poor confrontation between North and South. It is a diagnosis that the 'haves' do not particularly relish. Note how often the USA and the USSR unobtrusively stand together to resist the economic demands of the Third World. If Brandt is right, a fairer sharing of Earth's resources is essential to security. It follows that there is a strong case, practical and ethical (in the long run, are not the two the same?) for stigmatising the gross imbalance between expenditure on defence and expenditure on aid and welfare as both unwise and unjust.

The second, related theme referred to the morality of the use of, or intention to use, nuclear weapons. Of course, the cost of defence includes the cost of non-nuclear weapons and armed forces. It has been argued that to provide what the nations regard as adequate security by such means could be even more costly than nuclear armouries. The basis of the argument is doubtful, for the cost estimates for such countries as the UK assume a non-nuclear defence in a situation where the major powers remain nuclear-armed. Entirely apart from cost, in itself not a negligible consideration, there are at least two persuasive criticisms of nuclear armouries. One is strategic. There is no defence against nuclear attack. The end product of an arms race is not more security, but less. The other is ethical. The force used is out of all proportion to the end sought. The good that is hoped to be achieved cannot outweigh the evil wrought. There is no prospect of 'victory'; only the prospect of hazardous survival on a scarred planet poisoned by long-lasting radioactive pollution. The readiness to inflict such monstrous anguish is neither in accord with man's nature as a rational being, nor with moral principles. This line of ethical criticism is not pacifist, though the pacifist would accept it. It is application of the just war doctrine.

In the context of the discussion so far we come, finally, to the crunch question. What sort of security can we and should we reasonably hope for? I begin once more with the frequently reiterated Christian judgement that war is evil; maybe, except for nuclear holocaust, a lesser evil, but still evil. It is a commonplace that men and women everywhere fear it and long for peace. The fact is that at the same time they find it attractive. It offers a deeply satisfying sense of partnership and an exciting enterprise. People are thrilled and stirred — in this country; slot in other names for other nations — by the stories of the rout of the Armada, Trafalgar, Waterloo, the Battle of Britain. Some of us can remember the hardship and danger as the bombs rained down on our cities, but we remember also the heart-warming sense of comradeship, of being all in it together. We know that we ought to love peace, and we say that we do, but somehow in comparison it seems curiously tepid.

Fortunately, the attraction is fading. Future wars will not be gallant charges against the enemy or heroic stands in beleaguered garrisons. Instead, technicians will be using computers in steel and concrete bunkers deep underground. After about three hundred generations of inventing ways of killing our fellows that demanded courage, discipline and the support of comrades in arms, we have at last devised techniques that strip away all the romance and excitement. Something is needed to fill its place, and I doubt if it is going to be filled very quickly by the derring-do of spaceship commanders in naval-type battle with aliens from distant planets. But do we really need an alternative? Why not settle for a quiet life? Because, being human, we need causes that lift us out of the rut of humdrum littleness and make us feel that we are living to some purpose. In short, in the search for security we need an alternative to war.

The security of 'peace' as it is commonly understood does not provide a satisfying alternative, for the simple reason that it is not an alternative. The absence of armed conflict is truce. But peace as it is theologically understood is positive, not simply sheathing the sword but turning swords into ploughshares. Both war and peace involve the planned organisation of men, skill and resources, both make immense demands on endurance and the ability to manipulate the logistics essential to success. War in fact does. Peace in practice does not because it has not had a comparably precise and compelling objective. Humans are practical and aggressive, ready to meet the challenges they clearly see and feel that they can handle. Ask them to organise a bring and buy sale to raise money to help spastics, or to set up a chain of mobile clinics in the mountains of Haiti, or to put a man on the moon, and they will cheerfully complain and get on with it.

I have earlier suggested that, in our generation, 'one world' has acquired a new significance. Every generation is convinced that none before it ever had to face such peculiarly difficult problems as its own, and has thought so with good reason; but in none before our own, I believe, has there been such a speedy drive towards a crossroad of history. If I read aright the signs of the times we are not simply facing old problems in modern trappings. Never before has it been possible for man to destroy the planet on which he lives, as it is now. The geometric progression of population growth is reaching a level that casts a dark shadow over the future of all peoples. For the first time we have not only a global awareness of escapable poverty but also a realistic factual assessment of its extent. For the first time, though we may not yet have the will, we have the technical ability to conquer poverty.

Here, then, is the outline of a real alternative. The convergence of unprecedented developments makes positive peace-making a challenge, cause and choice entirely fitting what William James once called the 'moral alternative to war'. There have been other suggestions, ranging from Fourier's global culinary competions to sport; sentimental ideas advanced by those who have never witnessed the rivalry when cakes are judged in a village show or who think that the Olympic Games bring the nations of the world together in happy harmony. But an all-out onslaught on world poverty and deprivation fills the bill. It is as all-embracing as war. The problems involved, though solvable, are just as intricately complicated. There is a parallel need for perseverance and collective intelligence. The end in view is clear. The pressure for action grows in urgency.

It may be, I admit, that in all this there is too rosy a view of human nature, but I do not think that it is gross exaggeration. Most great causes (and bad ones) are sustained by the determination of an active five per cent, but the causes are won because the majority respond to the prodding and persuading. A call to co-operate in an enterprise that is difficult — 'blood, toil, tears and sweat' — but has a goal that is worth achieving secures a response.

In the full range of ethical proclamation, advocacy of a viable alternative must have a place, perhaps the primary place. My own grapplings with the concept of 'security' have dealt mainly with reasonable defence, with the conscientious argument about the Christian attitude to war. They have reflected the pros and cons of much contemporary debate. How can the worst excesses of war be restrained? How can an effective corpus of international law be established? How can the Gadarene rush of the arms race be reversed? What, when war comes, is the duty of the individual Christian? The argument runs round in circles. I begin to think that the way out is to stop limiting our debate to war, though it must be an essential element in the debate — and to bring into it the concept of an intellectually and spiritually satisfying alternative. Perhaps the ethics of security is most truly defined as the ethics of positive peace-making.

Notes

1. *The British Nuclear Deterrent* (London: SCM Press, 1963), p. 11: Resolution of the British Council of Churches and Report of a Working Group [of its International Department], October 1963. [Chairman: Kenneth Johnstone.]

2. *The Search for Security: a Christian Appraisal* (London: SCM Press, 1973), pp. 2-3: the Report of a Working Party on Defence and Disarmament of the Department of International Affairs of the British Council of Churches and the Conference of British Missionary Societies. [Chairman: the Reverend Edward Rogers.]

3. Ibid., p. 4.

4. H.J.P. Arnold, *Aid for Developing Countries: a Comparative Study* (London: The Bodley Head, 1962).

5. *North-South: a Programme for Survival* (London: Pan Books, 1980): the Report of the Independent Commission on International Development Issues. [Chairman: Willy Brandt.]

5 THE ETHICS OF RISK

G.R. Dunstan

> Sirrah, your father's dead:
> And what will you do now? How will you live?
>
> As birds do, mother.
>
> *Macbeth*, IV. ii. 29

That cannot be. Man, a product and part of nature, can no longer live in nature. He is grown up and gone away; nature affords no home now to his complexity. His life is sustained by artificiality; without it — without that which his mind has conceived and his hands have made — he would die; and that miserably.

Nature has its laws, and some are known. In the unknown lies what we call chance, or hazard, or *accident*, literally that which merely happens. There may be an ultimate in chance, a process still unmatched by law even if all were known. We call it *random* — a play upon the digits of infinity. Chance engaged with — chance faced, calculated, grappled with as a notional possibility — we call *risk*. Today a new science is being born, called 'risk accountancy'. This is not as the birds live.

> the poor wren,
> The most diminutive of birds, will fight,
> Her young ones in the nest, against the owl.
>
> *Macbeth*, IV. ii. 9

In Nature, instinct is the primary protector of vulnerable life — though between instinct and calculation, when your cat or your dog stays to measure an unlikely leap, it would be hard to draw a line. In Nature, survival depends upon adaptation to risk, in an infinity of mutual relation and avoidance.

Man's history is part of natural history; and he is part of nature still. His increased complexity has bought him no immunity; rather, he is the more vulnerable because of it. (Where there is radioactivity, for instance, the 'higher' and more complex the organism, the more lethal is a given dose.) As instinct weakens in man, intelligence takes over to protect against chance in nature. He fashions clothes to conserve body heat, for want of homeostasis and the bear's furry skin. He stores water, food and fuel, against seasonal change and uncertainty. He makes rules, conventions and whole technologies, to reduce random collisions on the road and in the air. He moves on, from guarding himself against nature to learning to exploit it – and so creates new dangers, a new dimension of risk. He exploits the wind, under sail. The more he can carry of an adverse wind, the more it is to his advantage; if he sails too far off the wind he may capsize. After sailing he learns to fly, pitting velocity and aerodynamics against the basic force of gravity. Today, his intelligence, his knowledge and his exploitive skill have carried him further than ever before into an engagement with the forces of nature, and so into a new dimension of risk. He has moved into the era of nuclear physics, and so of nuclear risk.

I leave on one side the risk of nuclear war. That is a subject in itself. The campaigns against nuclear armament are now eclipsed by the campaigns against nuclear energy, not in England only but in Europe also and in the USA. At the beginning of February 1980, upwards of 20,000 demonstrators, led by the mayors of their home towns, besieged the nuclear site at Plogoff, in Brittany, with slogans like *Non au nucléaire, oui au soleil!* and *Si vous acceptez le nucléaire, préparez votre cerceuil!*[1] After a year of intense resistance the project, the largest nuclear plant in France, was cancelled by M. Mitterrand, the new President of the Republic, in May 1981. Elsewhere there is civil disobedience and even sabotage. The anti-nuclear lobby recruits from a wide field: nuclear pacifists, environmentalists, back-to-naturists, civil libertarians, ecologists and wild-life protectionists, Green Peace voyagers, campaigners against bureaucracy and for 'open government' – and many more. The one word which they have in common in all their protestations is *risk*. Their appeal is to *fear*, moving in on the popular imagination a generation or so after the hell-fire preachers have moved away.

Even without such complications, the issues would be difficult enough. This is because the exploiting of nuclear physics engages with nature at so many points, each one of them with a science, a technology, a language of its own. There are the nuclear physicists themselves, of course, and the nuclear and chemical engineers; there are the medical radiologists, geneticists, oncologists, haematologists, cytologists, ranging widely over the body systems; there are ecologists, climatologists, geologists, seismologists and oceanographers, concerned with the environment at its widest extent, looking at a future still thousands of years away; and there are political and social theorists professing a concern for values and liberties in an imagined 'plutonium society'. Given the technical data which each group supplies, given the range of legitimate interpretations of those data, and given the difficulty which any one group of experts finds in understanding the technicalities of the others, to decide upon a policy, after balancing potential risks with potential benefits, must be extremely difficult indeed. The decision must be a political one, the responsibility of the government of the day. And, as things are now, that decision must command some degree of consent in the country, among the governed. To promote an informed debate on the ethics of risk would seem to make good sense.

The terms of the debate, and the relevant data, were set out — and superbly set out, if I may judge — in the Sixth Report of the Royal Commission on Environmental Pollution, of which the chairman was then Sir Brian Flowers, published in September 1976. The report provides a beginner's guide to radioactivity and radiobiology and to the generation of nuclear energy and the issues arising from it. It describes measures of national and international control, and the safety factors in the siting and management of reactors, in the handling and storage of plutonium and in the management of radioactive waste. It sets out the case for a steady development of nuclear generation, and for alternative or complementary strategies — the continued use of coal in conventional generators and the transforming of solar heat, winds, tides and waves into usable energy. If the commission erred, it erred on the side of caution — as may be expected from a body charged with the examination of threats to the environment. It concluded that the case for a major expansion of nuclear power, involving especially the development of fast breeder reactors, was by no means so clear-cut as its official sponsors supposed it to be. It favoured delay, in the hope that something better would turn up — a slowing down of the world's rapidly increasing energy use; a rapid and more economical development of alternative supplies — from sun, wind and water; and, perhaps, the development of a commercially feasible fusion technology out of our growing experience with fission. It reckoned with risks at every stage, even, at the end, with the risk attending its own policy of delay.

In the four and a half years which have followed, the debate has continued in the terms which the report laid down. From France, Germany and the USA, all countries with growing nuclear experience, and with vociferous anti-nuclear campaigns, tables of comparative risks have appeared: some comparing the notional risks from nuclear energy with those proven risks attending other sources, notably the mining of coal; some comparing the risks from radioactivity in nuclear power stations and the storing of waste with the radiation risks which we accept without much qualm in medicine and our normal walks of life;

some comparing nuclear risks in general with those of our accepted lethal indulgences, like smoking, driving a motor car, climbing mountains or crossing a road. My impression, from a superficial and lay reading of the literature, is that, despite the accident at Three Mile Island in the autumn of 1979, there is, among those best placed to make a reasoned estimate, a growing confidence that the risks in a nuclear energy programme can be contained; that the benefits outweigh the risks foreseen; and that to delay is more risky than to proceed. So it is that in January 1980, the British government was officially recommended to build a commercial fast breeder reactor, at a minimum estimated cost of £1,200 million, to be established by the year 2000. France is already ahead.[2] At the end of 1980 the first contracts were awarded for two new advanced gas cooler type (AGR) power stations, the whole estimated to cost £2,500 million.[3]

Risk accountancy, as now practised, begins with the first extraction of the relevant fuel or energy source, and continues through to the delivery of usable energy or power. On this basis, calculations in Britain, France and the USA agree in putting coal as the most dangerous energy source — dangerous in the actual death of miners, from accident and pneumoconiosis, and in deaths and disabling disease in the population attributable to an atmosphere polluted, among other things, with sulphur dioxide, sulphurous acid, oxide of nitrogen, benzpyrene and even radon, the radioactive gas most feared from nuclear accidents. Of the existing energy sources, oil is placed second in the danger table (120 men perished when an oil rig collapsed in the North Sea in the winter of 1980), nuclear reaction third and natural gas fourth. For the alternative technologies, Lord Rothschild (in the Dimbleby Lecture of November 1978) pronounced nuclear power to be safer than windmills, and that not rhetorically. In terms of present risks the facts are known: we know how many miners die each year in England, and how many are crippled — and even the most advanced technology cannot replace miners underground. Nuclear risks can only be calculated: so far there is not yet one known plutonium fatality in England from which to begin to extrapolate for the future. So R.H. Mole, a radio-biologist, can write in the *British Medical Journal*[4]

So, in relation to plutonium as to all exploitation of atomic energy, there is something new in our concern: argument, often heated argument, about whether some kind of harm that is not detectable is at a level that is acceptable or not acceptable.

The fear of radiation, and its cancer-producing potential, is, of course, at the heart of the debate. All the studies offer tables of how much radiation we take for granted already, not only with television and medical and dental x-rays, but also environmentally: growing up, for instance, in Truro or Aberdeen, walking on granite moors or at high altitudes or simply basking in the sun. Nuclear scientists can claim, with 2,000 reactor-years of experience behind them, that the radiation risk even to workers in nuclear plants is lower than we assume to be acceptable elsewhere. That count, of course, assumes normal working. Controversy surrounds the risk of accident or malicious interference.

First, it is established that, despite disseminated fears, an accident in a nuclear reactor would not simulate a nuclear explosion; neither could stolen plutonium be converted easily by terrorists into a home-made nuclear bomb. Secondly, it was calculated by a committee of the American Academy of Sciences that the chances of the most serious of accidents at a nuclear power station, that is of a melt-down in the reactor core and uncontrolled atmospheric discharge, were about one in 100,000 reactor-years; so, with 100 reactors working, there could be one every 1,000 years. The casualties of such an accident, if it happened, in terms of radiation-induced cancer, leukemia and genetic damage spread over the following 30 years, would in fact make a hardly significant statistical addition on a national scale to the incidence of those diseases already occurring, not least from cigarette smoking. That was written before the accident at Three Mile Island in 1979 — when the melt-down nearly happened, it is said, *but did not.*[5] Minor accidents are reported from time to time at Windscale, and recently cracks in the cooling systems at Bradwell and Dungeness. On any just assessment, accidents cannot be excluded in any development of a new technology, and each experience evokes stronger precaution. We did not abandon the railways in the mid-nineteenth century, when inadequate signalling on single-track lines produced enormous fatalities, nor jet-engined passenger aircraft when cracks around cabin windows plunged our first Comet into the sea, nor box girder bridges when an early model collapsed in the making.

It is acknowledged that uranium, and even more the plutonium produced in nuclear reactors, is dangerous stuff; and that plutonium and other ingredients in the spent atomic fuel continue dangerous for a very long time, some over a thousand years. It is claimed, however, that the danger can be contained: clad in steel and glass, the stuff can be stored deep in beds of salt or rock estimated by geologists to have been stable for millions of years. Indeed, such confidence is there that the policy of dumping the canisters in some rocky fissure in deep mid-Atlantic is discounted: scientists would prefer to store it where they can keep an eye on it and respond to change, either with new protection or perhaps for further use. The British government is spending £25 million in research into the best, i.e. the safest, provision for nuclear waste, including boring for stable and suitable geological beds.[6] Granted the need for security against theft of plutonium in transit or from store, it is suggested that the precautions taken would threaten our civil liberties, imprison us in the surveillance-state. In fact the monitoring processes are simple, and they are with us already, screening large numbers of people. We accept them at the door of the hospital wards where radium needles are in use; we accept them at airports for ourselves and our baggage before every flight.* In short, those who see no alternative to the development of nuclear energy as the world's *main* reliance for the foreseeable future would seem to have answered, with reasonable probability, the objections which the Flowers Committee properly raised. They do not, cannot, claim absolute certainty for their defence, but a moral certainty, a reasonable probability: and this, in a finite world, is all that we can properly expect.

Their case, however, demands more than developing simply as we are. It looks as though the bolder is now the safer course: that is, that reasons of safety as well as of economy urge the development of the fast breeder reactor as the next replacement for our present high-temperature reactors, in their varied designs. The reasons for this are relatively simple. Uranium exists in limited quantities, and supplies economically recoverable and politically available could run short fairly soon. Uranium mining is dangerous to miners, because of the carcinogenic action of dust particles upon the lung. Conventional reactors leave accumulating residues of plutonium to be processed and stored. The fast breeder reactor would make more economical use of the uranium, and would reuse much of the plutonium, so reducing demand and overall risk. It may be that this is the right interim policy, until fusion becomes industrially possible, rather than to perpetuate a perhaps obsolescent past. On the widest view the risk of not developing nuclear energy at all is probably the highest risk of all. Given the world's multiplying population, and widespread endemic poverty and hunger, and the rapid exhaustion not only of fossil fuels but of some essential minerals as well,

---

* A significant increase of 'material unaccounted for' would make it harder to falsify statistically a claim by terrorists to possess a critical amount, and so to dismiss as bluff a threat to use it.

we have to count actual deaths and deprivation against hypothetical risks; for poverty and hunger cannot be removed without greatly increased energy resources — irrigation and agriculture depend upon them as much as industry; and it looks as though energy in this quantity cannot be provided on a world scale without nuclear power. The risk of doing nothing is higher than the risks attending what we think we can now do.

I have attempted this crude analysis of a contemporary issue in order to illustrate my thesis that, challenging as are man's attempts to mini- mise natural hazards, that is risks from the elements untamed, the risks and therefore the challenges are greatly magnified as man extends his control over nature, exploits technically his increased knowledge of the natural order. It may well be asked, is this an exercise in *ethics* or in mere calculation?

As written, it is almost entirely a statement and arrangement of facts, calculations, disputed judgements and reasoned probabilities. Yet the very arrangement, and the conclusions expressed, themselves presuppose certain 'values' or moral assumptions, and are determined by them. Not the facts alone, but the facts considered in the light of the moral assumptions, exhibit the moral claims and are the ground of ethical judgements, imperatives or prohibitions.

It is a moral assumption that governments ought to provide reliable sources of usable energy. The assumption is grounded in human need, in the facts that populations are now too dense for each family to supply its needs from the cutting of faggots or from the collecting and drying of cow dung for fuel; and that the scale of energy sources now required, whatever the technology, puts the cost generally beyond the scope of private enterprise and that political considerations, particularly for nuclear power, make it expedient for governments to meet the require- ment. It is a moral assumption that the present generation ought to make provision for generations immediately to follow it; that it would be humanly irresponsible to exhaust available fossil fuels without developing the means for their replacement. It is a moral assumption that human beings, in their vulnerability, ought not to be exposed to avoidable risk. And when risk has to be weighed against risk — for example the risk of nuclear accident in an area of technological afflu- ence against the risk of disease and death from endemic poverty and starvation in countries deficient in energy resources — it would become a moral duty to accept (while seeking to minimise) the lesser, local, still incalculable risk, if that were instrumental to a lessening of the greater, already evident risk to the millions of the poor. This argument does not suppose that nuclear power must be the only major source of energy:

solar, wind or geothermal sources might be developed where they can be relied on. But a nuclear potential might well be the means of creating the technology and hardware necessary for the exploiting of those 'natural' resources, which otherwise might not be developed. Here we are, back to calculation; but, granted the moral assumptions just made, that calculation becomes a moral duty, an exercise in ethics.

Earlier in this essay I set on one side the risk of nuclear war. That was a literary necessity at that point, but perhaps an artificial evasion in the present world. Any discussion of risk in contemporary military and political planning − risk in the various nuclear 'postures' or strategies set against or in conjunction with 'conventional' means of warfare; risk in competitive armament or in unilateral or bilateral disarmament − must involve a high degree of calculation. The calculation, too, must be so technical as to be possible, at advanced levels, only for military specialists, and so politically sensitive as to be the preserve, at its critical points, of persons sworn to secrecy. It must cover the design, control, range, accuracy and destructive power of weaponry; the cost of manufacture, maintenance and deployment; the size and quality of the forces required to handle it; the consequences of its use or, indeed, in terms of deterrence, of its possession and preparedness for use. These consequences themselves are to be measured under several heads: consequences for intended military targets; for the area surrounding those targets, liable to contingent damage; for human life, animal life, organic life at various levels; for towns, cities, the artefacts and conditions of human culture and civilisation. The prospect of an all-out nuclear exchange invites a calculation about the survival of life itself. Granted that vulnerability to nuclear radiation increases with advances on the organic scale, so that human beings would perish while organisms far less developed in their evolution would survive, what would be the possibilities of life 'beginning again', in a new evolutionary effort, in a nuclear-devastated world? The calculation here becomes incalculable; only the imagination can play.

Calculating the consequences of disarmament, particularly unilateral disarmament, would appear to be as inconclusive. Ideally it would proceed on the basis of trust: sufficient sense of security would be generated for one country or allied group to take the first steps, safe in the expectation that no military advantage would be taken of this self-imposed weakness, and that the other side would follow in reducing its own military potential. That initial calculation of trust cannot be without risk. It is made no easier when we can scarcely trust the knowledge or information which we are given of one another: the streams of communication are so poisoned by propaganda that we know not whom to believe. We in Britain believe that we have some honest newspapers and radio communicators through whom we believe we gain a not too distorted picture of nations whom we have to regard as potential enemies; yet the calculations which we base on the information received are diverse. Some unilateralists proclaim that *if* Britain renounced all nuclear capacity we ourselves would be safe from nuclear attack, even in a nuclear war waged against neighbouring states. To others such a hope seems utter fantasy. In the record and perceived strategy of 'the other side' they see a readiness to exploit every weakness in pursuit of hegemony: the advance of control, by threat if possible and if necessary by force, over routes, resources, markets, peoples and territories; only a preparedness to resist and to retaliate will deter them. There is similar division over the consequences of either submission or defeat: some profess to believe that our liberties and the worthwhile characteristics of our way of life would survive, despite the evidence of countries already dominated; others take warning from that evidence and maintain a duty to resist, if necessary, in defence of the way of life. Mistrust, lack of faith or security, is a cardinal factor in the calculation and hence a major contributor to risk.

Calculation on this scale is new in the history of warfare, because of the new technology of warfare. But calculation *per se* is no newcomer to the ethics of warfare. 'A likelihood of success' has for long been one element in the calculus of the *ius ad bellum* in the traditions of the just war and the just rebellion; and that likelihood has depended on calculation. Is there not in the Gospel itself the aphorism of the king commanding a force of 10,000 sitting down first to consider whether to join battle with his adversary commanding 20,000? Or how, if not by calculation, do we apply the principle of proportionate good and harm in deciding whether or not to intervene (e.g. to defend Hungary or Czechoslovakia when invaded or Poland if invaded, or to try to end the Iran-Iraqi war) or whether a more just regime can be established after hostilities than the one to be overthrown?

In short, we may, if we will, dismiss calculation as mere politics and believe ourselves to work on the higher levels of ethics when we discuss the 'right' and the 'wrong', the 'inherently evil' and the 'conditional intention' — we may do this; but we should deceive ourselves if we thought that thereby we are advancing the cause of peace or making the risk of war more remote. For ethics is a practical art, a working at the morality of practice; and practice is concerned with fact, possibility, probability, consequence and therefore with calculation. The exercise is one in which theorist and practitioner must engage together: ethics is part of politics. And few of our contemporaries know this better than Sydney Bailey, in whose honour these essays are written; a man whose very conviction about the right and the wrong in war has carried him, for so many years, deep into the technical debate, and deep, therefore, into the confidence and affection of those practical men with whom the responsibility of decision lies.

I choose now another field in which the ethics of risk are debated in order to illustrate our ambivalence about risk: the field of medical practice, especially in the introduction of new medicines. It is not the function of the moralist to teach the doctors their business. His concern is with the pattern of mutual expectations in the society in which the doctors practise. The expectations are, or should be, the product of a common morality, shared beliefs about men and human relationships. They are statements, explicit and implicit, of the claims which we think it right to make upon one another and to meet. My thesis now is that in medical matters, especially concerning the linked potency and toxicity of medicines, our expectations and claims are in confusion and conflict because of our ambivalence about risk. In other areas of life we encourage risk; we live with risk, take unnecessary risks. In matters medical, pharmaceutical and cosmetic we incline to assume that we can have all that we want, without risk.

We encourage dangerous sports, mountaineering, pot-holing, motorracing and the rest. At a charity fete run by the students' union of my own college 20 or more children from a local primary school knelt in a row for a stunt motor cyclist to soar over them, and no one said it was odd. We continue to smoke, though disease from smoking costs the British hospital service an estimated £600 million a year. It is true that we are more safety-conscious in other activities. Having spent a quarter of a century expelling paternalism from the protection of our morals we take it back to protect our bodies: witness safety helmets, seat belts, Safety at Work Acts, control of fireworks, and firedoors in schools which pinch more fingers than (fortunately) they control fires. On medical practice, especially surgery, on new medicines or vaccines, cosmetics, food additives and domestic chemicals our attitude is different. It is assumed that these can be without risk. If harm occurs, it must be someone's fault. We sue.

The roots of this ambivalence are in our being. Life is dull without adventure. Had 'safety first' been built into our genetic code we should never have emerged from the swamp; neither should we now, without deep sea divers, get oil from the sea bed. We praise courage among the virtues, and courage takes risks. Our sense of the worth of man has risen, too. Greek philosophy and Roman law put a high value on the life of man – if free. Judaeo-Christian theology taught that all men, bond as well as free, were of infinite worth. Yet for centuries men's bodies could be mutilated, racked, ransacked, burned, not so much for the good of their souls as for the good, the protection, of the body politic, civil and ecclesiastical. It is not so now, except in war, terrorism and political tyranny; and this we condemn.

At the root of our concern for safety is this belief in the worth of man. He is too precious to be injured or contaminated by contrivances defective in design or management, or to have his children marred in the womb. This is to put it on the level of principle: the value of the human person, and the protection due to him, in our shared morality. The principle imposes a duty of care; its breach creates the tort or wrong of negligence, or worse.

At a more personal level we take our medicine in the expectation that it will do us good, not harm. We do not want to be hurt. Neither do we want those we care for to be hurt, or those around us. The common morality stands upon our common vulnerability.

But moralism also enters in. 'Why should it happen to me?' is still a common cry when misfortune strikes. It is a deep, ancestral response, an echo of the days before science taught us to relate event to cause, immediate, complex or remote; of the days when men believed blindly that if something happened God or the gods must have done it. The saucy recall this echo in the jargon of 'playing God' while the theologians try to silence it; theologians no longer believe in that sort of God. But a theological determinism now gives place to a scientific or technological determinism. Popular imagination has not come to terms with working unpredictability, even with randomness, sheer change, in the infinite range of organic possibilities within our biological constitution. The truth known to medical scientists has not yet possessed the rest of us, that, test and extrapolate as they will, for no pharmacological intervention can they predict absolutely a uniform response. Safety cannot be guaranteed. And if the medicines are powerful and they must be, to effect what we want them to effect – so the results are more catastrophic when things go wrong.

Without an understanding of this the immediate response to mischance is moralistic: someone must be to blame. This can be dealt with, if left to itself: enquiry can establish whether negligence or error of judgement occurred in the sequence of causes. But material loss may complicate the issue, for which compensation may be due. Moralism has clouded the law here also: the threat of damages is an instrument of discipline. The award of compensation has depended traditionally on proof of fault: no fault, then no award. This is a means, however blunt, of enjoining reasonable care. But it can be unjust to the victim when mishap occurs without assignable fault as, granted final unpredictability, it may. Some countries have moved to forms of 'no fault' compensation.[7] In Britain we hesitate. The Congenital Disabilities Act 1976 is still based on tort, and the Pearson Committee recommended strict liability in tort for damage from vaccines; yet it recommended also 'a new weekly benefit for all seriously disabled children whatever the source of their handicap'; and the government has begun to pay a lump sum of £10,000 tax free to children damaged as a result of vaccination encouraged and undertaken for the public protection as well as for their own. If a scheme of no-fault compensation were introduced for all such accidental handicap medicinally induced, the maintenance of standards and penalties for their infringement would be pursued by other means. Moralism would be less of an impediment to adequate compensation.

Another factor complicates the issue for the manufacturer of toxic medicines. It is human cupidity, the spur to litigiousness. Damages for impairment or handicap may be very high. And when, as in some countries, lawyers may take a percentage of damages won – the contingency fee – the added cost to the manufacturer of defending vexatious actions can be high. He is driven to ever more extensive testing of his products, at mounting expense in capital cost and animal lives, or he stands to lose heavily in damages and loss of reputation if fault is proved.

This has serious consequences. Costing has to take into account the synthesizing and discarding of new compounds in the initial research – 10,000 is the figure quoted for one new drug[8] – and then extensive toxicity tests and clinical trials. Together this may take 15 years and cost about £25 million before marketing.[9] A wide market must be assured to recoup all this; and a wider one – or the branding of a number of scarcely significant variants – to make a profit and investment for future research. Two results follow: The first is – as Dr J.M. Walshe found with his triethylene tetramine for the treatment of Wilson's disease[10] – that it is extremely difficult to get a drug manufactured when the predictable market for it is very small. The second is the flooding of world markets with antibiotics and their over-use, with the consequent raising of resistances which render them useless when they should be specific. The excuse for this is the recouping of cost. But the cost lies, not in the ingredients nor in the manufacture, but in the defences against commercial risk.

Even so, safety is not assured. Since 1964, under the Adverse Reactions Reporting System, doctors have been recording on a yellow card any adverse reactions they have noticed in patients for whom they have prescribed new medicines. Notifications run at about 6,500 a year; even so they are estimated to cover only between 1 and 10 per cent of all adverse reactions. The trouble is that it is hard to notice what you have no reason to look for: over 100,000 patients were given practolol, an extremely useful drug, before an association with the dry-eye syndrome could be established. The government, therefore, is trying a tighter method of post-marketing surveillance, using the Prescription Pricing Authority to sort prescriptions and to initiate monitoring by the prescribing doctors. The cost of the scheme, when fully developed, may rise from £10 million to £66 million – not to promote health, but to try to cut risk, to pay for safety.

There is yet another complication, born of ambivalent social attitudes. The public which indirectly requires all this assurance is also growing resentful of the use of animals in toxicity testing. Despite extravagance and errors in presentation, the animal lobbyists have a point. We have, whether by assignment or by usurpation, dominion over the animal world. This means that we must be good lords (*domini*) to them, not absolute tyrants. We can use animals experimentally only because they are biologically so near to us, in relevant respects, as to make the experiment informative, to yield reliable results. But that very proximity creates its own obligations. It creates a claim upon us, that we should extend to them the humane considerations with which we protect our own kind. So it is that the excessive use of animals, especially for non-essential, not immediately medical, experiments is increasingly called into question. A humane morality requires that laboratory use of animals be under moral control.

But not the use of animals only. We have the Helsinki Declaration and other ethical codes to control experiments on human beings. They still do not prevent testing on Puerto Ricans and other poor the contraceptive and other medicaments of whose safety we are not quite sure for ourselves. The IPPF journal, *People,* reported with deep disapproval in 1977 the trial of a synthetic prostaglandin abortifacient on ten women (only) in Sweden. It was then proposed to transfer the trial to 2,000 women 'in developing countries where the drug could prove useful because of the shortage of hospital facilities for abortion.'[11] It is perhaps another example of our ambivalent attitudes that the proposal evoked nothing of the protest, amounting to hysteria, occasioned by the trial of new smoking mixture on beagles or by other toxicity tests on rabbits and rats. On what principle may we put other people at risk in place of our wealthier selves simply because they are poor?

I conclude. I have pointed to inconsistencies in public expectation to which, if we are to take rational and ethical decisions, attention must be given. Men are vulnerable and infinitely varied in a world of finite resources in which we cannot have everything all at once, in which chance cannot be eliminated and in which all contradictions cannot be resolved. Absolute safety can nowhere be guaranteed. This is the essence of the matter. There is every imperative, human and economic, for the prevention of avoidable risk. Yet all risk cannot be eliminated, either in theory or in practice. An obsession with risk, unique in degree in the field of health, can impede progress in the service of health itself. The major advances in medicine have been in the face of risk, taken without regard for many of the ethical restraints accepted now. Somewhere we have to find a way between moral paralysis and moral insensitivity. Even to do nothing is to take a risk.

Notes

1. *Le Monde,* 5 February 1980.
2. *The Times,* 3 January 1980.
3. Ibid., 30 December 1980.
4. 17 September 1977.
5. *The Times,* 2 April 1980.
6. Ibid., 19 May 1980.
7. J.G. McK. Laws, 'Compensation' in *Dictionary of Medical Ethics,* A.S. Duncan, G.R. Dunstan and R.B. Welbourn (eds.), 2nd edn (London: Darton, Longman & Todd, 1977).
8. D.G. Davey, 'Testing New Drugs in the Laboratory', *J. Roy. Coll. Physicians,* vol. 11, no. 3, (1977), p. 219.
9. D. Smart, 'A Presidential Address to the Association of the British Pharmaceutical Industry', *The Times,* 18 January 1980.
10. J. Walshe, 'Drugs for Rare Diseases', *Brit. Med. J.,* vol. 3, (1975), p. 701. Cf. 'Drugs for Rare Diseases' (Leader), *Lancet,* 16 October 1976, p. 836.
11. *People,* vol. 4, no. 3 (1977), p. 45.

6 THEOLOGICAL REFLECTIONS ON COMPROMISE

John Habgood

All Government, indeed every human benefit and enjoyment, every virtue, and every prudent act, is founded on compromise and barter.

Edmund Burke on American independence

The reason that the right will continue to run away is partly that they have been running away for so long that it has become a habit, and partly that the flight to ignominy always consists of single steps; they are never asked to do anything that is more than an extension, and usually only a small extension, of something they have already done.

Bernard Levin on the right wing of the British Labour Party

If compromise is a major part of the art of politics, at what point should a politician stop compromising? When does the negative element in any compromise, the concessions and surrenders it implies, outweigh or undermine the positive value of the agreements or promises achieved through it? Are those who wave the banner of 'no compromise', and who stress the pejorative meaning of the word, the only true leaders and prophets, or are they merely being foolishly unrealistic?

Politicians live constantly with such questions and learn, more or less successfully, to keep upright on the slippery ground between statesman-like compromise and unprincipled surrender. It is not often that they look to theologians for support because there is a strong suspicion, whether justified or not, that theology already leans too far in the direction of absolutism for political comfort. Religious people seem to give the impression that there is something vaguely disreputable about compromise. This essay is an attempt to redress the balance, to indicate that there are elements within the Christian tradition which may be of greater usefulness to them than many practical politicians suppose.

A recent cartoon showed Moses receiving the Ten Commandments on Mount Sinai, and saying to God, 'I think they would go over better if we called them voluntary guidelines.' The joke does its work at a number of levels, in part pointing the finger at contemporary Christians

111

for loss of faith in absolute standards; in part acknowledging the sheer difficulty in actually applying such standards in the real world. It is an old moral dilemma. An apparently straightforward command, 'Thou shalt not kill,' has been interpreted and qualified and restricted in its application since the first day it was uttered. The Israelites had no compunction about killing their enemies or executing wrongdoers. They knew the difference between justifiable and unjustifiable homicide. Their massive elaborations of the law represented increasingly sophisticated attempts to uphold its inviolability while making it workable in practice.

Christian casuistry followed the same pattern. The more rigourous their beliefs about moral obligation, the more elaborate were the various expedients which practical moralists had to adopt in order to make life tolerable. The interpretation of the 'strenuous commands' in the Sermon on the Mount has always been a crux of Christian ethics. Those who have felt themselves impelled to 'give to those who ask' and 'turn the other cheek', literally and without any qualification, have almost always had to live their lives in some separated and specialised community, which by its very existence offers a measure of protection against the full force of the standards it professes.

The uneasy conscience of many good Christians about their failure to live up to the demands of the Gospel has its roots in the awareness that there is something hard and uncompromising at the heart of their faith, to which extreme moral reactions bear witness. The rich young ruler of Luke *18*, 18-23 was good by any ordinary standard, yet still felt his need of something more. Nor is it just particular stories, sayings or demands which create this unease. Religion itself, in any but its most complacent forms, has a tendency towards absolutism through the very nature of the claims made about God. Religious language is the language of extremes, because somehow it has to attain enough velocity to secure lift-off. The transition from earth-borne language to language about God has to be signalled by words which express a sense of finality and all-inclusiveness.

Consider the famous passage in Colossians where Paul's words about Christ take wings:

He is the image of the invisible God; his is the primacy over all created things. In him everything in heaven and on earth was created, not only things visible but also the invisible orders of thrones, sovereignties, authorities and powers; the whole universe has been created through him and for him. And he exists before everything, and all things are held together in him. He is, moreover, the head of the body, the church. He is its origin, the first to return from the dead, to be in all things alone supreme. For in him the complete being of God, by God's own choice, came to dwell. Through him God chose to reconcile the whole universe to himself, making peace through the shedding of his blood upon the cross — to reconcile all things, whether on earth or in heaven, through him alone.[1]

Note the repeated use of words like 'all', 'every' and 'complete' with the imagery of all-inclusiveness, balanced by equally decisive language at the opposite pole — the word 'alone'. Such language has echoes all the way through the Bible, and sets the tone for the believer's own life. In the previous paragraph Paul prays that his readers 'may receive from him [God] *all* wisdom and spiritual understanding for *full* insight into his will, so that your manner of life may be worthy of the Lord and *entirely* pleasing to him'.[2] The exaggerations, if that is what it is right to call them, like the use of hyperbole in the teaching of Jesus, are not mere exaggerations. They have a very definite religious function. But they carry with them the danger that this function will be misunderstood and the believer will find himself trapped by an impossible set of ideals and demands. To lessen the demand of the imperatives is to weaken the sense that the believer is confronted by nothing less than God himself. To accept them at their face value is to lose one's hold on ordinary human existence.

A strange book by Nigel Balchin, published in 1947, expressed on behalf of some of those who had lived through the 1930s and 1940s their sense of disillusionment with the exaggerated certainties of those who thought they knew where they were going. Entitled *Lord I was afraid*, it was a defence of the servant in the parable who hid his talent in the ground because he could not see any clear way of using it with integrity. In the final scene of the book, the hero is drowning in a latter-day flood and complains to Methuselah:

We stood at the cross-road of time, with all the sign-posts down. We saw error and ignorance and prejudice and stupidity go marching boldly down the roads away from somewhere and towards anywhere. The bands were playing and the flags flying. It would have been easy to follow. But we stood there, fumbling for our lost compass and our missing map — waiting for the stars to come out and give us a bearing; waiting until it was light; and in the end waiting because we had always waited. That was our failure. And we must drown for it. Yes, yes, we know. We have no complaint, and ask no mercy. It is for God to decide what sort of man he wants, and he has always had a partiality for the stone-slinging, ruddy-faced sinner who could slay you his ten thousands, and come straight home to a bout of hearty adultery, and then weep in his bed in repentance. But Michal, Saul's daughter, despised him in her heart, and so do we. We have slain no Goliaths, but Uriah's blood is not on our hands . . .[3]

If David, with his extremes and his excesses, is the archetypal believer, then Balchin's hero can stand for the archetypal compromiser, the man despised by the prophets for 'halting between two opinions', and condemned for dithering until all is lost.

But is the contrast really as stark as this? When all has been said about the necessary element of absolutism in religion, and when the weakness of mere indecisiveness has been exposed, is there not a middle ground on which compromise can be seen as the expression of faith? What follows is an attempt to spell out the limits of this middle ground, insofar as they are affected by three theological considerations.

I

Troeltsch made the point that a church-type Christianity can accept compromises far more readily than a sect-type. The ideal of the Kingdom of God 'requires a new world if it is to be fully realized', but it

cannot be realized within this world apart from compromise. Therefore the history of the Christian Ethos becomes the story of a constantly renewed search for this compromise, and of fresh opposition to this spirit of compromise. The Church in particular, however, as a popular institution, is forced to compromise; this she effects by transferring to the institution the sanctity and the grace of forgiveness proper to it as an institution . . .[4]

In other words, the more the church regards itself as possessing the objective treasures of grace, the less it need be damaged by the absence of personal holiness among its members, and the compromises into which it is forced by the pressure of events. The church is holy, but its holiness is compatible with its role as a school for sinners, rather than a society for saints.

A sect, on the other hand, in its pure form tries to realise the ideal of the Kingdom of God with the fewest possible concessions to human frailty. It admits little room for compromise and depends for its identity on the actual holiness of believers. It is therefore inevitably confined within strict limits and pushed out of the mainstream of social life.

The notion that compromises can be tolerated within some sort of objective framework of grace can usefully be linked with Reinhold Niebuhr's insistence that what he calls 'the paradox of grace' reveals the finiteness and sinfulness of all historical activities. Niebuhr would not, of course, have tolerated the idea of an 'objective framework of grace' somehow guaranteed by an institutional church, because any church, as part of history, falls under the same condemnation as every human endeavour, and is most to be condemned when its claims are greatest. But the context of grace, however received and known, allows and makes possible — indeed makes necessary — real admissions of ignorance, partiality and the distorting effects of sinful finite minds.

To live by grace is to have and not to have, because the having depends on God; it is to know and not to know; it is to act, and to admit the limitations of action, because only God can overcome the effects of human egotism. For Niebuhr one of the most disastrous mistakes Christians can make is to take the absolutist elements in Christian faith and translate them into programmes, and thus eventually into fanaticisms. This is not to say that strong convictions should never be turned into effective actions. On the contrary, firm action, not least within the political realm, is essential. But to acknowledge the limitations of action, and to act within a spirit of forgiveness and an awareness of grace, is to be freed from the paralysis engendered by a sense of our own inadequacies; and freed also from the intolerance which refuses to take seriously the convictions of others.

Political action, thus understood, is inevitably marked by compromise. Niebuhr has harsh words for the kind of sectarian perfectionism which was 'blind to the inevitability of the compromises in which it saw its opponents involved. It therefore poured the fury of its self-righteous scorn upon them without recognizing that their compromises were but the obverse side of responsibilities, which the perfectionists had simply disavowed.'[5] Too much tolerance, on the other hand, too great a willingness to compromise, may merely reveal another kind of irresponsibility, indifference towards the problems of political justice.

It is not surprising that Niebuhr's careful balance, his unblinkered perception of sin, and his strong sense of the realities of power should have given him a dominant position in Christian political thinking. Since his day the trickle of Christian political comment has turned into a flood, and politicised theology has dug much deeper into the practical implications of translating Gospel insights into political programmes. Christians who are prepared to get their hands dirty and to face the realities of political compromise are found in many theological traditions. But Niebuhr's warnings still stand, and mark out the territory within which such activity can retain its Christian roots. The paradox of grace defines the relationship of human beings to God, and every other relationship must derive its Christian quality from this primary one.

II

A second element in this attempt at map-making, defining the middle ground of faithful compromise, takes us back to the subject of religious language. The tendency, already mentioned, to push ideas and images to their limits is only one of its characteristics. Another is its obliqueness.[6]

Jesus spoke in parables. Straight answers to straight questions are rare in his teaching. His favourite method was to illuminate some problem by putting it in a fresh context, and then pass it back to the questioner. To reply to the question 'Who is my neighbour?' by telling the story of the Good Samaritan is to do more than provide a vivid illustration of some simple truth about neighbours being people in trouble. The story reverberates on many levels, can be interpreted in many ways and allows the hearer to identify himself with more than one character. There is a real sense, therefore, in which the hearer provides his own answer to the original question. An oblique shaft of light shows him where he stands and what he is. It helps to reveal God by conveying an awareness of multiple layers of meaning in which the hearer himself is involved.

Much communication between friends and lovers is indirect, allusive, only half-expressed. Its very inarticulateness can give it depth. It depends upon two people, not just on the speaker. To be addressed like a public meeting, as Queen Victoria discovered, is quite a different experience. So too God in communicating with us is present in the silences and reveals himself through the unspoken words. Obliqueness, far from being a disadvantage in religious discourse, may be the only way to express the inexpressible.

In St John's Gospel it takes the form of irony. The signs around which the story is constructed both reveal and conceal. They divide those who understand them from those who see only one level of meaning, and who express their incomprehension in words which themselves carry unrecognised overtones. When Pilate said of Jesus,

'Behold your king,' the ironic reverberations were endless.

But there is another process also going on in St John's Gospel, which C.K. Barrett refers to as 'dialectic'.[7] Ideas and images are taken up, thrown about, looked at first from this side, then from that, argued against, reaffirmed and combined, in ways which make the reading of the Gospel a somewhat bewildering experience. To follow the ramifications of an apparently simple word like 'work', or an idea like that of 'coming to Jesus' through this text is to be taken up into a conversation rather than to be confronted by straight exposition.

It is at this point that the relevance of these sketchy observations to the theme of compromise may begin to be apparent. If one of the modes of Biblical revelation is through the entry of its readers into a complex dialectical process in which they themselves are involved, then the notion that somehow amid the confusions of life there ought always to be some single line of action which can be identified clearly and indubitably as 'the will of God' begins to look less convincing.

There are times when it is possible to be morally certain that one does indeed know the will of God, just as there are aspects of Christian teaching which are not oblique. The command to love one another may have endless implications; but it means just what it says. There are other times, however, when the idea that there must be some uniquely right solution to every complex problem leads either to a fruitless search for perfection or to an intolerant defence of the chosen solution against every alternative. A God who reveals himself in hints and glimpses, who draws out a response from those engaged with him, must surely will that his creatures fulfil his purposes not by one route but by many.

In a sense this is so obvious that my excursion into Biblical exposition may seem an unnecessarily roundabout way of making a simple point. Yet the notion that the will of God must somehow be unequivocal exercises a curious fascination over Christian minds. It leads to the suspicion that the ordinary human processes of argumentation and bargaining which result in compromises, represent a falling away from the ideal. The inner voice whispering, 'This is the way; walk ye in it', seems a more appropriate guide to the life of faith than the hard-won conclusions of some committee. To acknowledge that obliqueness and dialectic may have their place in revelation, therefore, may help some Christians to place more value on their counterparts in ordinary life.

The acknowledgement must not be taken so far, though, as to evacuate the notion of the will of God of all content. Trying to discern the will of God is more than trying to come to a sensible compromise. Compromise, perhaps some unavoidable and agonising choice between evils, may have a part in it. But the reference to the will of God, like all references to the transcendent, adds a new dimension to decision-making. It is a reminder of the imperfection of all merely human processes of willing. It sets limits to the adequacy claimed for all merely human responses. Donald MacKinnon once wrote movingly of how

> a recollection of religious perspectives may restrain a man, in the sense of preventing him from seeing his choice as other than it is, as something which leaves many claims unacknowledged, that leaves him indeed with problems still to solve, claims however properly disregarded that he must yet somehow meet.[8]

The faith which allows us to accept compromises for what they are, must also point beyond them. And this leads to a third consideration in the attempt to map out some Christian limits.

III

Classical moral theology deals with compromise as the ultimate means of avoiding the choice between two evils. Personal morality was primarily in view, but the main principle elaborated seems to apply equally well to political choices. Compromise can be justified as a device for gaining time.

The essential context for justifiable compromise is that the evils envisaged in a straightforward and immediate choice must be equally unavoidable and undesirable. Moralists have sometimes gone to great lengths in trying to weigh values one against the other, and to work out some sort of balance sheet for the long and short term consequences of our actions. Such exercises have their place, whether they are done in traditional ethical terms or as some kind of cost/benefit analysis. But when, as often as not, no clear answer emerges, arbitrary choice or compromise may be the only alternatives left. 'A moral compromise, nobly undertaken and bravely endured', wrote Kirk, 'may enshrine a greater devotion of service and of faith than a reckless embracing of one alternative, even though the world calls the latter heroic and the former merely base.'[9] Only for a limited period, though.

Compromise, as Kirk understood it, is a device for deferring decisions to a more favourable time. It is not a settlement, but a staving off of the evil day in the hope that something else will turn up. In this respect it differs from the kind of statesmanlike compromise a politician might work for as a permanent means of resolving competing interests. When the context is a conflict between evils rather than between interests, compromise contains an element of connivance with evil, which is dangerous if it is allowed to continue unchecked, and eventually unnoticed. Such compromises harden into solutions which embody the evils from which they were intended to provide the means of escape.

The emphasis on forbearance, on not pushing ahead with decisions recklessly in order to appear decisive, is the main positive factor in compromise according to this analysis. Its main negative factor is the peril of compliance and complacency.

In our day nuclear deterrence provides the most momentous example of a choice between evils. It is interesting to note how at the height of the original Campaign for Nuclear Disarmament the plea was made by responsible Christian bodies for more time. David Edwards, writing in 1963 as the spokesman of the group which developed into CCADD,* said 'with a heavy heart I expect that nuclear weapons will remain in existence *for some years to come . . .*'[10] In the same year the British Council of Churches stated, 'The Council is convinced that these things are an offence to God and a denial of his purpose for man. Only the *rapid progressive reduction* of these weapons, their submission to strict international control and their eventual abolition can remove this offence.'[11] The implication is that a monstrosity can be tolerated for fear of something worse, but only if there is clear evidence that the compromise is a temporary one.

Eighteen years later, despite limited gains, the nuclear powers remain as firmly committed as ever to the use of such weapons, and the dangers of their world-wide proliferation have increased. The sense that time is running out, that a moral enormity can be accepted only for so long and no longer, is one of the factors underlying the resurgence of anti-nuclear feeling. Though traditional moral theology contains plenty of warnings against impatience, the belief that we ought to be moving faster, and in the right direction, has a strong claim on the Christian conscience.

The time horizon within which decisions have to be made is a matter of increasing importance within the political sphere, for two reasons which work in opposition to one another. On the one hand, the availability of instant news on a world-wide scale, and the possibility of instant reactions to events, puts pressure on politicians to define their attitudes long before it may be strictly necessary for them to do so. On the other hand, there is the fact that many of the processes on

---

* The Conference (later, Council) on Christian Approaches to Defence and Disarmament.

which the modern world depends have long lead times for their development and may call for decisions to be made many decades in advance. Energy policy is an obvious example. Politicians, therefore, find themselves caught between two time scales, and because the immediate pressures are likely to be stronger than the more remote ones, far-reaching decisions are frequently postponed.

Here again an awareness of moral time limits within which compromises are allowable may help to define the border between cautious flexibility and weak-willed procrastination.

Theological reflections can do no more than touch the margins of the complex problems with which politicians have to wrestle. The quality of the answers found, however, may depend rather heavily on the way in which politicians themselves, and those whom they represent, understand the limitations within which they are operating. An acceptance of the paradox of grace, for instance, may give the moral courage needed to take some decisive action, without the arrogance which then refuses to admit that it might be wrong. A sense of the complex dialogue in which God engages with his people may alert them to hitherto unrecognised voices in unexpected places. A recognition that God's infinite patience is held within the context of his ultimate judgement may give a sense of urgency to seize the creative moment when it comes. An acknowledgement that some otherwise messy compromises may nevertheless be faithful can help to reduce guilt and recrimination. And the admission that some may be unfaithful is a necessary safeguard against the ever-present danger of self-deception.

Notes

1. Colossians *1*. 15-20 (NEB).
2. Ibid., *1*. 9-10.
3. Nigel Balchin, *Lord I was afraid,* (1947), p. 320.
4. Ernst Troeltsch, *The Social Teaching of the Christian Churches* (1931 edn), p. 999.
5. Reinhold Niebuhr, *The Nature and Destiny of Man,* vol. II (1943), p. 242.
6. The point is well made in an essay by John Tinsley, 'Tell it Slant', *Theology,* vol. LXXXIII, pp. 163-70.
7. C.K. Barrett, 'The Dialectical Theology of St. John' in *New Testament Essays* (1972), ch. 4.
8. D.M. MacKinnon, *A Study in Ethical Theory* (1957), p. 264.
9. K.E. Kirk, *Conscience and its Problems* (1927), p. 374.
10. D.L. Edwards, *Withdrawing from the Brink in 1963* (1963), p. 18.
11. Quoted in *The Future of the British Nuclear Deterrent* (BCC, 1979), p. iii.

7 PATTERNS OF INTERNATIONAL COLLABORATION AMONG NON-GOVERNMENTAL ORGANISATIONS

J. Duncan Wood

The event which gave rise to the reflections in this essay took place in Geneva on 3 October 1979. On that occasion a distinguished company assembled at the headquarters of the International Labour Organisation to celebrate the fiftieth anniversary of a body which plays a modest but important role in Geneva's international life, the *Fédération des Institutions Internationales semi-officielles et privées établies à Genève*. Happily — and here we can trace the hand of Bertram Pickard, the most active of its founding fathers — the Federation's cumbersome title can be reduced to the pronounceable acronym, FIIG.

This is one of the three groupings of Non-governmental Organisations to which Bertram Pickard devotes some pages of his *The Greater United Nations*,[1] written at the end of his years of active service with and on behalf of the NGOs. His service was carried out in Geneva, and it is therefore not surprising that the other two groupings which he discusses are also based in that city. Of course, he was well aware of the existence of important NGO groupings elsewhere but decided to limit his examination to those of which he had direct personal experience. The present writer's international experience is, in some important respects, a continuation of Bertram Pickard's: limited to Geneva and deeply involved in the life of its NGO community. This essay, therefore, has a similar perspective to his and will consider the same institutions as they now appear a quarter of a century later.

FIIG

FIIG was born on 25 June 1929 after nearly four years of gestation. The scene of its birth, the Quaker Centre at 5 Place de la Taconnerie in the shadow of Calvin's cathedral, was also the place of its conception. The Quakers, seeing in the League of Nations an instrument for promoting the peaceful settlement of disputes, which they had consistently advocated since their origin in seventeenth-century England, had established what they somewhat grandiloquently called an 'embassy' in

Geneva to watch over and, if possible, promote the progress of the new world organisation. At first their centre was staffed by short-term volunteers, and it was one of them, Margaret Lester, who noted that the Quakers were not alone in recognising Geneva's new international importance. 'There are', she wrote to London on 3 November 1925,[2] '43 international organisations with headquarters in Geneva, many of which are working for our ideals.' In a later letter (22 December 1925)[3] she expressed regret at the tendency of these organisations to be over-jealous guardians of their particular interests; she thought that the provision of a meeting ground might help them to realise that 'they can do their own work better if they can be sure of the friendly help of the others.' These considerations led her to initiate a regular series of lunch meetings for what we would now call the NGO community.

Margaret Lester was not the only Quaker in Geneva to think along these lines. Inazo Nitobe, Japanese Under-Secretary-General of the League of Nations, was also a member of the Society of Friends. Acting with discretion and in his personal capacity, he urged the Quaker head-quarters in London and Philadelphia to maintain Margaret Lester's initiative by appointing permanent representatives in Geneva. Their appointees, Bertram and Irene Pickard, arrived in June 1926.

Lengthy negotiations, in which Bertram Pickard took a leading role, were needed to create the formal structure of FIIG out of the informal programme of lunch-meetings; they have been fully described elsewhere.[4] There is no indication that Inazo Nitobe took any part in them, but his initial contribution does invite some comment and speculation. As under-secretary-general he was responsible for the League's International Bureaux Section, that is to say its external relations with other inter-national bodies which, it must be remembered, were independent creations not co-ordinated into anything resembling the UN family. Fortunately for him, this was not an uncharted field, for there already existed in Brussels the *Union des Associations Internationales* which published a yearbook of international organisations. Without the assist-ance of the Brussels Union he could not have carried out his League assignment. The Union had been founded in 1910 by Henri LaFontaine and Paul Otlet, who not only saw that organised internationalism, already rapidly growing, needed a central focal point for the exchange of information, but also nourished the vision that a grouping of inter-national organisations could provide the intellectual and philosophical framework for a new and peaceful world order, the whole being, as it were, greater than the sum of its parts. There is no way of telling whether Inazo Nitobe had caught this vision, but there is evidence that the founders of FIIG had in mind not only the provision of agreed common services to member organisations but also the possibility that, by coming together, these organisations could contribute to the harmonious growth of the international community. These two aims, the practical and the visionary, inspire all NGO groupings and give rise to much healthy controversy within them.

Throughout most of its 50 years FIIG has concentrated on practical services. It did, on occasion, represent its members' interests at the League, notably by securing for them 'reserved seats with an assured access to documents and delegates'[5] at the Disarmament Conference of 1932, thus foreshadowing arrangements made for NGOs by the UN and, incidentally, removing a cause of friction among its members who had been contending with one another for such privileges. But with the advent of the UN the care of such questions passed into other hands, and in fact the principal service that FIIG has rendered to its members is to act as their spokesman in negotiations with the Genevese authorities on such vital material questions as the provision of office space and the taxes payable by foreign employees.

FIIG's membership includes NGOs with headquarters in Geneva, the Geneva offices of NGOs and voluntary agencies with headquarters elsewhere, and some – such as the International School – operating exclusively in Geneva but with an international outreach. Common to all of them is their establishment in Geneva, the international composition of their staff and their status as non-profit-making organisations; in other respects, they display a great variety of size, structure, aims and functions. The business which they pursue together through FIIG is conducted by officers and committee members serving in a voluntary capacity; and the running expenses are met by a membership fee based on a fixed amount per organisation, plus a fee based on the total number of employees each organisation has in Geneva, an arrangement which provides an equitable sliding scale and recognises the fact that individuals as well as organisations enjoy the benefits of co-operation.

To the lasting credit of Geneva, it contained in the 1920s a number of influential citizens who recognised that the NGOs were an essential part of the new international community centred in their city. One of them, Guillaume Fatio, worked closely with the founders of FIIG and was instrumental in establishing cordial relations between them and the authorities which continued with mutual benefit until the mid-1960s. By that time, a new generation of Genevese was more conscious of the burdens of internationalism than of its glamour. Their city was suffering from over-rapid growth. Some of the blame could indeed be attributed to the international community, then in full expansion following the decolonisation of Africa; but other factors were involved, including the decision by a number of American and multinational companies to make Geneva the centre of their European operations. Growth produced high prices, especially for housing, of which there was an acute shortage. Rising resentment found a ready-made scapegoat in the international officials, long regarded as parasites because they paid no taxes yet enjoyed the amenities provided by tax-paying citizens who were less well paid. A new party, the *Vigilants,* appeared on the political scene to exploit popular discontent.

The *Vigilants'* opportunity came when the UN Conference on Trade and Development of 1964 decided to become a permanent body with headquarters, preferably, in Geneva, threatening a further invasion of tax-exempt bureaucrats. It happened that the Cantonal budget for 1965 included a small item of 50,000 francs as a contribution to the *Fondation des Immeubles pour les Organisations Internationales* (FIPOI), a Swiss fund to finance further international buildings. The *Vigilants* organised an Initiative to challenge this item on the budget and a referendum had to be held. Feelings ran high during the weeks preceding the vote on 4 April 1965, for what was at stake was Geneva's future as an international city. Only citizens could decide this issue, though it chiefly concerned non-citizens, members of the international community who faced the gloomy prospect of having to move to one of the many other cities which were promising them a warmer welcome. In the event, they were reprieved: the *Vigilants* secured 25,806 votes but 31,813 voted against them – not a famous victory for internationalism, especially when account is taken of the abstentions which amounted to more than 60 per cent of the electorate.

Swiss referenda serve not simply to decide issues; they are also a form of opinion poll valuable to a government based on the principle of broad consensus. The Genevese authorities were able to make their contribution to FIPOI but had also to take note of a body of opinion hostile to the tax-exempt status of international officials. The only possible sop to this opinion was a drastic cut in the tax concessions previously accorded to foreign employees of the NGOs. The authorities regretted this, but they and FIIG had to bow to the storm. Worse was to come. The *Vigilants'* Initiative heralded a whole decade of national debate concerning proposals, associated with the name of James Schwarzenbach, to reduce the foreign population of Switzerland as a whole. The most widely debated of the successive referenda on this issue – that held on 6 and 7 June 1970 – gave Schwarzenbach and his associates

46 per cent of the vote. Again, the government felt bound to recognise the strength of anti-foreign feeling and imposed severe restrictions on the issue of work permits. Again, so far as Geneva's international community is concerned, it was the NGOs who had to bear the brunt of these new limitations: each new work permit, even if it were required for a foreigner replacing one who had departed, became the subject of lengthy negotiation.

These circumstances made it more than ever necessary for the NGOs to have an organisation 'to protect the common interests of its members in relation to their activity in Geneva and to seek to resolve problems which may arise out of this activity'.[6] Membership of FIIG has become an essential safeguard for any NGO with a permanent office in Geneva. From 72 in 1965, FIIG's membership had risen to 100 in 1978; and these 100 organisations employed 1,555 foreigners — 50 per cent more than were registered in 1965 — a tribute to FIIG's success in protecting its members' common interests.

This success justifies the confidence of FIIG's founders in the practical utility of co-operative action by NGOs. It also justifies the hope that such co-operation might contribute to the harmonious growth of the international community. FIIG has been able to defend the important principle that the staff of international institutions should be internationally recruited, a principle which applies equally to inter-governmental and to non-governmental organisations. The Genevese authorities have done their utmost, within the limits set by Berne, to respect this principle, valuing — as did their predecessors of the 1920s — the contribution of the non-governmental element to the international community. This community cannot live in a vacuum; it has to operate from chosen bases, of which Geneva remains one of the most significant. The malaise of 1965 revealed that, in addition to material facilities, a base of operations must offer the psychological benefit of a secure home; it revealed, too, the need to break down the barriers of mutual incomprehension which had separated foreigners from the Genevese. Since then many members of the international community, both from the UN family and from FIIG, have found the way to collaborate with the Genevese in a variety of cultural, religious and philanthropic activities, to their mutual enrichment. Yet there are still many Genevese, of a generation which belittles the value of administration and uses the word 'bureaucrat' as a term of abuse, who fail to see the relevance of the intergovernmental institutions housed in the great palaces of concrete, chrome and glass which form so conspicuous a feature of their landscape. Most of FIIG's members work closely with one or other of these institutions and can help to bridge the gap between them and the population at large by presenting the human face of internationalism.

ICVA

Though the second of Bertram Pickard's NGO groupings, the Standing Conference of Voluntary Agencies Working for Refugees, no longer exists under that name, he would recognise that it has bequeathed its purposes and an important part of its title to its descendant, the International Council of Voluntary Agencies (ICVA). It is not easy to draw a clear distinction between a voluntary agency and a non-governmental organisation. Both are non-governmental, being managed by private citizens and funded by voluntary donations; both are non-profit-making and pursue particular objectives, social or cultural, scientific, religious or philanthropic. The objectives of voluntary agencies are essentially philanthropic, at least in origin, but their truly distinctive character is their pursuit of these objectives through practical programmes designed to meet human needs − in other words, they are operational. This distinction, however, is not clear cut, for there are many organisations, such as the World YWCA, which combine the operational programme of a voluntary agency with the 'non-operational' activities of a consultative NGO. The latter, as defined by the UN, are international bodies composed of a number of national affiliates that are autonomous within their own national frontiers; this is not necessarily the case with voluntary agencies, which may be national bodies, operating beyond their own frontiers not through affiliates but through dependent offices. Though they do not satisfy UN criteria, there is no reason to deny such agencies a place in the international community: ICVA's experience has been that national initiatives can make an important contribution to international thinking.

These different types of organisation, national and international, were represented in the Standing Conference, which was recognised as their spokesman by the International Refugee Organisation and by its successor, the Office of the UN High Commissioner for Refugees, with which it enjoyed consultative status. When IRO was dissolved at the end of 1950 the governments assumed that its work was completed and that UNHCR would not need to conduct operational programmes on behalf of refugees. Until the assumption was shown to be false, the members of the Standing Conference provided the High Commissioner with an essential operating arm. The close partnership established in those early years continues to this day.

The immediate post-war years were a period of massive migration, notably of European refugees to new homes overseas. Responding to a widespread interest in the problems of migrants, the UN and ILO convened in 1950 a Conference of NGOs Interested in Migration. The conference had results that must be considered normal: first, the participants felt that it had been so useful that it should be reconvened and, secondly, they found that they had touched on so many problems that effective follow-up required the services of a paid secretariat. Thus, a new organised grouping was created, holding a full conference every two years to consider the papers produced by working parties in the interim. The membership of this conference overlapped to such an extent with that of the Standing Conference that, in Geneva at any rate, it was sometimes difficult to determine which of the two bodies had convened a particular meeting.

The merger of these two parallel groups was brought about by Dr Elfan Rees on his return to Geneva early in 1959 from the Thirteenth UN General Assembly, where he represented the Commission of the Churches on International Affairs (CCIA). That Assembly had given its blessing[7] to the British proposal for a World Refugee Year, a decision which called for the undivided support of all organisations concerned for refugees. The two groups pooled their resources in the International Committee for World Refugee Year. The new body concentrated on the concern of the Standing Conference but adopted the other partner's device of a full-time secretariat: at Elfan Rees's suggestion, Dr Michael Potulicki was invited to prolong a distinguished career as an international civil servant by becoming the new committee's Secretary-General. Under his direction, ICWRY, which had a larger membership than its two parent bodies, made a notable contribution to the success of World Refugee Year, the first and (so far) the most effective[8] of the various 'Years' that the UN has instituted.

As World Refugee Year drew to a close, the voluntary agencies began to consider ways of continuing the close co-operation which it had stimulated. The desire to stay together was widely shared but owed much to the enthusiasm of the Director of the Geneva office of the American Joint Distribution Committee, Charles Jordan, whose brutal murder in Prague in August 1977 – probably by Syrian agents – deprived Geneva's international community of a vital and colourful personality. He must be counted among the founding fathers of the International Council of Voluntary Agencies, formally launched on 6 March 1962 as a permanent body in the hope that, by continuing their collaboration, the agencies could keep alive in the world at large the heightened humanitarian awareness that had marked World Refugee Year.

ICVA, like ICWRY before it, has its full-time secretariat, of which Michael Potulicki remained in charge until his retirement in 1969. In pursuit of its aim 'to promote the development, growth and improvement of Voluntary Agencies and their activities throughout the world', ICVA has provided services to its members. Dr Potulicki instituted several: the exchange of information on current programmes through the periodical *ICVA News;* the more ambitious publication, in collaboration with OECD, of a directory of development programmes sponsored and funded by voluntary agencies, valued at that time at $1,000 million; the organisation of periodic conferences at which the member agencies can take a fresh look at the range and complexity of the human needs they are called upon to meet.

ICVA's Commission on Refugees has performed a service, not only to the agencies but also to those whom they assist, by maintaining a close working relationship with the Office of the UN High Commissioner for Refugees. Together, the Office and the agencies — both individually and, through ICVA, collectively — disbursed the large fund for the indemnification of refugees who had suffered Nazi persecution for reasons of nationality. This difficult task, involving a response to thousands of claims from all over the world, continued throughout the 1960s; it was part of the unfinished business of World Refugee Year, which had set out to solve the European refugee problem. If it did not quite achieve this objective, the Year proved, nevertheless, to be a watershed, for after it the centre of the refugee problem moved to other continents. The international community has been faced with a tragic series of refugee emergencies: the Tibetans, the Tutsis from Rwanda and many other refugees in Africa, the massive exodus of Bengalis in 1971, the Ugandan Asians in 1972, the Chileans in 1973, the Cypriots in 1974, the Kampucheans, the 'boat people' and many more. The response to these emergencies has been marked by a steadily growing consensus that there can be no limits to humanitarian concern, neither geographical nor political — for these new refugee movements are attributable to persecution by regimes of every tendency and colour. The agencies have played an important part in creating this consensus, at the international level by regular statements addressed through ICVA to the High Commissioner's Executive Committee, and at the national level by maintaining a climate of opinion favourable to generous governmental aid. Some governments have recognised the important role of voluntary agencies in this respect by inviting their officers to be members of their official delegations to the Executive Committee.

Refugees are often termed victims of 'man-made' disasters. A comparable consensus exists where the victims of natural catastrophes are concerned. For them, too, Geneva is the focal point for international aid, through the UN Disaster Relief Organisation for intergovernmental and the League of Red Cross Societies for voluntary assistance. These two bodies have the means and the expertise to assess the immediate needs of disaster victims. This does not mean that they need necessarily exercise a monopoly over the provision of aid, but it does mean that others who wish to help should act in close consultation with them. In this way the response the public makes through its preferred channels can be co-ordinated into a single operation. ICVA does not play a direct role in such operations, but discussions among its members have led to the institution of the valuable monthly meetings at League headquarters where representatives of intergovernmental organisations, the International Committee of the Red Cross and voluntary agencies exchange information on current disaster situations, both natural and man-made, some of which are unknown to the public and all of which tend to continue longer than the public response to them.

Work which ICVA members undertake on behalf of refugees and victims of disasters is centred in Geneva; participating agencies must be represented there or be within easy access. ICVA's membership, however, is world-wide and includes a large number of agencies whose primary concern is social and economic development. Thus, ICVA has a wider field of interest, and a wider membership, than its predecessors. This is logical since the humanitarian sequel to natural disasters, which have a tendency to afflict developing countries, or to such refugee emergencies as that which occurred in Bengal in 1971, is to engage in long-term programmes of rehabilitation. A concern for development arises naturally from a concern for emergency relief.

Nevertheless, the two concerns have not always lived happily side by side. Development is a relatively young discipline whose content and application are not universally agreed; as yet, there is no consensus on its principles. Divergences of view on this subject came to light early in ICVA's history when, on 14 January 1964, its governing board considered an application for membership from the International Planned Parenthood Federation. The board was swayed by the doubts expressed by the Catholic agencies concerning the relevance of this organisation to ICVA's field of interest, and it was some years before the question of population found a place on the agenda. Whether or not it is concerned with this delicate question, any development programme involves making choices which, in the last resort, are political. Within a world-wide and heterogeneous body such as ICVA, political choices are divisive, the more so when some of them are made by national agencies responding to a particular national outlook. A choice that appears unexceptionable to one agency may seem dangerously revolutionary to others who fear that, if approved at an ICVA meeting, it may offend their contributors or even endanger their charitable status. ICVA's Commission on Social and Economic Development (COSED) has provided a useful forum for the exchange of views but has not yet produced consensus, still less an organ for co-ordinating the agencies' programmes in this vast and important field.[9]

The existence of COSED, and its implications in respect of membership and programme, is in large part responsible for the internal problems that ICVA has encountered. Some of its keenest and most influential supporters have seen in ICVA the spearhead of the voluntary movement throughout the world, offering a means of practical expression to the growing sentiment of universal brotherhood. From this point of view, ICVA's strength lies in its having a permanent secretariat to follow up the decisions of its meetings and, if necessary, take initiatives to promote its purposes. It was this concept that led to the acquisition by ICVA of consultative status with the Economic and Social Council in Category I, thus giving to many of its members access to the UN which they would not otherwise have enjoyed.

On the other hand, there are influential member agencies that have their own access to the UN and would not wish another body to speak on their behalf. From their point of view it is improper for ICVA to set itself up as an organisation apart from the members that compose it. This view found expression when the UN High Commissioner conferred on ICVA the Nansen Medal Award for distinguished service to refugees. The public ceremony was held in the Council Chamber at the Palais des Nations on 10 October 1963, when the medal was handed to Charles Jordan, then ICVA's president, and the acceptance speech was delivered by his Quaker predecessor; but this was followed on 7 November by a further ceremony which made it clear that the award had in fact been made to each and every one of the voluntary agencies who were working for refugees long before ICVA had been thought of. Thus, ICVA was not the true recipient but merely a convenient channel for distributing the honour to all those who had earned it.

There is a world of difference between a 'spearhead' and a 'convenient channel'. The latter does not require an independent secretariat able to take initiatives; it may not even require a secretariat at all. Some of those who take this more limited view of ICVA's function are also among the important contributors to its budget, a budget which is modest enough by intergovernmental standards yet constitutes a burdensome addition to the overheads of members, which has to be justified to contributors who tend to regard administrative costs as an expensive luxury. It would be possible for these agencies to 'cut ICVA down to size' by withholding their contributions, but they have not done so since one does not lightly or easily call a halt to 20 years of co-operative effort. Consequently, the two different concepts of ICVA's purpose continue to live side by side, held in equilibrium by the opposing forces of sovereignty and solidarity.

CONGO

The full title of Bertram Pickard's third NGO grouping is 'Conference of Non-Governmental Organisations in Consultative Status with the Economic and Social Council of the United Nations', for which, fortunately, the acronym CONGO is now in common usage. It owes its origin to a group of 18 NGOs who had acquired the consultative status provided for in Article 71 of the UN Charter. They met first at Lake Success in September 1947 and brought their concept to fruition at Geneva in 1950. Prominent among its promoters were Dr Howard Wilson of the Carnegie Endowment for International Peace, John Ennals of the World Federation of United Nations Associations, Dr Elfan Rees of CCIA and Dr Gerhard Riegner of the World Jewish Congress, still actively associated with CONGO after three decades of service. Three formative conferences were needed, and as all of them took place in Geneva it can be assumed that the experience of FIIG was transmitted to the new body; indeed, the first of these conferences, held in 1948, was chaired by Georges Thélin of the International Union for Child Welfare, who was then FIIG's president.

The Third General Conference in 1950 adopted precise objectives for the new grouping: to hold periodic meetings to study consultative arrangements; to improve the material possibilities for consultation; and to take such steps towards improving them as are approved by two-thirds of the members. CONGO was to be a trade union to defend the rights and, if possible, improve the working conditions of its members. Membership was, and still is, open to all NGOs having consultative status (of whatever category) with the Economic and Social Council (ECOSOC) and to NGOs having consultative or equivalent relations with any of the Specialised Agencies. CONGO's present membership amounts to less than a quarter of the total — now of the order of 800 — eligible under this definition, but does include a much higher proportion of those organisations which maintain regular contact with the UN; it has also to be remembered that some specialised agencies, notably UNESCO, have their own active NGO conferences, not all of whose members feel it necessary to join CONGO.

The periodic meetings foreseen in 1950 have taken place every two or three years and are now called 'Assemblies'; with one exception (New York, 1952), they have been held in Geneva, usually just prior to the summer session of ECOSOC. The meetings elect the president for the ensuing two- or three-year period and a number of organisations to serve on the executive committee, which was formerly known exclusively by its French title, 'Bureau', but has now been given an English title, 'Board'. The other officers, elected from among the members of the Bureau/Board, all serve, as does the president, in a voluntary capacity, often making a hidden contribution to CONGO's running costs by using the office time and manpower of their organisations in the discharge of their duties. Only in 1976 was it felt necessary to make budgetary provision for secretarial assistance to the president.

Thus, CONGO resembles FIIG rather than ICVA in its administrative arrangements. It differs fundamentally from both in that it cannot be based exclusively in Geneva since the consultative arrangements, which are its concern, apply equally in New York: CONGO has to function in two cities simultaneously. Until recently, its solution to this problem was to alternate the presidency between the two centres of UN activity and to ensure that the elected organisations could name representatives to each of two co-equal Bureaux, one in Geneva and one in New York.

Unfortunately, like some intrepid aviators of the 1920s, the founders of CONGO underestimated the width of the Atlantic. Finance is one factor which makes transatlantic communication difficult. Europeans still tend to regard New York as a faraway place at the end of an expensive journey; recently, US citizens, who used to flock to Geneva for summer meetings, have begun to find the journey costly. The use of sophisticated forms of telecommunication has been restricted by budgetary considerations. There have been occasions when language was a barrier to understanding between a French-speaking officer in Geneva and an Anglophone opposite number in New York. Nor is it simply a question of linguistics. The two Bureaux have been subjected to different influences: in Geneva, from the interplay of different nationalities within the Bureau itself, affected very little by the politics of a self-effacing host country; in New York — where the Bureau has been a more homogeneous group, with a higher proportion of US citizens — from all the political and social pressures of a dynamic and volatile nation. Organisations have not always exerted the same influence in the two cities, being represented in one by a full-time officer, in the other by a part-time, and possibly ill-informed, volunteer. Issues which seem urgent in New York may appear trivial in Geneva — and vice versa. For all these reasons it often proved difficult for the two Bureaux to reach a decision save after months of transatlantic exchanges.

CONGO's Eighteenth Assembly in 1976 decided to end this bicephalous system by establishing a single Board, based in Geneva, which would meet once a year in New York. This new arrangement may solve the problem of decision-making by placing it firmly in one spot, but it ignores the awkward fact that, whereas history has put the centre of the NGO world in Europe, the UN has placed it in America. The chief of the NGO Section of the Secretariat has always been based in New York and the important meetings of ECOSOC's Committee on NGOs are held there. Since many other bodies meeting at UN Headquarters take decisions affecting the consultative relationship, it is difficult to see how New York can be permanently relegated to a subordinate role in CONGO's operations. A long-term solution to the problem will necessitate a greater participation in NGO work at New York of non-US citizens and, above all, a warmer welcome to representatives of NGOs based in Eastern Europe.[10] This requires an operation in New York not unlike that which FIIG has successfully performed in Geneva. At the same time, it is important for nationals of other countries to recognise that US citizens are just as capable as they are of rendering loyal and effective service to the international community.

These internal problems have not prevented CONGO from carrying out the mandate of its Third Conference. It is valued by the UN secretariat as a recognised channel for the discussion of NGO needs and has been instrumental in securing proper access to delegates and documentation and the provision of facilities for NGO meetings. All NGOs, whether or not they are members of CONGO, benefit from these arrangements, which they could not have negotiated individually. Most of the founder members of CONGO regarded such services as an adequate return for their subscriptions. They did not wish the Conference to become involved in matters of substance — indeed, in such matters, they insisted on retaining unimpaired their sovereign independence. This is not simply a sign of organisational pride and prejudice: many NGOs were created to promote certain principles or doctrines which do not readily lend themselves to negotiated compromise.

The first test of the exclusion of CONGO from matters of substance came when ECOSOC decided,[11] on the proposition of the United States, to convene a conference of NGOs interested in the eradication of prejudice and discrimination. The organisation of this conference was the responsibility of the UN secretariat which, desiring to meet the wishes of the participants and finding it impossible to consult the (then) 252 consultative NGOs individually, turned to CONGO's New York Bureau for assistance. The Bureau felt it right to assist in matters of procedure, although — or perhaps because — it was not responsible for convening the conference.

Just prior to the opening of the conference, held in Geneva from 31 March to 4 April 1955, the World Veterans Federation announced that it would include in its delegation M. Vincent Auriol, the former French President — the obvious choice to preside over the assembled NGOs. He brought to his task all the arts of persuasion and cajolery which had stood him in good stead when presiding over the Fourth Republic. An initial shower of draft resolutions from one or other of the 97 NGOs represented was reduced to four orderly documents, which were adopted with unanimous acclaim. It was, as some participants reflected after the event, a splendid public condemnation of sin — but perhaps little more, save an agreement to request another conference to pursue the subject further.

Prior to the event the Bureau had expressed the hope that 'this new form of consultation . . . might prove so useful that the conference would mark a new step in the development and evolution of the consultative process'.[12] This was just what some organisations feared. The Catholic NGOs, for instance, were resolutely opposed to 'collective consultation', fearing that it would result in their particular point of view being submerged in an ocean of generalities. Procedures for the convening of a second 'discrimination conference' were due to be initiated at the Commission on Human Rights early in 1957, by which time international tension had been heightened by events in Suez and Hungary. It did not seem to the Catholic NGOs that this was the time to be involved in a display of solidarity — in whatever cause — with organisations from whom they might differ profoundly on the main issues of the day. Accordingly, they spoke out strongly at the Commission against holding a second conference at that time and persuaded the delegates that its convening was inopportune.

This event dominated CONGO's Seventh Conference in July 1957. The non-Catholic NGOs, Protestant, Jewish and secular, angry with their

Catholic colleagues for having acted unilaterally, pushed through a resolution in favour of a second discrimination conference. They then provoked the first contested election for the presidency, for which the previously designated candidate had Catholic support, by persuading the Quaker secretary to stand. His election by a small majority put him at the head of a divided body. The main source of division, the second discrimination conference, was removed from the arena by being entrusted to a highly informal planning committee, which ensured that a conference was held, to satisfy the majority, but in conditions which enabled the minority to participate. Catholic NGOs were among the 84 organisations attending this second conference, held in Geneva from 22 to 26 June 1959, a much less flamboyant affair than the first but providing a better opportunity for serious discussion and exchange of views. Though rated a success, it had no sequel, and when the subject of discrimination appeared once more on the NGO agenda it had a rather different social and political context.

CONGO did not meet again for its Eighth Conference until 1960, by which time the personality and actions of Pope John XXIII had begun to revolutionise relations between his Church and the rest of the world. A wide range of NGOs had meanwhile indicated their belief in the continuing value of CONGO, and the conference was able to unite in reaffirming the original objectives. It also agreed on a small step in the direction of 'collective consultation'. Provision was made for CONGO's president to convene, at the request of six member organisations, a meeting of NGOs interested in a specific item under discussion at a current session of ECOSOC or one of its organs. Once assembled, such a meeting elected its own president and formed an *ad hoc* committee, for the duration of the UN session, to plan common tactics and possibly prepare a joint written statement or name one of its members as spokesman, all of which measures were rendered desirable by the increase in UN membership, which meant that more time had to be given to governmental and less to non-governmental speakers. Use was made of this device for joint discussion of such questions as slavery.

The problem of joint action on matters of substance arose more acutely when the General Assembly, in designating[13] 1968 the 'International Year for Human Rights', called for the participation of NGOs. Deeming this to be an exercise in consultative relationships — and assuming human rights to be everybody's concern — the New York Bureau became directly involved in activities relating to the Year. In Geneva an independent initiative was taken by Sean MacBride, then Secretary-General of the International Commission of Jurists, who, as early as

14 May 1966, convened a number of NGOs for a preliminary discussion which led to the formal establishment, on 3 August, of the Standing Committee for Human Rights Year. This committee, which had no connexion with CONGO, organised a large NGO conference in January 1968 to inaugurate the Year and was active throughout the year in encouraging activities at the national or international level. In several respects this proved to be a landmark in the development of the NGO community.

In the first place, Sean MacBride insisted on making his committee as representative as possible of all NGO interests and included all three trade union organisations. The full participation of the World Federation of Trade Unions, which has its headquarters in Prague, was the first step in a process which, in a short space of time, brought the Marxist or 'Eastern-based' NGOs into much closer contact with, and participation in, the NGO community in Geneva. The return of the Women's International Democratic Federation (East Berlin) to consultative status, the acquisition of consultative status by the World Peace Council (Helsinki) and the participation of the World Federation of Democratic Youth (Budapest) in the preparation of the World Youth Assembly of 1970 were all part of this process which led, in 1972, to the election of some of these NGOs to the bureau of CONGO.[14]

Secondly, as with World Refugee Year, the International Year for Human Rights had provided valuable experience in NGO co-operation. Continuing co-operation was clearly required to tackle the problems which the Year had revealed but left unsolved. Happily, an agreement of its Eleventh Conference enabled CONGO to be used as a 'launching-pad' not only for the temporary *ad hoc* committees foreseen in 1960 but also for more permanent, independent bodies. This procedure was used at the Twelfth Conference in 1969 to approve the creation in both Geneva and New York of Special[15] NGO Committees on Human Rights and Development. Almost as an afterthought, on the suggestion of Gertrude Baer of the Women's International League for Peace and Freedom, the creation of the Special NGO Committee on Disarmament was approved. At first this committee was unique to Geneva where it inherited the work and membership of a previous informal NGO group which had organised a seminar for NGOs on disarmament in March 1966.

Thirdly, an important item on the programme for Human Rights Year was a big governmental conference held in Teheran in May 1968. This was the first of a series of world conferences held under UN auspices which were a notable feature of the 1970s. Teheran provided a warning to NGOs that — even in a matter so close to their hearts as human rights — they could not automatically expect to enjoy at conferences convened by the General Assembly all the rights which their status with ECOSOC conferred upon them. Prior to the conference, Sean MacBride had presented to the Standing Committee in Geneva a draft resolution on the Protection of Human Rights in Armed Conflicts, a question of whose urgency the public had been made acutely aware by the Vietnam War. This resolution, endorsed by members of the committee, was translated and reproduced in Geneva and taken by its author in bulk to Teheran where no facilities were available for processing NGO documents. In spite of these handicaps, it formed the basis of the most — perhaps the only — significant outcome of the conference, a resolution on Respect for Human Rights in Armed Conflicts, which was subsequently endorsed by the General Assembly.[16]

This had long-term repercussions in Geneva. The fact that the UN was seized of the problem gave added interest in the updating of international humanitarian law. This is the special province of the International Committee of the Red Cross which, after lengthy consultation with government experts, produced two draft additional protocols to the Geneva Conventions for submission to a Diplomatic Conference on International Humanitarian Law Applicable in Armed Conflicts, convened by the Swiss government in Geneva in February 1974. During the autumn of 1973, a group of 20 NGOs from the Human Rights and Disarmament Committees met together to prepare a detailed memorandum commenting on the drafts. The Swiss government recognised the value of their work and granted to the members of the group rights in relation to the Diplomatic Conference comparable to those enjoyed under UN auspices. At the end of a very long exercise, terminating only in 1977, it could be reported that 'some of the points in the memorandum were reflected in Conference decisions'.[17]

A similar approach was adopted to the Plenipotentiary Conference on Territorial Asylum, which met in Geneva in January 1977. During the summer of 1976 a working group of the Special NGO Committee on Human Rights met to prepare a commentary on the text of the draft convention which was to be put before the conference. When the conference opened it became clear that the Soviet delegation did not wish it to reach a conclusion; as part of their filibustering tactics they challenged the right of the NGOs to attend, and NGOs did not enjoy all the rights normally accorded to them by ECOSOC. Fortunately, the working group had circulated its commentary to all delegates before the conference opened, and it had considerable influence on such conclusions as the conference was able to reach before its time ran out.[18]

These exercises in expressing humanitarian principles in acceptable treaty language are an important collective use of NGO expertise — one of the objectives of the consultative relationship. Similar work continues at Geneva in other aspects of human rights. Such an approach is appropriate when governments have reached the stage of treaty-making. Most of the big world conferences of the 1970s were convened at a much earlier stage in the discussion of the topics assigned to them; they required a different approach by NGOs, for which the 1972 Stockholm Conference on the Human Environment provided valuable initiation. The organisers of this conference encouraged NGOs to participate but had so enthusiastic a response that it was impossible to accommodate all of them in the official conference hall. A separate forum[19] was therefore arranged as the focus of NGO activity, related to, but separate from, the governmental meeting. This experiment was repeated at the UN Conferences on Population (Bucharest, 1974), International Women's Year (Mexico City, 1975), Habitat (Vancouver, 1976) and, most recently, the Conference on the UN Decade for Women (Copenhagen, 1980) where the forum attracted 8,000 participants.

Opinions are divided on the effectiveness of these forums or tribunes.[20] Some NGOs feel that their separate meetings have given publicity to the topic under discussion by providing more wide-ranging, and much more interesting, discussions than those conducted by government delegates. Those who hold this view stress the educational value of the forum approach, both for their own members and for the public at large. Others fear that these separate meetings, often held at some distance from the governmental ones, distract NGO attention from what the governments are doing — or, more likely, not doing — to promote the cause which brought them together; in their view an 'integrated' approach, concentrating the attention of NGO observers on the main conference, is more effective. This was used at the World Food Conference (Rome, 1974) and UNCTAD IV (Nairobi, 1976) with some success.[21]

A common feature of the NGO activity at each of these conferences has been the publication of a conference newspaper, an idea also born in Stockholm with the daily, *Eco,* which (like its successors) was the responsibility of a small group of NGOs. The dedicated and specialised group which has followed the marathon UN Conference on the Law of the Sea has published *Neptune* in both Geneva and New York. At Rome and Nairobi, ICVA sponsored the publication of *Pan* and *Cosmos.* Some of these publications have been widely read by delegates: *Planet* at Bucharest achieved a circulation of 5,000. Newspapers are thus a new form of NGO statement, though, being unofficial, they are not translated into all the working languages. On the other hand, being free of Secretariat control, they can be more outspoken: *Pan* achieved the distinction of displeasing the US and Soviet delegations on successive days.

These large conferences were convened by the General Assembly and much of the preparatory work for them was conducted in New York. This gave CONGO's New York Bureau an important role in initiating negotiations for NGO participation and in setting up the committees in which the interested NGOs met to plan their activities. Geneva played a subordinate role in these preparations, save for International Women's Year when transatlantic co-operation proved no easier in a matter of substance than it had been in matters of procedure. For all these conferences the case for NGO participation was greatly strengthened by the existence of demonstrable NGO interest in and knowledge of the subject. The experience of one of the NGO committees established in 1969 will illustrate the point.

When the Special NGO Committee on Disarmament was established in Geneva as an official but independent entity, it invited into membership some organisations which were not, and could not be, members of CONGO, since at that time a concern for disarmament did not qualify them for consultative status with ECOSOC. The subject was not yet in the mainstream of NGO thinking, being regarded by some as 'dangerously political'. The next act of the committee – on 19 February 1970 – was to adopt a resolution drafted by its Quaker chairman on Chemical and Bacteriological Warfare. The text urged – in the terms of General Assembly Resolution 2603 (XXIV) – 'all States which have not already done so to accede to the Geneva Protocol of 1925'. Since it only asked governments to do what they had already approved, it was easy for some 50 NGOs, many of them non-members of the committee, to endorse this resolution before it was transmitted to all governments. Alongside a similar exercise conducted at the same time by the International Committee of the Red Cross, this action of the committee helped to make 1970 a record year for new accessions to the Protocol.

The committee next turned its attention to organising a conference on disarmament for NGOs, held in Geneva at the end of September 1972. This was an opportunity for NGOs to familiarise themselves with the subject and for some national NGOs to participate for the first time in an international gathering which spanned the ideological divide.

In June 1973 a sister committee, the NGO Committee on Disarmament at UN Headquarters, was established under the chairmanship of Dr Homer Jack. The two bodies co-operated in preparing for the First Review Conference of the Non-Proliferation Treaty in 1975. Unfortunately, it proved impossible to produce a statement on which all members of both committees could agree, but a very positive achievement was the acquisition of a form of consultative status at the review conference, giving recognition and facilities to the NGO observers.

This foreshadowed a much more significant achievement in relation to the Tenth Special Session of the General Assembly, known to the NGOs as the SSD – Special Session on Disarmament. From the start, the SSD Preparatory Committee, meeting in New York, opened its meetings to NGO observers, whose persuasive arguments led it to propose that NGOs be allowed to address the Special Session on the conclusion of the general debate. Since this was an unprecedented extension of the consultative arrangements to the General Assembly, it was appropriate that the president of CONGO should share with the two NGO committees the delicate task of selecting the organisations which addressed the Committee of the Whole on 12 June 1978.[22] The 'integrated' approach to a big UN meeting could not go further than this. The other activities organised by the NGO community at the SSD were designed to assist visiting delegations in following the debates: maintaining a Disarmament Information Bureau in a storefront opposite UN Headquarters and publishing daily the *Disarmament Times*, a newspaper which, though no longer a daily, continues to appear on a regular basis.

Disarmament is only one field of NGO interest. Similar initiatives have been taken in other fields, leading to a proliferation of organs for NGO collaboration and leaving CONGO, like ECOSOC, surrounded by adult, independent offspring. There are some who would like to assert the primacy of CONGO in this extended NGO family by making the special committees an integral part of its structure, thus giving it a direct interest in matters of substance and possibly enabling it to become 'the voice of world public opinion'. This concept of CONGO's future takes up the vision of one of its founders, Dr Howard Wilson, who remarked at the Second Conference in 1949 that the NGOs had all felt that they were 'marching forward in a movement more important than ourselves',[23] it even recalls the more distant dreams of Paul Otlet and Henri LaFontaine. But it would be a final break with the limited objectives set in 1950.

The time for such a step is not yet here. It would take a very bold man to assert that the consultative relationship is now secure for all NGOs for all time. The experience of the Plenipotentiary Conference on Territorial Asylum is not unique, and there have been attempts to downgrade the NGOs generally or to exclude specific ones from participation in UN meetings. It would not be to the benefit either of the

NGOs or of the UN if the recent development of collective consultation led to the exclusion of individual NGOs who have their own opinions to express. So long as there is a need to protect the right of NGOs to express their views on matters of substance, it can best be met by a body uncommitted to any opinion on such questions.

Nor is it easy to assert that on any of the great issues of the day there is a discernible world public opinion to be voiced, other than the universal yearning for peace and justice. The outstanding feature of the NGO world is its diversity, but in its present composition it does not fully mirror the diversity of outlook and opinion in the world at large. We need not be distressed if the world speaks with many voices, for the great human problems of the day are too complex to be settled by some easy, uniform solution. Over the past three decades the NGOs have learned to live with discord and they cannot yet expect to reduce it to a comfortable harmony.

There is, however, one point on which harmony might be possible. The NGOs of which we have been speaking are all related, in one way or another, to the UN and must be assumed to share a common belief in its purposes. These purposes have been betrayed by member states which see in the UN not an instrument for international collaboration but a device to advance their national interests; which regard appointments to the Secretariat as national perquisites rather than openings for international service; which have wasted the time of every one of the big conferences called to consider problems affecting the future of the human race by the intrusion of local, temporary and irrelevant political issues. National interest has taken precedence over international responsibility, bringing to the verge of collapse the world order of which the founders of the UN dreamed in 1945. The NGOs are an integral part of this world order, the only part which could call on governments to abandon their sterile military confrontations and to give priority to the real problems facing the human race as a whole. To persuade governments to think less about sovereignty and more about solidarity is a daunting task and is certainly beyond the field of competence of the three groupings discussed in this essay. The experience of FIIG, ICVA and CONGO may, however, have its contribution to make to the renewal and revitalising of the hopes and aspirations which once launched the United Nations in the name of 'We, the Peoples'.

Acknowledgements

I am indebted for assistance in tracing documents or verifying facts to MM.
Amerding and Malempré of UNESCO; Edith M. Ballantyne, president, and Lee
Weingarten, secretary of CONGO; Douglas Deane; Miss Anne-Marie Hertoghe;
the Librarian, Friends House, London; Sean MacBride; Irene Pickard; Dr Gerhard
Riegner and the staff of the World Jewish Congress; Cyril Ritchie, president of
FIIG; Peter Whittle, Quaker House, Geneva.
The views expressed in this essay are, of course, entirely my own.

Notes

1. Bertram Pickard, *The Greater United Nations* (New York: Carnegie
Endowment for International Peace, 1956).
2. Friends Service Council archives. Geneva correspondence.
3. Ibid.
4. 50th Anniversary booklet, published by FIIG, Palais Wilson, Geneva.
5. Pickard, *The Greater United Nations.*
6. From statutes adopted in 1929.
7. GA Res. 1285 (XIII), 5 December 1958.
8. Judged by popular participation; almost as successful in this respect was
the International Year of the Child (1979), which originated with Canon Moerman
of the International Catholic Child Bureau, Geneva.
9. Some agencies, finding that ICVA could not, as they had hoped, provide
an 'umbrella' for their rehabilitation programmes in the southern Sudan, joined a
separate body for this purpose, Euro-Action Acord.
10. In the early 1950s the welcome was glacial; some NGO representatives
were frozen out by their inability to obtain US visas. CONGO had to intervene on
their behalf, insisting that the Headquarters Agreement should apply as much to
NGO representatives as to government delegates. But the memory of those days
lingers on.
11. Res. 546 (XVIII), 6 August 1954.
12. CONGO Document B-NY/54/UN Prej. Conf./1.
13. GA Res. 1961 (XVIII), 12 December 1963.
14. Previously, 'equitable distribution' of membership had taken into account
different interests represented by religious, women's and youth organisations,
and categories of status. To accommodate ideology the bureau was increased to 20.
15. Unfortunately, in New York, where they have less regard for linguistic
niceties, the old title *ad hoc* was retained for these new committees though it has
long since ceased to be appropriate.
16. GA Res. 2444 (XXIII), 19 December 1968.
17. CONGO Document NGO/GA-14/Doc. 7-F, para. 4.
18. Ibid., Annexe.
19. At Stockholm there were in addition three informal NGO gatherings in
progress simultaneously. The extensive NGO interest aroused by this conference
has led to the creation of a permanent NGO organ, the Environment Liaison
Centre, working with the United Nations Environment Programme (UNEP) in
Nairobi.
20. The name given to the NGO gatherings at Bucharest and Mexico City.
21. For a full discussion of NGO activity at world conferences, see the draft
paper by Angus Archer, 'New Forms of NGO Participation in World Conferences',

prepared for a UNITAR colloquium, 14 October 1976.

22. For an account of the origin and organisation of this event, see the article by Barrett Hollister, 'NGO Day – How it all Began', *Disarmament Times*, no. 16, 12 June 1978.

23. CONGO Document MN40/23/49.

8 COMMONWEALTH AND UNITED NATIONS: EXPLORATIONS IN COMPARATIVE INTERNATIONAL ORGANISATION

Nicholas A. Sims

Students of international organisation owe Sydney Bailey a number of debts. In the key area of United Nations studies his contribution has been of especial importance, and not just for the meticulous scholarship of his books on the various Principal Organs and his monographs on UN issues, the strong background in constitutional analysis which he has brought to them, or simply his gift for making the complicated readable. Going beyond that, he has also demonstrated that it is possible to take the factual, empirical skeleton of international institutions[1] and make these dry bones live: which, in an area of study where the factual emphasis has tended to be played down in favour of relatively abstract theorising, is no mean achievement. Writing on (like teaching) international organisation is indeed wide open to the insidious onset of a dry formalism that not all can resist: it could hardly be otherwise, given that 'the first characteristic of the subject of international organisation is that it is concerned with the development of formal structures in international society'.[2]

What saves Sydney Bailey's work from this fate is, I suggest, the combination of two noteworthy qualities in his writing. The first is a keen sense of the political. 'It is only in books', he says, 'that a neat distinction can be made between policy and administration';[3] and the chapter on the UN Secretariat's internal organisation from which that quotation is taken demonstrates most effectively the advantages of bringing a sense of politics, as well as a sense of history, to the understanding of such matters.

The second is a concern for the uses to which international institutions may be put. They do not exist unto themselves, but the impression is sometimes given in academic writing and teaching that they do (much to the detriment of their popularity among students as subjects for study). Sydney Bailey never falls into this trap. He is with those who are interested in seeing international institutions as (among other things) 'indications of a growing international order, that is, of a strengthening consensus about appropriate rules of procedure and management in the international system'.[4] What is more, he has kept that perspective

144

before him as an adviser to government[5] and in his many-sided work, in Quaker, ecumenical and other non-governmental (NGO) contexts, as a consistently helpful influence in such NGOs' policy formation on international affairs.

Sydney Bailey's contribution to our better understanding of international organisation does not end with his writing and policy advice. He has actively promoted the study of the subject through such bodies as the Institute for the Study of International Organisation (of which he was a Council member) at the University of Sussex and, established on a more lasting basis, the UN Institute for Training and Research.[6] Since the latter has added to its central interest in the peaceful settlement of disputes the study of relations between the UN and other international institutions, it may be not inappropriate to devote this essay to the theme of comparative international organisation, in drawing some parallels and noting some contrasts between the UN and the Commonwealth in certain aspects of their institutional development.

The United Nations and Regional Organisations

When the United Nations came into being, international organisation on a regional basis was almost unknown apart from the inter-American system. Yet the tension between regionalists and globalists was one of the principal themes of the Charter-drafting process in 1944-5, and a whole chapter of the Charter (albeit one of the shorter ones) was devoted to regional arrangements, with their relationship to the UN outlined in articles 52-4. The credit for this section is generally[7] given to those (a high proportion) of the UN's founder-members who also belonged to the inter-American system and who gave notice, in the Act of Chapultepec adopted when the Conference on International Organisation was about to meet at San Francisco, of their intention to move on from the heritage of Bolívar to new institutions – in the event, the Rio Pact of 1947 and the Bogotá Charter of 1948 which created the Organisation of American States.

Yet within a few years the international scene was to be crowded with new regional organisations of all kinds, behaving to a greater or lesser degree in the spirit of chapter 8 of the UN Charter. The League of Arab States (1945) narrowly antedated the UN; it was followed by the Organisation of American States (1948), the Council of Europe (1949), and later by the Organisation of African Unity (1963) and the Association of South East Asian Nations (1967), not to mention the North Atlantic

Treaty Organisation (1949) and the other institutionalised military alliances that followed it. And this was only the tip of the regionalist iceberg. The multi-functional (or general) regional organisations brought into being by such documents as the charters of Bogotá, London and Addis Ababa have been overtaken in weight of numbers, although not necessarily in visibility, by the profusion of specialist bodies each with its narrowly defined function — from the European Organisation for the Safety of Air Navigation to the South Pacific Bureau of Economic Co-operation. At the same time, the emergence of politico-economic amalgams in quest of regional integration, such as the European Communities, has complicated the scene still further.

The United Nations co-operates with regional organisations at many levels, from the ceremonial to the practical. The most important of the general ones — the European Communities, the League of Arab States, the Organisation of African Unity, the Organisation of American States — enjoy the highest status, with permanent observer offices in New York and Geneva. They are accepted as quasi-participants in UN affairs at the level of the Security Council and the General Assembly, although the extent to which they can operate there as entities distinct from their own member states is both uneven and uncertain. In that sense they are at a disadvantage in comparison with the permanent observers of, say, the Palestine Liberation Organisation or the South-West Africa People's Organisation, who are freer to conduct themselves as ambassadors in all but name of member states-in-waiting, on a par (in practice) with the permanent representatives of 'proper' governments.

Beyond Regional Organisations: the Commonwealth and Others

Beyond the strictly regional organisations, however, there are three others that the UN allows to enjoy observer status on an equally permanent basis, although up to 1980 they had not followed the regional bodies in establishing offices in the UN cities. These are the Council for Mutual Economic Assistance (CMEA), the Organisation of the Islamic Conference and the Commonwealth.

The first two have strong regional affiliations. The CMEA, sometimes called Comecon, until recently consisted exclusively of the Soviet Union with its East European and Mongolian neighbours. In the last few years, however, it has extended full membership to more distant countries in Asia (Vietnam in 1978) and Latin America (Cuba in 1972), and has extended observer status to Angola, Ethiopia, Laos and South Yemen. In so doing it has forged an institutional link between the geographically concentrated states-parties to the Warsaw Treaty and the geographically dispersed *penumbra,* or Soviet-inclined fringe, of the non-aligned movement. As for the Islamic Conference, its potential (and to some extent actual) significance in linking the Arab heartland of Islam with the more populous non-Arab countries in which Muslims predominate is obviously considerable in terms of coalition formation within UN institutions.

That leaves the Commonwealth. By no stretch of the imagination could an organisation with 15 member states in Africa, 11 in the Pacific, 9 in the Caribbean, 5 in Asia, 3 in Europe and 1 in North America be described as regional. Yet its membership is world-wide only in the sense of being scattered: its 44 members are fewer than those of the largest truly regional organisation (the Organisation of African Unity) and even if all belonged to the UN (which several of the smallest do not) they would still constitute less than 29 per cent of the total UN membership, now 154.

The Commonwealth is as *hors série* as any organisation could be. Its supporters delight in emphasising its unique character, while its de-tractors tend to see in that very resistance to classification evidence of lack of substance.

In some respects the nearest counterpart to the Commonwealth is the *Agence de co-opération culturelle et technique,* which links nearly 30 states of the French-speaking world. There are certain similarities, for sure. The *Agence,* like the Commonwealth, appointed a Canadian as its first Secretary-General, and looked to the Third World for his successor – picking a Nigérois while the Commonwealth found its man in Guyana. Again, technical co-operation between rich and poor countries in a context of shared cultural attributes is central to the functioning of both organisations. Their relative similarity has been officially recognised, with reciprocal visits of Secretaries-General to each other's headquarters.

And yet the differences are at least equally striking. The principle on which the *Agence* rests is linguistic. Alongside France and some of its recent ex-colonies it groups African countries that were colonies of others (Burundi, Rwanda, Zaire), European countries that were never colonies (Belgium, Luxembourg, Monaco), and three members of the Commonwealth whose experience of French colonial rule lies far in the past (Canada, Mauritius, Seychelles). By the same token, *La Francophonie* itself is not a constitutional relationship, but the expression of linguistic identity (with the *Agence*, it has been argued, an 'outpost' rather than its main institution).[8]

The Commonwealth, on the other hand, rests much more lightly on the linguistic principle. Although English is an official language (if not always the only one) in most Commonwealth countries, the most populous and powerful English-speaking country – the United States of America – is not a member, and never has been. So it would be a colossal mistake to regard the Commonwealth as *Anglophonie* institutionalised.

It is the peculiar genius of the Commonwealth to have transcended its origins, which lay in the bilateral relationships of each of a number of former colonies with Britain, so as to become a multilateral association: one which would more likely than not survive a British withdrawal were that ever to occur. The Commonwealth has evolved from a constitutional formula into an international organisation. Therein lies one of its claims to uniqueness.

The Commonwealth and its Secretariat

It has been a remarkable evolution, and one which is insufficiently appreciated. This is the consequence of a scholarly literature which has remained until recently biased towards an anachronistic view of the Commonwealth. However necessary it remains to understand the Commonwealth in its historical context; however intellectually attractive the traditional debates over the political theory (almost, at times, the metaphysics) of dominion status, external association, divisibility of the Crown, the *inter se* docrine[9] and much else besides; we need nowadays to examine the Commonwealth more directly as a species of international organisation. In this new perspective its multilateral character is taken as central to the analysis, rather than tacked on as a postscript to the history and political theory of a set of constitutional relationships with a Britain in imperial decline.

Margaret Ball made a start with her book *The 'Open' Commonwealth*[10] in shifting the perspective so as better to do justice to the contemporary Commonwealth, and other important contributions have been made by, for example, Richard Leach[11] and Margaret Doxey[12] following their researches in the Secretariat in 1970 and 1974 respectively. Bruce Miller's authoritative *Survey* volume[13] has also done much to help. There remains a need for more studies of international organisation in the Commonwealth which, from the vantage-point of the 1980s, can treat the Secretariat (and all that flows from it) as a mature institution rather than a novelty.

Why the Secretariat? Because, at the risk of appearing to commit *lèse-majesté*, it has to be said that since 1965 the Secretary-General has very largely replaced the Head of the Commonwealth as the unifying personality, and the Secretariat has — more obviously — replaced the Commonwealth Relations Office of the British government as the unifying bureaucracy holding together the 44 members of this world-wide association. This is not to suggest for a moment that the Head of the Commonwealth has become an irrelevance: it is indeed, a tribute to the skill and sensitivity with which the Lady in question has occupied that role for nearly thirty years, and to her ability to keep it distinct from her role as Britain's (and 14 other Commonwealth members') head of state, that its perpetuation is not in jeopardy. But it is in the Secretariat, above all, that the Commonwealth's claim to be an international organisation, and its interest as a unique form of international organisation, alike reside.[14]

The Secretariat, then, constitutes the obvious point of departure for any exploration of the Commonwealth phenomenon in terms of comparative international organisation. How similar is it to other international structures, for example those of the United Nations system, where the concept of an international civil service has grown up?

The Secretariat and the Agreed Memorandum of 1965

Margaret Doxey found the Commonwealth Secretariat in 1974 very different from the UN. It could not expect to be spared the problems inherent in the very enterprise of making an international secretariat work, 'but in many ways it has been able to minimise them'. She instanced the common language and (more surprisingly) the preference for temporary over long-term appointments as helpful factors, and went on in a passage crucial to our understanding of the Secretariat:

But the Secretariat not only benefits from a common working language, but also from what may be called the common 'style'. Style is an elusive quality, but it is one which most senior members of the Secretariat tended to stress in personal interviews, and for that reason alone it is worth trying to capture some of its meaning. It has, of course, nothing to do with the kind of panache which admirers have attributed to the Kennedy administration of the early 1960s: there is no flavour of 'Camelot' about Marlborough House. Commonwealth style, which probably derives in the main from comparable education and administrative experience, is perhaps a way of looking at problems and a recognisable approach to dealing with them. It deals in common sense rather than political rhetoric, prefers informality to protocol and performance to theory. Described thus (and imperfectly) it may sound the antithesis of style: low-key, pragmatic, sensible.[15]

The Secretariat was set up in 1965 on the basis of a consensus reached by the Heads of Government the previous year that such a development was desirable in principle. Its genesis has been well analysed by Richard Leach.[16] It was left to a group of senior officials, led by the Secretary of the British Cabinet, Sir Burke Trend, to draft a memorandum; and this, accepted by Heads of Government in 1965, remains the constitutive document of the Secretariat. Its minatory tone, as if fearful of the adoption of the 'UN model' for the new Secretariat, may be grasped from the following sections:

4. The Secretary-General and his staff should approach their task bearing in mind that the Commonwealth is an association which enables countries in different regions of the world . . . to exchange opinions in a friendly, informal and intimate atmosphere. The organisation and functions of the Commonwealth Secretariat should be so designed as to assist in building on these fundamental elements in the Commonwealth association. At the same time the Commonwealth is not a formal organisation. It does not encroach on the sovereignty of individual members. Nor does it require its members to seek to reach collective decisions or to take united action . . .

6. The Secretariat should not arrogate to itself executive functions. At the same time it should have, and develop, a relationship with other intra-Commonwealth bodies.

7. The Secretariat should have a constructive role to play. At the same time it should operate initially on a modest footing; and its staff and functions should be left to expand pragmatically in the light of experience, subject always to the approval of Governments.

Why this excess of caution? The answer probably lies in the hesitations which some in the 'old Commonwealth' entertained at the prospect of a new institution which the 'new Commonwealth' might turn to its own, sectional purposes. Certainly the impetus for a Secretariat came in the early 1960s from Africa, Asia and the Caribbean; ironically, it was Australia, which long before had urged without success the desirability of a Commonwealth Secretariat, that now found itself most doubtful as to its wisdom.[17] Sir Burke Trend and his colleagues reflected these doubts in their drafting. The Agreed Memorandum of 1965 left no room for uncertainty about the nature of the Secretariat: by defining its functions in such heavily negative terms it ruled out any suspicion of an 'Afro-Asian' engine that would take Commonwealth governments in certain directions whether they wanted to or not.

Richard Leach comments on the looseness of terminology in the Agreed Memorandum, making the point that 'Secretariat' and 'Secretary-General' seem to be used interchangeably; and he sees this as evidence of an intention to build the Secretariat around its chief officer, which corresponded in practice to Arnold Smith's description of it as 'my Secretariat' and his strongly personal mode of operation.[18] What is at least equally remarkable, as regards looseness of terminology, to this observer is the apparent confusion in paragraph 4 between formal organisation and encroachment on sovereignty. It seems to be implied there that the reason the Commonwealth does not encroach on the sovereignty of its members is that it is not a formal organisation – as if 'formal' meant 'supranational'. On the contrary, if it were not a formal international organisation already, the creation of the Secretariat made it one, by endowing the Commonwealth with a visible bureaucracy responsible to no one government but to the membership as a whole.

The personalities of its first two Secretaries-General have simply confirmed this development. It may therefore be appropriate to look next at the evolution of their political role and to ask whether there are similarities with UN experience.

The Political Role of the Secretary-General

What do we find when we examine the political role of the Secretary-General in the two organisations? It would be impossible to emulate the depth and breadth of understanding of the Secretary-General's political role in the UN which Sydney Bailey has demonstrated in his writings. So let us move quickly from the Thirty-eighth Floor to Marlborough House.

Neither Arnold Smith nor Shridath Ramphal has had to contend with the institutional tension between the Security Council and the

General Assembly; or balance restrictive interpretations of the Charter against permissive; or develop a 'vacuum doctrine' to justify political interventions which may not adequately be covered by the provisions of Articles 98 and 99.

On the other hand, they *have* had to weigh up the political consequences of any intervention in terms of how it will affect the attitude of member states' governments towards the Secretariat and, accordingly, towards their own role thereafter. Will there be repercussions? Will influential governments accuse them − privately, if not publicly − of exceeding their proper function? Will their decision latitude suffer, so that they are less well placed to act as they would wish to act in subsequent crises?

Another similarity has been the remarkable florescence of an acknowledged political role on a constitutional foundation of equally remarkable flimsiness. The Agreed Memorandum of 1965 is more negatively worded than the Charter of 1945 in regard to the Secretary-Generalship; but neither reads as if the actual evolution of that office had been foreseen by the authors of the founding documents. Nor is that their fault. Representatives of governments are no more able to see into the future than the rest of us.

The central thread in the explanation of how both UN and Commonwealth Secretaries-General have developed their political role is, I suggest, the concept of *good offices*. This concept has the merit, a considerable merit in international relations, of combining flexibility and imprecision. In the exercise of good offices there is room for a sometimes necessary blurring of technical distinctions. Article 33 of the Charter recommends a number of methods for the peaceful settlement of international disputes, starting with 'negotiation, enquiry, mediation, conciliation, arbitration, judicial settlement'. Not a mention of good offices (although the recital of methods is, expressly, not meant to be exhaustive), which if one insisted on assigning it to a place in this spectrum would presumably find itself associated with the earlier (and more voluntary) methods rather than the later (and more binding) ones. But it may be that its very omission from the text of the Charter − in common with other such now-accepted terms of UN discourse as peace-keeping, preventive diplomacy, decolonisation and the veto − has been helpful in UN practice rather than unhelpful.

The first two Secretaries-General of the Commonwealth have made the exercise of good offices a hallmark of their service. Arnold Smith had barely arrived at Marlborough House before his namesake Ian, having been quite properly dismissed from his premiership by the governor of Southern Rhodesia, declared the colony independent and launched it on the 14-year rebellion of 'UDI'. The Organisation of African Unity recommended its member states to break off diplomatic relations with the United Kingdom, which it held responsible for the failure to prevent or subdue the rebellion. Although the OAU recommendation was by no means universally adopted, Ghana and Tanzania were among those which did break off relations with London, and by January 1966 the future of the Commonwealth appeared threatened as seldom before. In this desperate plight it was, by common consent, the good offices of Arnold Smith which more than anything else held the Commonwealth together through the emergency meeting of Heads of Government at Lagos and the atmosphere of suspicion and recrimination which soured relations between Britain and many of its Commonwealth 'partners' in Africa.

The other crisis in which Arnold Smith is known to have performed a clearly political function, serving the interests of Commonwealth cohesion as well as of peace-making, was the Nigerian civil war of 1967-70. What especially threatened the Commonwealth in this case was the decision of two member states (Tanzania and Zambia), as well as three non-member states (Gabon, Haiti and the Ivory Coast), to grant diplomatic recognition to the Republic of Biafra — as the former Eastern Region of Nigeria styled itself after it broke away from the Federation. Support for secession could not be construed otherwise than as an unfriendly act towards Nigeria. When it is remembered that Pakistan left the Commonwealth, in 1972, precisely over the issue of some member states' sympathies for the secessionists of Bangladesh, the magnitude of the threat posed to the cohesion of the Commonwealth by support for Biafra is apparent. It would be quite wrong, however, to give the impression for a moment that the immense human tragedy of 1967-70 should be measured in terms of its effect on the Commonwealth, or that the primary motive impelling the Secretary-General to lend his good offices to the quest for peace in Nigeria was one of institutional self-preservation. Far from it: the motive was, first and foremost, humanitarian, and political in so far as the attempt to bring any intermediary endeavour to bear on the parties to a war always and necessarily involves politics. The Commonwealth acted, through the person of its Secretary-General, for the sake of the suffering people of Nigeria, as did many other organisations and individuals.

Shridath Ramphal succeeded Arnold Smith in 1975, when the latter had completed his second five-year term of office. (Since the Commonwealth possessed no Security Council or General Assembly, it was left to the most senior of the Heads of Government, Tengku Abdul Rahman of Malaysia, to take soundings among his colleagues in 1970 prior to Arnold Smith's reappointment.)[19]

The new Secretary-General had an equally strong personality but a very different background. He had been a politician, not a diplomat; his experience of international relations arose from his tenure of the Foreign Ministry among many other Ministerial portfolios in the course of his governmental career in Guyana. While Foreign Minister he had chaired the Non-Aligned Movement when it met in Georgetown at the level of foreign ministers (which is intermediate between its Co-ordinating Bureau and its Heads of Government 'summits').

In exercising his good offices between member states in dispute Shridath Ramphal has acted no differently from (frequently) the Secretaries-General of the UN and (less frequently) Secretaries-General of other international organisations: witness Joseph Luns of the North Atlantic Treaty Organisation in the 'cod wars' between Britain and Iceland or Habib Chatti of the Organisation of the Islamic Conference in the more recent, and much bloodier, war between Iran and Iraq.

It is perhaps just unfortunate, from a British point of view, that in 1979-80 this political function of the Commonwealth Secretary-General has most often meant warning the British government more or less discreetly that some course of action on which it has embarked or which it may be contemplating has implications for Commonwealth relations which should make it think again. This appears to have been Shridath Ramphal's main role during the constitutional conference at Lancaster House which paved the way for Zimbabwean independence — though he was not alone in urging the British government to dismiss from its mind any thought of going back on the agreement reached at Lusaka by the Commonwealth Heads of Government. By reiterating the Commonwealth dimension of the Lancaster House agenda he was able to reinforce certain trends in the negotiation (which was one of the most unusual and difficult in the history of decolonisation) and discourage others. In so doing, though, he was bound to find himself acting in closer political proximity to certain Commonwealth governments than to others.

The pattern repeated itself in the case of the New Hebrides, as it moved uneasily from the status of a British-French condominium to independence as Vanuatu. Secession was threatened, and more than threatened on the island of Espiritu Santo; the central government in Vila found little but vacillation in London and Paris; the metropolitan governments seemed unable to agree on what to do about the redoubtably televisual Jimmy Stevens and his rebellion, or even on whether to delay the granting of independence. In these circumstances, a significant appeal was made to the Secretary-General. It came from the prime ministers of two neighbouring countries, both members of the Commonwealth: Papua New Guinea (PNG) and the Solomon Islands. Their perceived interest lay in seeing the New Hebrides brought speedily to independence, without dismemberment, for the alternative would undermine the norm of territorial integrity and – more practically – threaten to revive secessionist tendencies in outlying islands, such as PNG's Bougainville. (That secessionist tendencies in outlying islands are not confined to the South Pacific is all too apparent from such examples, in the 1970s, as Gran Abaco and the Bahamas, Carriacou and Grenada, and – successfully, with the backing of France's veto in the Security Council – Mayotte and the Comoros.) The outcome of their joint appeal to Marlborough House was that the Secretary-General issued a statement on the urgency of keeping the New Hebrides intact and not delaying independence. In effect he begged the condominium governments to stop dithering. This appeal may have had some success as regards the date of independence, although it was left to friendly PNG forces, promptly called in by the newly independent Vanuatu, to restore the central government's authority in Espiritu Santo and bring the rebels to trial. As an exercise of good offices, the whole process saw the Secretary-General seeking to defuse a growing crisis in intra-Commonwealth relations by urging one side (Britain) to see the strength of the other's case.

The most recent bilateral dispute in which the Secretary-General has involved himself is of a quite different character. It concerns the 'patriation' by the British Parliament to Canada of the British North America Act which, anachronistically enough, has remained the sole location of Canada's constituion for 114 years. The *principle* of 'patriation' is not contested: indeed, the wonder is rather that it has taken so long for Canada to request it. What has given rise to difficulties, amounting (at the time of writing) to a sadly worsening climate of misunderstanding and apprehension, is the Canadian government's apparent desire to have Westminster also enact a Charter of Rights for Canada and a particular amending formula for the constitution *before* 'patriating' the Act, and the awareness of British MPs that the bulky package does not come to Westminster with the united support of the Provinces but against vociferous protest from several of them. Even if some British MPs are thought to be over-receptive to Provincial lobbying, it remains the case that there is a genuine unwillingness at

Westminster to be forced into an invidious choice between, on the one hand, making constitutional changes that ought properly to be made in Canada *after* 'patriation' and, on the other, seeming to reject a request from the government and parliament of a friendly state. Neither course appears consistent with the mutual respect and concern for non-interference which should govern relations between sovereign states. It is a choice that should never have to be made — and with sensitive statesmanship it may yet, just possibly, be avoided.

In a speech on 11 December 1980, Shridath Ramphal rather surprisingly asserted a Commonwealth interest in the matter. He did so on the grounds that for the British Parliament to do other than acquiesce in whatever request eventually arrived from Ottawa would be to cast doubt on the received wisdom of Commonwealth relations since the 1931 Statute of Westminster, now approaching its fiftieth anniversary.

The issue of the 'repatriation' (*sic*) of the Canadian constitution, now being so vigorously debated in Canada, is resonant of that assertion of equal status fifty years ago. It is, of course, no part of the Commonwealth's business to intervene in Canada's domestic arguments. But the Commonwealth cannot be wholly detached from those issues which the repatriation proposals throw up for relations between the parliaments of Ottawa and Westminster . . . There are no residual 'colonial' responsibilities that interpose Britain between the Government of Canada and its people or between the Governments of Canada and of its Provinces; but there are responsibilities as between Canada and Britain.

For my own part, I would be surprised if in this matter the British Parliament were to do anything other than respond in terms to a request duly made by the Parliament of Canada for modification of the British North America Act. I would not expect the Parliament at Westminster to imply in any way that there is less to celebrate in 1981 than the Commonwealth widely believes.[20]

The handling of the 'patriation' affair so far can give no cause for rejoicing to those who care for the health of British-Canadian relations. But whether it really offers any threat to the wider Commonwealth is doubtful. And whether it is wise for the Secretary-General to make pronouncements on the bilateral difficulties of member states in which he implicitly takes sides is also open to question: for does it not tend to diminish the residual capability of the Secretariat to exercise good offices?

To be fair to Shridath Ramphal, the same speech contained one of those strikingly felicitous phrases that have become the hallmark of his eloquence. 'In the years ahead,' he declared, 'there will be need to preserve a balance — to ensure that Britain's relationship with the Commonwealth does not swing from dominion to detachment, but steadies to a sense of fraternity.'

The most valuable political contribution that can be attributed to the present Secretary-General transcends the notion of good offices as commonly understood. It lies in his effort to convince the richer countries of the world that their future is bound up with that of the poorer, through a global interdependence that implies a common interest. He has used all the resources of his office to amplify that message, and it is well known that he and Edward Heath were largely responsible for the final draft of the Brandt Report.[21]

Can the Commonwealth, as a microcosm of the world, help the world towards North-South consensus? That was the purpose of the three McIntyre Reports, *Towards a New International Economic Order*, produced by a Commonwealth Group of Experts in the mid-1970s;[22] the first report was specifically aimed at influencing the Seventh Special Session of the UN General Assembly, where it was well received, and the second at reconciling the various groups at UNCTAD IV in Nairobi. That was still the special role of the Commonwealth, according to the Nicosia Meeting of Senior Officials in November 1980.[23] In one of his earliest articles on this theme, Shridath Ramphal explained why:

Nehru . . . once summed up his faith in the association as one that could bring to a troubled world 'a touch of healing'. Today, that Commonwealth combines within itself nearly all the elements involved in the current international dialogue. It is a Commonwealth of developed and developing nations, rich and poor, semi-industrialised and essentially agricultural communities. It is a Commonwealth of plural forms of government, of varied political ideologies, of many religions. It is a Commonwealth whose members occupy places of prominence within most of the world's great groupings of states. It is a Commonwealth that is truly a sample of the world community. What higher function can so unique a family of . . . states fulfil than to strive to bring to our modern world, weakened by poverty, that touch of healing?[24]

Dissimilarities in Structure and Institutional Experience

When the late Professor S.A. de Smith warned that comparisons between the UN and the Commonwealth 'would not be profitable if formulated in constitutional terms',[25] he had in mind the UN's possession of a Charter, a legal personality, an executive organ (the Security Council) and the International Court of Justice. He might have added, with as good reason, the General Assembly, the other two Councils, and the formidable committee structure that has blossomed under the too-permissive auspices of ECOSOC and the Assembly.

It is still true today that there are great dissimilarities in most of these respects. Leaving aside the problem of legal personality, which the Agreed Memorandum should have resolved, we can readily agree that the Commonwealth has no equivalent to the Security Council or the International Court; its Agreed Memorandum of 1965 is 'a series of guidelines, not a charter';[26] while the Singapore and Lusaka Declarations which sometimes appear in reference books as if they were constitutive documents are really nothing of the kind but rather heady affirmations of principle, with no bearing on the organisation of the Commonwealth.[27]

The central organ of the Commonwealth is its Heads of Government Meeting (CHOGM), which owes its relative informality of title to the informality of style deliberately introduced by Churchill in the Second World War as a reaction against the grandeur of pre-war Imperial Conferences. Whether the informality of style has remained constant since then is doubtful; at the Singapore CHOGM of 1971, in particular, there were complaints that the former intimacy of the occasion had been lost, and Pierre Trudeau was credited with restoring it when he chaired the 1973 meeting. But that is a strictly relative fluctuation: compared with the formality of UN occasions the Commonwealth's are informal to a degree. Meetings are not geared to the adoption of decisions or resolutions, and the responsibilities involved are generally very different. 'In the Commonwealth approach to international affairs generally, there is more "consultation" than "co-operation" and there is no question of seeking concerted political action.'[28]

There has never been much of a committee structure on the political side of the Commonwealth, as distinct from the considerable range of bureaux and committees in non-political fields which institutionalised Commonwealth co-operation on a functional basis before the era of the Secretariat and were brought into relation with the Secretariat, as necessary, after the Sherfield Report of 1966.[29] There is nothing akin to the comprehensive coverage that the UN committee system gives (or gives the appearance of giving) to the problems of the world.

The essence of Commonwealth relations is consultation. Below the CHOGM level, departmental Ministers consult in Commonwealth-wide meetings on a regular basis. The best known, because it deals in relatively 'high politics', is the annual meeting of Commonwealth Finance Ministers which takes place immediately before the annual meetings of the Bretton Woods institutions. There are also regular meetings of education, Food, Health and Law Ministers, and matters can be referred to the appropriate group of ministers between CHOGMs. An example is the proposal for a Commonwealth Human Rights Commission made by Sir Dawda Jawara, President of The Gambia, which was processed through Commonwealth Law Ministers as well as an advisory group set up by the Secretary-General.

These arrangements recall the Council of Europe in their combination of Ministerial consultation and functional specificity. They are not resolution-oriented, like many meetings in the UN system, or regulation-oriented, like many in the European Community system. Indeed it may well be that the appeal of the Commonwealth is not altogether dissimilar from that of the Council of Europe. It is low-key, practical, functional and consultative; it has no pretensions to supranationality; it is straightforwardly international, threatening no one's sovereignty; its members know where they are with it; it does not offer them the promised land but neither does it make excessive demands on them.

Only two general-purpose organs exist below the CHOGM level, and both are composed of officials, not Ministers. It will be recalled that the Agreed Memorandum was prepared for Heads of Government in 1965 by Sir Burke Trend and other Cabinet Secretaries or their equivalents. This became a regular meeting, held in the alternate years between CHOGMs, with different governments providing facilities. The Meeting of Senior Officials is more than a mere agenda committee, in as much as it receives advisory committee reports (such as the Wilson Report on the Commonwealth and its NGOs,[30] which was considered by the Meeting of Senior Officials at Kuala Lumpur in 1978) and may approve changes in the structure of the Secretariat which need inter-governmental consideration but are not of sufficient moment to await the next CHOGM. It also reviews developments in the year since the most recent CHOGM over the whole span of Commonwealth issues. States are generally represented by their Cabinet Secretary or the Permanent Secretary of the Prime Minister's Department or Presidency, as the case may be; sometimes, however, the representative is a senior diplomat, as when the Director-General of the Cyprus Ministry of Foreign Affairs

(Ambassador George Pelaghias) presided over the 1980 meeting in Nicosia.

The other general-purpose organ composed of officials is the meeting of Commonwealth High Commissioners in London (to which is added a senior official of the Foreign and Commonwealth Office to represent Britain). The original purpose of this body, under paragraph 42 of the Agreed Memorandum, was to act as a Finance Committee through which the annual budget for the Secretariat would be submitted to governments for their approval; under paragraph 34 the same group of dipomats was to appoint the Deputy Secretaries-General — of which more later. Richard Leach, writing in 1970, saw the Finance Committee as a significant constraint on the pace at which Arnold Smith could develop the Secretariat: even a 'handicap'. This was because 'the High Commissioners, or some of them, in turn rely on fiscal advisers who are as often as not "Treasury types", who do not see the difference between the Secretariat and an ordinary agency of their own governments. Thus the budgetary recommendations they have prepared for home government approval have all been minimal . . . The result is that the Secretariat has not been able to do a great many things it might have with a more adequate fiscal base.'[31]

The idea of using the largest available *corps diplomatique* of Commonwealth representatives for this purpose may have been one of the factors militating in favour of London as the seat of the Secretariat. Ease of communication, which is connected, was another. Although some international organisations have attracted their own *corps diplomatique* of permanent representatives (the UN twice over, in Geneva and New York; the European Communities, NATO, OECD, etc.), others have taken advantage of existing bilateral representation. The (Bangkok) Council of the South-East Asia Treaty Organisation, for instance, was composed of its member states' Ambassadors to Thailand, and an earlier parallel is afforded by the role of Ambassadors to the Netherlands in the stand-by system of the Permanent Court of Arbitration at The Hague. To take advantage of the High Commissioners in London rather than appoint separate permanent representatives to the Secretariat made good sense, and not only for reasons of economy. Most of the High Commissions in London were among the larger missions maintained by their governments; their calibre of diplomatic staff was generally high because London was regarded as an important posting; for many, bilateral relations with the British government were already combined with other responsibilities, such as relations with neighbouring countries (in which it was not thought necessary to establish separate embassies), by means of multiple accreditation.

The Finance Committee's members, wearing other hats, were soon to become the Commonwealth Sanctions Committee, as the British government sought Commonwealth help in imposing economic sanctions on the illegal regime of Ian Smith in the rebel colony of Southern Rhodesia. Subsequently, this committee broadened its scope and is now the Commonwealth Committee on Southern Africa. It has co-ordinated much active Commonwealth diplomacy in the region, concerned not just with Zimbabwe (as Southern Rhodesia was to become) but also with organising support for Zambia and Mozambique — even though the latter was not a member — to compensate them for the economic damage sustained by them during the imposition of Rhodesian sanctions, and with offering Commonwealth assistance (and the prospect of membership) to Namibia.

Here we encounter parallels with UN action, political and economic, in pursuit of majority rule for the territories of southern Africa. In the end it was a Commonwealth Monitoring Force, not the projected United Nations Zimbabwe Force, which assisted in the transition of Southern Rhodesia to independence. The economic compensation efforts mounted in favour of Mozambique and Zambia by the Commonwealth have direct parallels in UN activity, as of course do the economic sanctions that gave rise to these countries' trade problems. Namibia and Zimbabwe have seen UN and Commonwealth funds opened for their students in exile, and it has even been suggested that the International Affairs Division of the Commonwealth Secretariat, exhilarated by the experience of Zimbabwe, will be keen to play a similar pre-independence role (or rather roles) in Namibia should the opportunity arise: in which event one would expect the UN Transitional Assistance Group, which has been cooling its heels for so long already, to welcome the addition of a Commonwealth component in a suitably subordinate position.

The validation of exercises of self-determination is another function in which Commonwealth and UN experience runs together. In 1967 it was the Commonwealth, not the UN, which supervised the Gibraltar referendum, and Commonwealth teams of observers monitored elections in two African countries during 1980: first in Zimbabwe and then, less happily, in Uganda. The Zimbabwe exercise was headed, significantly, by an 'old UN hand', Rajeshwar Dayal, who had been one of Dag Hammarskjöld's representatives in the Congo (now Zaire) twenty years before. More often, however, it has been the UN that has found itself involved in supervising or monitoring the exercises of self-determination, whether by plebiscite, referendum, election or (as in the case of Bahrein) simply consultation. Belize, for which – like Cyprus – the Commonwealth set up a ministerial committee in the 1970s to organise diplomatic support, may afford an opportunity for UN-Commonwealth co-operation in validating its option for independence against Guatemalan claims to the territory. UN involvement in Sabah and Sarawak, when they entered the new federation of Malaysia in 1963 rather than join the larger part of Borneo which formed part of Indonesia, had rather the same function.

In spite of this evidence of common experience the Commonwealth and UN are still poles apart in their institutional structure, the Secretariats aside. And this basic dissimilarity extends beyond the General Assembly, Security Council and committee structure of the UN, which it has been asserted have no counterpart in the Commonwealth, to several major spheres of activity in which there is no UN-Commonwealth overlap whatever. We shall now turn to an area of comparison in which there are more similarities between the two organisations, and we shall start by asking the fundamental question applicable to every international institution: *cui bono?* Do all benefit equally, some disproportionately or some not at all?

Similarities: Disproportionate Benefits, Development Orientation and Regionalism

Membership of the Commonwealth, like membership of the UN, has brought disproportionate benefits to its weakest and poorest members. This disproportionality is no accident. It is a mark of solidarity, or community spirit, among peoples that the relatively prosperous are prepared to help their disadvantaged brethren: a mark of solidarity which may be found to some extent in several international organisations, but pre-eminently in the UN and Commonwealth systems.

When Papua New Guinea was approaching independence in 1975, its experience of Australian tutelage was such that Michael Somare and his government sought multilateral assistance in the administrative development of their country as it proceeded through the intermediate stage of internal self-government to the full assumption of international personality on independence. So the Commonwealth Secretariat was called in. It organised a special programme of administrative support for the transition to independence.

This and subsequent programmes – from the provision of expertise in legislative draftsmanship for newly independent islands in the Caribbean

and the South Pacific to the emergency training of Zimbabwe's diplomatic service — recalled, albeit in a lower key, the special programmes
organised by the UN Secretariat for states that had come to independence
in unusually difficult circumstances. Dag Hammarskjöld's OPEX*
assistance to Somalia in 1960, and even more critically the UN's role,
beginning in the same year, in alleviating the trauma of Congolese
independence, indicated a co-ordinating function for the international
Secretariat which was to be repeated in the following decade with East
Pakistan's violent transformation into an independent Bangladesh.

The similarity persists through the history of promotion of regional
institutions. After the creation of the Economic Commission for
Europe in 1947 all the subsequent regional economic commissions
created by the UN Economic and Social Council have been designed
fairly and squarely to promote the development of poor countries: in
Latin America, in Asia and the Far East (later renamed the Economic
and Social Commission for Asia and the Pacific), in Africa, and most
recently in Western Asia. The Specialised Agencies of the UN system
range from the highly centralised to the highly devolved, but in those —
like the World Health Organisation — which have chosen a strongly
regional structure, the development orientation is also to the fore. So
too in the Commonwealth system the growth of a regional level of
organisation has taken place within the context of development co-
operation. This has given rise to such Commonwealth institutions as the
regional health secretariats for West Africa and East, Central and Southern
Africa respectively, and more recently the CHOGRM (Commonwealth
Heads of Governement Regional Meeting) framework for co-operation
among Commonwealth members in Asia and the Pacific. The Commonwealth has had an equally important role in promoting institutions that,
although consisting largely of Commonwealth members, now enjoy an
autonomous existence, such as the Caribbean Community (formerly the
Caribbean Free Trade Area, CARIFTA) and the South Pacific Bureau
for Economic Co-operation. In every case the fundamental concept is
one of co-operation for development involving self-help by the poor
countries in a region which attracts support from richer countries, and
the Commonwealth like the UN system provides the all-important
means for the expression of this underlying solidarity.

Where the Commonwealth has not followed the UN example is in
trying to formalise criteria for the allocation of member states to such

---

* Operational, Executive and Administrative Personnel (a UN programme of technical assistance approved by the General Assembly in 1958).

categories as 'least developed' or 'most severely affected'. The experience of the UN in the 1970s suggests that attempts to develop such categories are doomed, if not to failure, at least to persistent distortions from political pressures which call seriously into question their validity as guidelines for international action. Here the relative informality of the Commonwealth has favoured instead a common sense approach, which eschews purposeless exercises in classification.

Central to the development orientation of the Commonwealth is its Fund for Technical Co-operation (CFTC), which was established at the Singapore CHOGM in 1971 after the Secretariat's early efforts in this field (e.g. seeking to help Botswana diversify its export markets so as to reduce its economic dependence on South Africa) had gradually become more formalised under the Nairobi Plan and other titles. CFTC assistance comprises four main programmes, covering (a) the supply of experts, advisers and consultants; (b) the training abroad of developing country personnel; (c) specialist advice to governments on legal, economic, fiscal and statistical matters; and (d) export promotion assistance. It also supports the work of the regional institutions already mentioned and funds two divisions of the Secretariat.

Is the CFTC comparable to any UN programme? 'Old Commonwealth hands' used to have a tendency to react with incredulity to any suggestion of similarity, the reason being that they saw the relatively informal, small-scale nature of Commonwealth co-operation as vastly superior to what they regarded (perhaps unfairly) as the over-administered but ill-co-ordinated sprawl of the United Nations Development Programme and other UN funds. Whether such a reaction would be common today is more doubtful. The 'restructuring' exercise of the mid-1970s brought the prospect of a much-needed degree of coherence into the economic and social sectors of the UN. The CFTC, for its part, grew rapidly during the 1970s from an initial budget of £400,000 to £13,500,000 by the end of the decade: still very small beer, of course, by comparison with many UN budgets.

Granted that there is a Commonwealth tradition which may lay claim to a distinctive style of operation, we can none the less recognise certain similarities in structure and function between the CFTC and the technical co-operation programmes of the UN. There is no fixed scale of contributions: Commonwealth governments, like member states of the UN at pledging conferences for the various programmes and funds, make up their minds from year to year. There is a Board of Representatives, with one member from each participating country, meeting twice a year to set CFTC policy, and a smaller Committee of Management.

The managing director of the CFTC ranks as an Assistant Secretary-General, which closely parallels the organisational pattern of the UNDP and other major programmes (such as UNHCR and UNICEF) whose executive heads are graded as high officials of the UN Secretariat and have a dual responsibility, to the Secretary-General as well as to their own executive committee or the equivalent governing body. It is a piece of administrative theory which, in the UN context, has not prevented altogether the strains one may think incidental to the life of any organisation with quasi-autonomous and separately funded progeny.

Financing

The financing of Commonwealth activities resembles quite closely that of the UN in structure, though not in scale. There is the same division between a regular budget out of which the central costs of the organisation are met and supplementary budgets out of which specific programmes are funded. The former is met by all member states according to a system of agreed shares, or scale of contributions, which meets specified criteria; the latter are subject to the vagaries of national policy preferences (as both the United Nations Development Programme and the Commonwealth Fund for Technical Co-operation have learned to their cost since the United Kingdom's change of government in 1979). It would be too simple to say that the former are 'mandatory' and the latter 'voluntary', although it stands to reason that members of any organisation, international or not, have in principle a stronger obligation to pay the basic subscription than any supplement: too simple, because for one thing the notion of 'mandatory' duties is entirely foreign to the Commonwealth tradition, while for another the issue of which UN budgets are 'mandatory' and which 'voluntary' is a vexed question in itself.

Confining ourselves to the regular budget, from which the Commonwealth finances its Secretariat, we find two outstanding similarities to that of the UN. First, the criteria for determining each member's contribution are population, national income and capacity to pay. Second, the application of these criteria gives rise to an extremely skewed distribution of percentages, in which the majority of members are paying at one or other of the two lowest permitted rates and a small minority are paying higher, unequal percentages of the budget.

Thus, in the UN through the triennium 1980-2, the scale of assessment provides for 70 member states to contribute at the lowest rate of all (.01 per cent) and another 9 at the next lowest (.02 per cent). This leaves only a minority of states (72 out of 151)[32] to pay at higher rates, including 10 at .03 per cent. So many very poor states have joined the UN that the minimum rate has twice had to be halved, from .04 per cent in 1972 and down from .02 to .01 per cent in 1978. On the other hand, the accession to membership in 1973 of the two German republics and the willingness of Japan around the same time to pay a higher percentage of the budget enabled this shift to take place (and enabled the USA to reduce its contribution from one-third to one-quarter) without crippling the organisation.

The scale of assessment for the present triennium is headed by the following 8 members, which contribute between them no less than 71.54 per cent of the entire budget:

	%
United States of America	25.00
Soviet Union	11.10
Japan	9.58
Federal Republic of Germany	8.31
France	6.26
United Kingdom	4.46
Italy	3.45
Canada	3.28

All the other assessments are for less than 2 per cent. Compare this with the Commonwealth's budget for the Secretariat. Here the two lowest rates are .75 and 1.5 per cent.[33] In the year 1976-7, when these rates corresponded to £13,571 and £27,141 respectively, the top contributors were:

	%	£
Britain	30.00	542,826
Canada	19.29	349,037
Australia	8.73	157,962
India	7.29	131,906
New Zealand	1.69	30,579

Every other member on a *percentile* assessment paid 1.5 per cent (14 members) or .75 per cent (16 members). Together these 30 member states contributed only £597,110 towards the total budget of £1,810,420.

In 1973-4, when the total budget was £847,920, Britain's 30 per cent share had been the same, India's considerably higher (9.66 per cent) and those of Canada, Australia and New Zealand broadly similar (19.19, 9.16 and 1.99 per cent respectively) to what they would be three years later. At that time, 13 members paid at the 1.5 and 14 at the .75 per cent level. The independence of Grenada, Papua New Guinea and the Seychelles over the next three years skewed the contributions structure still further, and this trend has continued since 1976-7 with the admission of new members from the Caribbean and Pacific regions. Meanwhile the annual budget has risen to £3,247,126 in 1980-1. India's contribution has fallen to 4.3 per cent, while the other percentages have changed little. The phrase *'percentile* assessment' is necessary because in one respect the Commonwealth has departed from the UN pattern of contributions. In 1968 a new category of special membership was introduced for Nauru, which was joined by Tuvalu in 1978 and by St Vincent and the Grenadines in 1979. These three special members enjoy all the rights of ordinary members of the Commonwealth except that they cannot take part in Heads of Government Meetings. In return, they are exempted from the percentile assessment, paying instead a fixed sum of £1,000 a year. The financial advantage to Nauru of this bargain can be calculated as having increased from about £6,350 in 1973-4 to £12,571 only three years later, and nearly doubled again by 1980-1.

Why has such a scheme found no place in the UN's financial arrangements? The answer probably lies in its link with the vexed question of associate membership and *its* implications, psychological rather than legal, for the norm of sovereign equality which is so highly prized in contemporary international society. Whereas the three special members of the Commonwealth are indubitably as independent as the other 41, associate membership of the UN (under whatever name it was introduced) might carry with it a question-mark over the international status of those countries that accepted it. It is perhaps more acceptable for the Commonwealth to adopt a category of special membership precisely because the UN has not. Any country that wants confirmation of its international status through UN participation will want full unqualified membership; and this includes St Vincent and the Grenadines. Other countries, which have not sought UN membership, are unlikely to be attracted to associateship either: these include both full members of the Commonwealth (Tonga, Kiribati, Vanuatu) and special members (Nauru, Tuvalu).

Staffing

Just as there are quite close resemblances between the UN and the Commonwealth in their financial structure, although the sums involved are very different, so the same can be said of their staffing. While the officials of the UN Secretariat have long been numbered in their thousands, the total staff of the Commonwealth has grown only from tens to hundreds — 345 by January 1980. The expansion of the senior staff, in the grades of assistant director and above, can be traced easily through successive editions of the *London Diplomatic List* from 21 in 1969 to 35 in 1974 and 53 in 1979. (In addition, 5 senior staff held overseas postings in 1979.)[34] Most of the expansion can be attributed to the growth of the Commonwealth Fund for Technical Co-operation and the creation of new divisions within the Secretariat, such as the CFTC-funded Food Production and Rural Development Division, which was set up in 1975 on the initiative of Judith Hart and other Development Ministers in the follow-up of the World Food Conference at Rome. The changing composition of the UN's senior staff in terms of titles and functions reflects a similar expansion of divisions, programmes, funds and other entities concerned primarily with aspects of economic and social development, accompanied by a growing complexity of organisation as quasi-autonomous units have proliferated alongside those sections that come more directly under the authority of the Secretary-General.

One of the closest resemblances between the two organisations in regard to staffing is their concern to balance two very different criteria in making appointments. In paragraph 35 of the Agreed Memorandum, the Commonwealth borrows wholesale from the UN Charter the language of Article 101.3, simply conflating its two sentences into one:

> The paramount consideration in the selection of staff and in the determination of conditions of service will be the necessity of securing the highest standards of efficiency, competence and integrity, due regard being paid to the important of recruiting the staff on as wide a geographical basis as possible within the Commonwealth.

In May 1979, using the Secretariat's own listing of nationalities, 10 members of the senior staff came from Britain, 6 from New Zealand, 5 from Canada and 3 from Australia; 14 from Asia (including 7 from India); 9 from Africa; and 8 from the islands of the Caribbean, Mediterranean and South Pacific. Altogether 21 different nationalities, or just under half of the nationalities of the Commonwealth, are represented among the senior staff.

Paragraphs 39 and 40 of the Agreed Memorandum, on legal personality, immunities and privileges, correspond closely to Articles 104 and 105 of the Charter.

The Agreed Memorandum also echoes the UN Charter in declaring that

> All members of the Secretariat, whatever their origin, must be strictly impartial in the discharge of their functions and place loyalty to the Commonwealth as a whole above all other considerations.

There is, moreover, a tacit recognition of the hard facts of UN experience[35] in the first part of the same paragraph (paragraph 37):

> All persons appointed to the staff of the Secretariat must be subject to clearance to the extent that their own Governments raise no objection to their suitability for employment.

The Second Echelon

One contrast in UN and Commonwealth organisation which is of special interest concerns the second echelon of the Secretariat. Here politics and public administration make an intriguing mixture, with which we may bring these explorations in comparative international organisation to a fitting conclusion.

In his book on the UN Secretariat Sydney Bailey is particularly illuminating on the problem of the second echelon over the first sixteen years of the organisation's history.[36] It is a complicated story, told with characteristic lucidity, and it reveals two interwoven themes. One is the perpetual difficulty of marrying the most efficient departmental structure for the Secretariat to a politically acceptable distribution of senior posts among key nationalities. The other is the frequency of attempts, by one device or another, to 'plant' a very select second echelon on the Secretary-General so as to circumscribe his freedom to consult with whomsoever he wishes — whether by introducing a 'sub-*troika*' principle or by requiring the Secretary-General to make especially intensive use of a particular group of senior officials for consultation (a Cabinet, in effect, in the British rather than the French sense of the word). What all these attempts have had in common is a desire to politicise the second echelon and use it to limit the decision latitude of the Secretary-General.

The success of UN Secretaries-General in resisting these attempts has upheld, in form at least, the basic principle of Secretariat organisation enshrined in Article 101.1 of the Charter. Every post in the Secretariat, however senior, is in the gift of the Secretary-General. He acts 'under regulations established by the General Assembly', but the appointments he makes are not subject to its approval, or anyone else's.[37] Sydney Bailey has pointed out that this marks a certain development from the Covenant of the League of Nations, which (in Article 6.3) required the approval of the League Council for staff appointments made by the Secretary-General.[38]

The 'sub-*troika*' proposal was put forward by President Kwame Nkrumah of Ghana and President Sékou Touré of Guinea in 1960. It made little impact just then: the General Assembly was too busy repudiating the Khrushchev proposal which would have replaced the secretary-general by a *troika* of three officials chosen from East, West and non-aligned countries respectively. The 'sub-*troika*' idea would have effected a compromise between the *status quo* and its critics by applying the principle of tripartite representation to the second echelon while preserving the unity of the Secretary-Generalship itself. It found its way, as a minority view, into the report of the 1960-1 Committee of Experts on the Secretariat,[39] when three of the eight experts — Omar Loutfi (permanent representative of the United Arab Republic), Alex Quaison-Sackey (permanent representative of Ghana) and C.S. Venkatachar (High Commissioner of India in Canada) — 'proposed that the Secretary-General should appoint three Deputy Secretaries-General, taking into account the main political trends. These Deputies should be men of eminence and high attainments, distinguished in public affairs, and should serve for one term only.'[40] This was a slightly less radical proposal than that of the two Presidents had been: 'taking into account the main political trends' would be compatible with Article 101.1, since it did not actually remove the power of appointment to the second echelon from the Secretary-General. Nevertheless, it was still too radical for the generality of the UN membership.

U Thant and Kurt Waldheim have in their turn retained their freedom from the organisational constraint of specified deputies over the past 20 years. There is, true, a single post of Director-General for Development and International Economic Co-operation, which the General Assembly inserted *above* the second echelon in 1978 as a consequence of the protracted exercise in restructuring the economic and social sectors of the UN, but the Director-General has specific responsibilities outside the political mainstream, and a period of service (four years) that is shorter than that of the Secretary-General, while — most important of all — his appointment is as much in the latter's gift as is every other staff position in the Secretariat. The second echelon remains a large and diversified class of officials variously graded as Assistant or Under Secretary-General or with titles of equivalent seniority. In 1979 the 'Under Secretaries-General, Assistant Secretaries-General, and Officers of Equivalent Rank' totalled 47 at Headquarters and a further 23 around the world. (Even so, some politically sensitive jobs such as the Directorship of the Human Rights Division are not yet included in this category.) This arrangement of the second echelon is much more favourable to the Secretary-General's position in the organisation than having a 'sub-*troika*' or even half a dozen deputies would be. It is significant that there is still no grade of Deputy Secretary-General, the term used by President Nkrumah and by the three dissenting experts in 1960-1.

Is it, then, too fanciful to see an echo of the 'sub-*troika*' idea in the provisions laid down just four years later for Deputy Secretaries-General of the Commonwealth? Ghana and India after all provide a link between the UN experts and the origins of the Commonwealth Secretariat. Be that as it may, the Agreed Memorandum of 1965 prescribes that the Deputy Secretary-General (economic), and the second Deputy-Secretary-General if it proves necessary to have one at all, shall 'be appointed by Commonwealth Heads of Government acting through their representatives in London'.[41] Although 'all members of the staff of the Secretariat will be responsible only to [the Secretary-General]',[42] his power of appointment applies only in the third echelon (Assistant Secretary-General) and below. Even there, the Agreed Memorandum draws a distinction between senior and junior staff: the Secretary-General 'will have discretion . . . to appoint senior staff to the service of the Secretariat, from among panels of names submitted by Commonwealth Governments, who need not feel themselves limited to Government servants in submitting nominations',[43] but he 'has authority to make appointments of junior staff'.[44]

In form, this Commonwealth model of Secretariat organisation marks a significant departure from the UN model. In practice, even as regards the crucial second echelon, it is doubtful whether the difference has proved a major constraint on the Secretary-General's freedom of action. Several factors tend towards this verdict. On the UN side there is the phenomenon of certain Secretariat departments being seen as 'baronial fiefdoms' to which particular governments effectively see appointed their own nationals, so that, for example, the Under Secretary-General heading the Department of Political and Security Council Affairs is invariably a Soviet national. The extent of this phenomenon, its consequences for inefficiency and duplication in departmental structures and its incompatibility with the common sense meaning of the Charter, have been the subject of a valuable monograph by a former delegate to the General Assembly.[45] On the side of the Commonwealth, the strong personalities of the first two Secretaries-General, their longer tenure of office (not expressly provided for in the Agreed Memorandum)[46] and a prudent rotation of nationalities in the Deputy Secretary-General grade have all combined to minimise the effect of the original provision for governmental appointment of Deputy Secretaries-General. It remains a latent, if unlikely, counterweight that governments *could* bring to bear on a maverick Secretary-General, but one which if ever used would surely reduce the Secretariat to institutionalised deadlock.

The balance of nationalities near the top of the Commonwealth Secretariat, as further down, has been maintained without recourse to the pre-emption of particular posts by particular governments which has disfigured the UN or to the introduction, at the opposite extreme, of a systematic rotation scheme. In practice, the two Deputy Secretaries-General have always come from different continents from each other and from the Secretary-General; while the existence of one, and since 1971 two, posts of Assistant Secretary-General has enabled all the major areas of the Commonwealth to be represented near the top of the tree most of the time. So far, successive Deputy Secretaries-General have been nationals of Ghana, Ceylon, Britain, India, New Zealand, Australia, Nigeria and Canada. The British Deputy Secretary-General was Sir Geoffrey Wilson (now Chairman of Oxfam), who held the post in 1971 between the permanent secretaryship of the Ministry of Overseas Development and the chairmanship of the Race Relations Board, both roles in British public life with strong Commonwealth overtones; earlier in his distinguished career he also managed the Colombo Plan, involving development co-operation in Asia among several Commonwealth countries.

With one exception, these Deputy Secretaries-General have entered the Secretariat in that grade: they have been recruited to the second echelon from outside, not promoted from within. (Comparison of senior staff lists at regular intervals since 1969 shows only one or two moves upward within the Secretariat involving even the fourth and fifth echelons, e.g. the present Director of the International Affairs Division was in 1974 an Assistant Director there.) The exception is Emeka Anyaoku, whose career is worthy of note for its very uniqueness. He entered the

Secretariat in its early days as one of several Assistant Directors in the International Affairs Division, became Director of that Division, then Assistant Secretary-General and eventually Deputy-Secretary-General in charge of international affairs, legal co-operation, information, applied studies in government, administration and conference services. The aspect of Commonwealth policy with which he was most closely identified in the Secretariat's early years was Rhodesia, as he was secretary to the Commonwealth Sanctions Committee; but his career to date has spanned many other aspects and may be thought to offer evidence for the feasibility of an alternative mode of staffing to the prevalent one, which relies on short-term secondment from governmental or other outside employment. It calls to mind the careers of long-term international civil servants in the UN Secretariat, where although a minority they have always been a sizeable minority, of whom Under Secretary-General Brian Urquhart is perhaps the best-known representative. It was at the UN, significantly enough, that Emeka Anyaoku gained experience of international organisation (as a diplomat in the Permanent Mission of Nigeria) before the Commonwealth Secretariat was formed. An earlier Deputy Secretary-General, A.L. Adu, gained his as a Ghanaian civil servant seconded to be Secretary-General of the East African Common Services Organisation.

We have deliberately been comparing Commonwealth and UN theory and practice, but before leaving this exploration of the second echelon in their Secretariats it may be worth remarking on a non- (or quasi-) regional international organisation that, although very different in purpose, appears none the less to have demonstrated a comparable concern for balance in its staffing at that level. The Organisation of the Islamic Conference in 1979 had Deputy Secretaries-General for political cultural and administrative/financial affairs who were respectively of Turkish, Moroccan and Pakistani nationality. Given that the Secretary-General was a Tunisian, it can be readily appreciated that the four nationalities reflected a balance between Arab and non-Arab, or looked at another way between African and Asian, which conformed to the political and psychological imperatives of cohesion in the 42-member organisation. As the organisation has only been in existence since 1971 it is too early to establish a firm trend.[47]

There is a hint of the same concern for balance, as a special application of the principle of equitable distribution of jobs among nationalities, in the understanding that accompanied the creation of the new post of UN Director-General for Development and International Economic Co-operation in 1978: to wit, that this job should always go to someone from a less-developed country so long as a national of a developed country held the Secretary-Generalship, and vice versa.[48]

How far can this concern be taken without overshadowing the paramountcy, affirmed in both the UN Charter and the 1965 Agreed Memorandum, of personal qualities as criteria in the selection of staff? It may be argued that the battle for personal as against national criteria was lost as long ago as 1933, when Joseph Avenol succeeded Sir Eric Drummond and the second echelon of the League Secretariat was reorganised to restore the balance of nationalities then perceived as politically desirable.[49] Others would take a more sanguine view. At least the flexibility common to the UN and Commonwealth structures (despite the differences we have noted) protects them from unconditional surrender to the principle of nationality: their founding documents remain, however inconveniently for some, pledged to the subordination of that principle to the 'paramount consideration' of 'securing the highest standards of efficiency, competence and integrity'.

These considerations are bound up with one of the fundamental challenges to the very concept of international organisation. Is not 'international loyalty' a contradiction in terms? An international secretariat is not immune to the usual strains and stresses of all bureaucratic life or to the habitual dilemmas of public administration, but it adds to these the peculiar difficulties of an international civil service in the making.[50] It is an enterprise fraught with problems: so too are others that seem likewise to 'go against nature' in search of a higher interest, whether the peaceful settlement of conflicts, the international protection of human rights, the limitation of war or the promotion of disarmament. Fortunately, however, there will always be those who refuse to be deterred by the obvious difficulties from engaging in such enterprises, and for them the writings and examples of Sydney Bailey provide continuing sustenance and encouragement.

Notes

1. 'International institutions' and 'international organisation' are used in this essay to mean *inter-governmental* bodies. On international *non-governmental* organisations (NGOs), see the essay by J. Duncan Wood in this book.
2. Paul Taylor, 'The Development of Theory of International Organisation: the Four Phases of Writing' in R.C. Kent and G.P. Nielsson (eds.), *The Study and Teaching of International Relations* (London: Frances Pinter, 1980), p. 59.
3. Sydney D. Bailey, *The Secretariat of the United Nations*, rev. edn (London: Pall Mall Press, 1964), p. 61.
4. Taylor, 'Four Phases', p. 61.
5. In his capacity as a member of the UN Advisory Group and the Advisory Panel on Arms Control and Disarmament, which advise Ministers at the Foreign

and Commonwealth Office. (The titles of both advisory bodies have varied since they were first set up by Lord Caradon and Lord Chalfont respectively in 1964).

6. He wrote the first ISIO Monograph and the first UNITAR Peaceful Settlement Study: see p. 203.

7. E.g. H.G. Nicholas, *The United Nations as a Political Institution,* 5th edn (London: Oxford University Press, 1975), p. 10; or in greater detail, Ruth B. Russell, *A History of the United Nations Charter: the Role of the United States 1940-1945* (Washington: Brookings Institution, 1958), pp. 688-712.

8. S.K. Panter-Brick, 'La Francophonie' in W.H. Morris-Jones and Georges Fisher (eds.), *Decolonisation and After: the British and French Experience* (London: Frank Cass, 1980), pp. 340-1.

9. This doctrine asserts that the relations of Commonwealth members among themselves (*inter se*) have a special legal quality that renders them less fully international in character than their relations with non-members. 'The *inter se* doctrine', as S.A. de Smith once memorably put it ('Fundamental Rules – Forty Years On', *International Journal* (Toronto), vol. 26, no. 2 (Spring 1971), p. 350) 'may have been born a dying duckling; it has long been a dead duck, dignified only by tardy obituary notices.'

10. M. Margaret Ball, *The 'Open' Commonwealth* (Durham, North Carolina: Duke University Press, 1971).

11. Richard Leach, 'The Secretariat' in special issue, 'The Commonwealth of Nations',*International Journal* (Toronto), vol. 26, no. 2 (Spring 1971), pp. 374-400.

12. Margaret Doxey, 'The Commonwealth Secretariat', *Year Book of World Affairs 1976* (London: Stevens, 1976), pp. 69-96.

13. J.D.B. Miller, *Survey of Commonwealth Affairs: Problems of Expansion and Attrition 1953-1969* (London: Oxford University Press for the Royal Institute of International Affairs, 1974).

14. This does not exclude the possibility that the Commonwealth could correctly have been described as an international organisation even before the advent of the Secretariat: e.g. Tom Soper called it a 'functional organisation', in *Evolving Commonwealth* (Oxford and London: Pergamon, 1965), p. 126, 'to which members wish to belong partly because they have got into the habit of doing business together and partly because they recognise it is in their best interests to do so.'

15. Doxey, 'Commonwealth Secretariat', pp. 81-2.

16. Leach, 'Secretariat', pp. 374-9.

17. Ibid., pp. 377-82. J.D.B. Miller, *The Commonwealth in the World,* 3rd edn (London: Duckworth, 1965), p. 79, identifies the further irony that the Secretariat, 'a dream of early supporters of the idea of Commonwealth unity ... should have had to wait for concrete proposals until 1964, when "unity" was a thing of the past'. One fear (p. 296) was that African states would use it 'as an annexe to the OAU'.

18. Leach, 'Secretariat', p. 387.

19. Ibid., p. 390, footnote 35, referring to the reappointment which the Tengku announced on 7 March 1970, says that 25 heads of government were in favour, 1 against, and 2 undecided: they are not, however, identified.

20. 'The Commonwealth in the 1980s: the Need to Care', Focus Lecture 1980, p. 9 (text issued by Commonwealth Secretariat).

21. *North-South: a Programme for Survival* (London: Pan Books, 1980): the Report of the Independent Commission on International Development Issues. Chairman: Willy Brandt.

22. *Interim Report,* 23 July 1975; *Further Report,* 2 March 1976; *Final Report,* 14 March 1977; by a Commonwealth Experts' Group.[Chairman: Alister

McIntyre (Secretary-General of the Caribbean Community).] All three reports were published by the Commonwealth Secretariat with a foreword by the Secretary-General.

23. *Commonwealth Currents,* February 1981, p. 4.

24. Shridath S. Ramphal, 'The Other World in This One', *Round Table,* no. 261 (January 1976), p. 71.

25. de Smith, 'Fundamental Rules', p. 348.

26. Leach, 'Secretariat', p. 377.

27. The Declaration of Commonwealth Principles (Singapore, 1971) and the Declaration on Racism and Racial Prejudice (Lusaka, 1979) were both adopted by Heads of Government and given publicity by the Commonwealth Secretariat through its information output since.

28. Doxey, 'Commonwealth Secretariat', p. 85.

29. Lord Sherfield was chairman of the Review Committee on Intra-Commonwealth Organisations: see the first *Annual Report of the Commonwealth Secretary-General* (26 August 1966), pp. 15-16 and the *Second Report of the Commonwealth Secretary-General* (1966-8), p. 71.

30. *From Governments to Grassroots* (London: Commonwealth Secretariat, 1978): Report of the Advisory Committee on Relationships between the Official and the Unofficial Commonwealth. [Chairman: Sir Geoffrey Wilson.]

31. Leach, 'Secretariat', p. 391.

32. There were 151 member states of the UN when the contributions scale for the present triennium was agreed. The figures in this section are taken from the *United Nations Handbook 1980* (Wellington: New Zealand Ministry of Foreign Affairs, 1980), pp. 190-2, an admirable work of reference published regularly, to its credit, by one of the UN's smaller member states.

33. 'At their last meeting [September 1966] Heads of Government reduced the 1.5% minimum rate of contribution to .75% in the case of those member countries whose populations are less than one million' (*Second Report of the Commonwealth Secretary-General,* p. 72): another parallel with UN experience, in halving minima.

34. An adviser on multilateral trade negotiations, Geneva; a CHOGRM consultant, Fiji; the Directors of the Commonwealth Regional Youth Development Centres in Guyana, India and Zambia.

35. Dag Hammarskjöld, *The International Civil Servant in Law and in Fact* (Oxford: Clarendon Press, 1961), pp. 15-17.

36. Bailey, *Secretariat.*

37. Hammarskjöld, *International Civil Servant,* pp. 12-13; Bailey, *Secretariat,* pp. 23-6.

38. Bailey, *Secretariat,* p. 95.

39. Sometimes known as the Georges-Picot Committee, from the name of its chairman, Ambassador Guillaume Georges-Picot, a former Assistant Secretary-General; it was established under GA Res. 1446 (XIV) of 5 December 1959.

40. Bailey, *Secretariat,* pp. 71-2.

41. Agreed Memorandum, para. 34. (The text is taken from *The Commonwealth Secretariat,* published by the Secretariat under the Commonwealth Information Programme in 1974, pp. 27-38.)

42. § 32.

43. § 35.

44. § 36.

45. Theodor Meron, *The United Nations Secretariat: the Rules and the Practice* (Lexington, Massachusetts: D.C. Heath, 1977).

46. The Agreed Memorandum, § 38, only fixes a maximum initial term of office, five years, and a less definite minimum of 'preferably not less than three'.

It applies these limits to 'senior officers, including the Secretary-General and Deputy Secretaries-General' and exhorts the Secretary-General 'to have regard to the need to stagger appointments in order to avoid a complete change of senior staff at any one time'. In practice, however, there have already been seven Deputy Secretaries-General during the tenure of the first two Secretaries-General; most of the Deputy Secretaries-General have held office for five or six years, as against the (reappointed) Secretaries-General with ten years each.

47. The *Europa Year Book 1980, Volume I: International Organisations* (London: Europa Publications, 1980) has been my main source of topical information on this and other regional and quasi-regional organisations mentioned in this essay.

48. The first holder of this office is Ambassador Kenneth Dadzie, previously permanent representative of Ghana and Chairman of the UN *Ad Hoc* Committee on the Restructuring of the Economic and Social Sectors of the UN system. It should be noted that no mention was made of the understanding in the authorising resolution, GA Res. 32/197 of 20 December 1977, or in its Annex summarising the recommendations of the *Ad Hoc* Committee; its status, therefore, remains informal.

49. James Barros has vividly described the political pressures surrounding the League Secretariat's reorganisation in 1933 in his book *Betrayal from Within: Joseph Avenol, Secretary-General of the League of Nations 1933-1940* (New Haven and London: Yale University Press, 1969).

50. Bailey, *Secretariat*, p. 61.

9 THE NEW INTERNATIONAL DIPLOMACY: A PERSONAL COMMENT (1980)

Hugh Caradon

Changes at the United Nations

When I was in New York recently I went to see Sir Anthony Parsons, the United Kingdom Ambassador to the United Nations. I knew him well since he had been with me in the United Kingdom Mission to the United Nations when I had been a Minister of State in charge of the Mission from 1964 to 1970.

As we talked about current problems and personalities at the United Nations I realised how much had changed since I left New York in 1970. There had of course been many changes in the personalities. Only very few of those I had known best were still there. Under-Secretary Brian Urquhart was one. Although he still looked young he had been in the United Nations from the beginning, and now as a senior and most respected under-secretary he continued to exercise a specially important and lively influence particularly in Middle Eastern and African affairs.

Robert McNamara was still in the key international post of President of the World Bank, but his impending retirement has since been announced; and Rafael Salas was and still is doing an outstanding job in charge of the United Nations Fund for Population Activities. But most of those I had known best, like Paul Hoffman of the United Nations Development Programme and Under-Secretary Ralph Bunche, had long since gone. And nearly all the representative Ambassadors were new to me (Andy Young for instance being a very different United States representative from Adlai Stevenson, who had been the United States Ambassador when I first arrived at the United Nations).

But the changes since my day were by no means limited to a new team of international diplomats and officials.

One development which Sir Anthony mentioned casually but which came as a surprise to me was that Arabic is now an official language of the United Nations (in addition to English, French, Russian, Chinese and Spanish). I realised what this meant in terms of expense with all speeches and thousands of documents having to be translated into Arabic — evidence of the new importance of the Arabic-speaking nations.

A New Development in the Security Council

Another surprising development was in the procedures of the Security Council. In my day in the 1960s a great deal of work was done in private consultations with individual Ambassadors or regional groups but with a recognition that the full public meetings of the Council were of dominant importance. The fact that after the intensive negotiations outside the Council it was necessary to go back to the Council for a final decisive debate brought things to a head, to a conclusion.

Now I was told there has been a remarkable change. A room has been prepared next to the formal Security Council Chamber. The new room is a replica of the Chamber itself – the same placing of president and members, the same provision for simultaneous translation, much the same rules of procedure. But with one essential difference. In the proceedings in this new room there is no record kept, there is no report, no audience, no *Hansard*. The members can give their views, state their positions, make their proposals, search for agreements, with a freedom impossible under the old system of set recorded speeches. And as a result it is sometimes possible to arrive at a consensus which enables the president to go back to the formal meeting of the Council merely to announce an agreed conclusion without the need for further debate or vote.

Looking back at the years I spent in the Security Council I was fascinated to learn of this new development. It seemed to me to hold out new prospects of successful international negotiation, to open the way to greater agreement, to facilitate genuine search for concerted international action. I particularly liked the thought of the American and Russian Ambassadors – or Foreign Ministers even – exchanging ideas without rhetoric and without the need to get the prior instruction or approval of their governments before every public pronouncement.

I wonder if my wishful thinking is being justified by results. And a doubt entered my head. In my day we got results in the end by the necessity of meeting the deadline of public debate in the Council. I began to wonder if instead of the compulsion of the public Council debates there might be a temptation to go on indefinitely in the private discussions in the room next door. There is always a temptation to delay, to put off difficult decisions, and I thought that under the new system they might be put off too long.

We shall have many opportunities to judge the new system by results – in the Middle East and Africa and elsewhere – and we can hope for the best.

All-important Economic Relationships

There was another new development at the United Nations the great importance of which Sir Anthony specially emphasised. He told me, what I had begun to realise before, that nowadays economic issues replace political questions in the priorities and purposes of most delegates. It is the economic relationships between the wealthier industrialised nations and the new nations of Asia and Africa and Latin America which are now uppermost in the interests of the majority. Even ideological differences between West and East are now secondary. The United Nations will have to face the great issues of disarmament and wrestle with racial conflict in Africa and continue the search for peace in the Middle East, but the United Nations will also be the forum for a world-wide economic confrontation between North and South. This is the issue which will increasingly overshadow others, and there is good reason to expect a time of increasing frustration and tension and bitterness. On the one hand there is the emphasis in the Brandt Report on the economic interdependence of rich and poor countries, the need for massive aid from rich to poor, not only to benefit the poor but to create new markets and to free trade to avoid world-wide recession in rich as well as poor nations. On the other hand there is the tendency amongst the industrialised nations to concentrate on their own internal difficulties of inflation and unemployment and even to turn to seek salvation in protection. The Brandt Commission called for a summit conference to tackle these problems but there still seems to be no enthusiasm for such an approach from the richer nations, and little or no evidence of any original radical economic thinking.

Men like Willy Brandt and Robert McNamara see the desperate need but the two super-powers are obsessed with their own military and diplomatic competitive policies and they, together with European powers, concentrate on selling arms to the rest of the world, to countries that cannot afford them while many of the Third World countries slide into internal destitution and confusion and conflict.

The United Nations has succeeded in past decades in establishing a whole range of organisations to deal with economic development.

I know the work of the United Nations Development Programme and the United Nations Fund for Population Activities best, having worked for those organisations in Africa and Asia. I have a respect for their achievements and their able present Directors, Bradford Morse and Rafael Salas. The creation of these international organisations is a positive achievement of great value, but what is now needed is a new lead, a new advance, a new inspiration in world economic affairs. This is surely the main international challenge of the 1980s.

An Encouraging Example: the Law of the Sea

I turn to a more encouraging prospect. The world may not be rising to its opportunities on land. It is doing better in regard to the sea.

We have been hearing recently that when the Third United Nations Conference on the Law of the Sea (UNCLOS III) returns to Caracas to conclude the negotiations it began there in 1974, there may well be agreement on a new regime governing the wealth of the oceans. It has taken a long time and many sessions of UNCLOS III but it now seems that a major international success may be within reach. This, I would like to hope, gives us justification for belief in the potential effectiveness of international action.

My mind goes back to the time when fifteen years ago Ambassador Pardo of Malta put forward a new subject for debate in the UN General Assembly. I remember the irritation expressed then that a small country should raise a new subject so soon before the General Assembly was to meet. What was it that Ambassador Pardo wanted to discuss? The question of the deep sea bed, he said. Consternation. What could little Malta possibly want to propose on such a subject? But Ambassador Pardo was not to be discouraged. He said that he understood that there were riches in the deep sea bed. Yes, no doubt, but what did he want to say about them? Ambassador Pardo said that he wished to propose that the riches of the deep sea bed should not be used only to make the rich nations richer or to benefit the great corporations but should be declared now to be 'the common heritage of all mankind'. Further consternation. But Ambassador Pardo was not to be diverted or prevented. Throughout the meeting of the General Assembly that year he pressed his case. In the end we all had to vote on it. I do not forget the historic day when the General Assembly voted by 99 votes to nil that the riches of the deep sea bed should be the heritage of all mankind.

What happened then? All the nations of the world with access to the sea grabbed the maximum. The three-mile limit became the 200-mile 'exclusive economic zone'. The United States Congress threatened to go ahead with exploitation of the deep sea bed alone.

Year after year international negotiations on the Law of the Sea took place. Questions of rights of maritime passage and fishing complicated the discussions, but now it appears that there is international agreement that an international authority should be set up to exercise authority over exploitation of the minerals of the deep sea bed. The last unexploited asset of the world is to be put to international use.

We may hope that the story to be told after the final session in Caracas will justify Ambassador Pardo's original initiative and will show that the international interest can prevail over selfish national and commercial power.

Elliott Richardson, the US representative at the Law of the Sea Conference, has spoken in ecstatic terms about this outstanding achievement of international negotiation. Yes, and we may be forgiven for hoping that the same purpose and spirit will be forthcoming in the great debate on international economic policy to be undertaken as the main enterprise of this decade.

Individual Leadership and Personality

My recollection of Ambassador Pardo's initiative on the deep sea bed provides a good example of the important part which individuals can play in international affairs. And when we talk of the new international diplomacy we look round to see what new individual leadership we can expect in these days of general disillusion and cynicism. Personalities still matter most. How long will the old men of the Kremlin survive, Brezhnev and Gromyko? What will the elections of 1980 and 1981 have done for United States and French and German leadership? Will Mugabe be enabled to sustain the promise of his first year in office? In the Middle East perhaps more than anywhere the personalities will predominate – Sadat, Hussein, Begin, Arafat. Can anyone adequately succeed the leadership of McNamara at the World Bank? Will Lord Carrington, with the exceptional qualification of the expectation of several years of office ahead of him, increasingly lead the New Europe?

It is still of first importance that the so-called permanent representatives should be of high personal qualities, resourceful and original, with effective influence with their own governments. The United Kingdom is indeed fortunate to be represented now, and we may hope for several years ahead, by an Ambassador of the calibre of Sir Anthony Parsons.

The Future

I have spoken of the changes which have taken place at the United

Nations in recent years, of the new emphasis on economic affairs, of the importance of the new diplomacy in New York. In turning to the future we must anxiously consider what prospect there is for effective action in and through the United Nations to tackle in time the more dangerous and more complex issues of today.

I like to preach the gospel of the effectiveness of the independent international initiative. So often when there is a dispute, a confrontation, a deadlock, it is worse than useless to hope that the two conflicting contestants will agree of their own accord.

Merely to bring them together is often to invite perpetuation of the impasse, or even the worsening of animosity. What is essential is an impartial intervention, the preparation – after intensive discussion with both sides – of a plan, a proposition, which neither side could propose but which both in the end can accept.

That is what we attempted for the Middle East in the Security Council in 1967 when we worked on the preparation of Resolution 242; that is what the Greek and Turkish Foreign Ministers achieved at Zurich in 1960 in the Cyprus agreement; that is what the Commonwealth Heads of Government Meeting at Lusaka in 1979 did for Zimbabwe. All three were independent, international initiatives.

Surely that is what we can hope to see in regard to Namibia and Cyprus and the Middle East, and perhaps in Afghanistan too, and also in the great economic issues in following up the first initiative of the Brandt Commission.

On the future of the sea it was the little country of Malta that took the initiative. In a recent session of the Law of the Sea Conference it was said that the moving initiator was Tommy Koh of Singapore. Sometimes it can be one country or one group of countries which can take the lead: the European Community members (the Nine) are in a strong position to take international action, particularly in the Middle East.

In so many confrontations the drift has already gone on far too long. The necessity for independent initiatives is desperately urgent. The United Nations provides the means but the UN organisation is not self-starting. The time has surely come when the existing machinery should be put to work.

World dangers are mounting. The danger of a race war in Africa may have been diminished or diverted or postponed by the success of the Commonwealth initiative over Rhodesia, but the danger may be revived over Namibia and South Africa – a race war involving all Africa and the wider world too. An even greater danger exists in Arabia, the danger of a religious war with the Moslem world united on the issue of the future of the holy sites of Islam in Jerusalem and the plight of the Palestinians. And both these issues unless dealt with in time might well find the super-powers of East and West supporting different sides. Indeed they have already started to do so.

The dangers are world-wide. The solutions have to be international. The United Nations is the instrument. It is the task of international diplomacy to stop the drift to disaster by urgent international initiatives, initiatives to put the international instrument to work.

We should remember Adlai Stevenson's warning. He used to say, 'Never mock the weakness of the United Nations lest we mock ourselves.'

It is not only a matter of courage to tackle dangerous problems. Courage is certainly essential but it is also a matter of attitude, of intention, of purpose, of a restless determination to escape from drift and deadlock, a readiness and an eagerness to search for justice as a foundation and insurance of peace.

These are the qualities we hope to find in a new generation of true internationalists, to turn from 40 years in the wilderness of the cold war of ideological confrontation between West and East to a promised land of new constructive co-operation between North and South.

APPRECIATIONS

1 SYDNEY BAILEY'S WORK IN QUAKER PERSPECTIVE

W. Grigor McClelland

I

'In connection with Religious, Political and Social work it is to be remembered that there may be no better way of advancing the objects one has at heart than to strengthen the hands of those who are effectively doing the work that needs to be done.' So wrote Joseph Rowntree in 1904 to the Trustees and Directors of the Trusts he was then setting up. It is a natural but significant step from 'strengthening the hands' to using a Trust's financial resources to free someone completely from the need to satisfy the usual requirements of institutional employment so that he can use his talents in the ways that seem to him best calculated to serve the general good. Such 'liberation' has in fact been carried out by the Joseph Rowntree Charitable Trust from its earliest days, particularly in the interests of nurturing the Society of Friends (a church without a paid ministry) or of furthering the cause of international peace. The same memorandum stated that 'it would be quite suitable for large sums to be appropriated' to support collaboration 'with competent investigators and workers upon . . . the question of our Foreign policy and Imperialism'.

Of course, the step of liberating someone in this way on a permanent basis to work without institutional framework and within only the broadest of agreed guidelines is seen by Trustees as somewhat momentous — less like appointing from a field of candidates to an established three-year research fellowship than like committing oneself to a marriage partner.

Within a small body like the Society of Friends, however, there is a network of personal contacts that at times have the character of 'knowing one another in that which is eternal'. When Sydney Bailey joined the service of the Trust in 1960 a number of Trustees had had first-hand contact with his work for some years. He and the present writer had been introduced, as fellow members of the Friends' Ambulance Unit (FAU), by Brenda (then his fiancée) in early 1945. At that time Sydney had returned for health reasons from service with the FAU in China and was pursuing his writing career as editor of the *FAU Chronicle,* an indispensable fortnightly house journal in a far-flung organisation of idealists. He subsequently joined Stephen King-Hall as editor of the celebrated *News-Letter* and from 1948 to 1954 was Secretary of another King-Hall venture, the Hansard Society, and editor of its journal, *Parliamentary Affairs*. Most of his early books and other writings were therefore about parliamentary government in the United Kingdom and overseas, and this of course turned out to be an immensely sound foundation when he turned his attention to the 'parliamentary diplomacy' and constitutional procedures of the United Nations.

When, years later, Commander Sir Stephen King-Hall published *Defence in the Nuclear Age* (London: Gollancz, 1958) and as a former military man lectured an audience of brass-hats on the merits of non-violent resistance, many who knew the power of Sydney's quiet per-suasiveness saw the hand of Sydney in this.

Whilst with the Hansard Society, he was already involved in corporate Quaker initiatives for peace. He was a member of the East-West Relations Committee, a small group of concerned Friends whose work led amongst other things to the Friends' Mission to the Soviet Union in 1951 and to the similar mission to China in 1955. This work involved collaboration with Friends in the United States and some other countries; deputations to British officials and Ministers; contact with diplomats from the non-aligned countries as well as from East and West; interpretation to Friends and public opinion generally of a point of view free from the emotional distortions of the cold war; and painstaking, committed and objective study of the issues. The committee was at the London end of an international Quaker network that included the Geneva Centre, the work of the American Friends' Service Committee based in Philadelphia and the Quaker United Nations Program (QUNP) in New York. It was to New York that Sydney and Brenda moved in 1954 when he left the Hansard Society and joined QUNP. Friends' status as a non-governmental organisation provided privileged access to the United Nations, and 'Quaker House', an easy walk from the UN building, provided an informal homely setting for discussion with delegates and officials. Sydney's four years in QUNP were followed by two further years in New York as a research fellow for the Carnegie Endowment for Inter-national Peace.

Roger C. Wilson was at this time chairman of the Rowntree Trust, and at the Trustees' September 1959 quarterly meeting he raised the question of the Trust being involved in Sydney's future work. In December he reported interest from Sydney in exploring the proposal, and in March 1960 Sydney met Trustees in York for a substantial discussion. From the outset work in both Quaker and non-Quaker contexts was envisaged. In the first, Sydney felt particularly drawn to the task of relating the crusading and reconciling aspects of Quaker concern for peace. In the second, he was 'anxious to continue and develop his present writing on the approach, work and inter-relationships of the leading organs of the UNO'. At the same time he welcomed 'the fact that the Trust did not appear to make a sharp dividing line between Quaker and non-Quaker interests'.

Looking back after 20 years it is easy to underestimate the uncertainties at this time about Sydney's future service. Despite the difficulties (at the time) of UK exchange control, should that service continue to be based in New York where so much of his raw material was ready to hand? If in London, what should be the relationship of the Baileys to any counterpart of the New York 'Quaker House' that might be established (a development to which they both attached considerable importance)? Given that various London Quaker committees and individuals attached to them were already active in fields that Sydney had made his own, might there be unfortunate repercussions from the injection into the situation of a high-powered freelance reporting only to an independent York Trust, itself responsible to no one?*

At their June meeting, Trustees met both Sydney and Brenda, who had decided to return to London on the basis of the Trust's offer. Whilst they themselves did not wish to act as wardens of such a place, Sydney had been pursuing the question of a London 'Quaker House' and on 24 April 1960 had prepared a memorandum to the chairmen and secretaries of the four London Quaker committees principally concerned. 'The implementation of the Quaker concern for international peace', it began,

> has increasingly, in recent years, brought Friends into direct touch with members of the diplomatic community. Diplomats shoulder heavy responsibilities and face grave and perplexing problems; many of them welcome association with concerned Friends who, in an understanding and patient spirit, will face with them the fundamental problems of international relations. Friends have no ready-

---

* He was shortly to write: 'Friends have not been hesitant to remind me of the difficulties which may arise because the Trust liberates Friends for full-time service independent of official committee channels. I have tried to accept the advice offered to me in a spirit of Christian charity, but I confess that (with one possible exception noted later) I have not been able to discover what these difficulties are in practice.'

made solutions to these problems, but we do adhere firmly to certain principles which should guide individuals and governments. Quaker contacts with diplomats have taken a variety of forms, but a number of general statements about these contacts seem to be valid. First, diplomats spend most of their time away from home; many of them, while leading busy lives, are quite lonely and value disinterested friendship. Secondly, diplomats have to spend a great deal of time attending to the formalities of protocol; they appreciate the informality of Friends. Thirdly, diplomats are constricted by the constant need to exercise discretion; they value the opportunity of candid discussion with people who do not represent governments and will not publicise what is said. Fourthly, diplomats have few opportunities of testing out new ideas and emerging policies by frank discussion with disinterested and concerned persons without official associations. Finally, there are occasions — though these are rare — when diplomats value help in making informal contacts across political barriers.

This memorandum was followed in the next six months by a number of discussions in which the Baileys took a leading part, and their presence in London was seen as a cardinal consideration. With the Trust's financial assistance, William Penn House in Balcombe Street, Marylebone, was opened in February 1962.

Despite the open and fluid nature of liberation by the Trust, it is the custom to set out in writing, for formal acceptance and future mutual guidance, the general understandings that have been entered into and agreed. In the Baileys' case this did not happen until 22 January 1962, when the then Trust Secretary wrote that Sydney's work

in general terms will lie in the field of personal service, including literary and interpretative work in regard to international affairs, with particular reference to the work of the United Nations Organisation, the development of informal and friendly contacts with diplomats and others of the kind that the work at Quaker House, New York, and now at William Penn House, London, calls to mind, and the reconciliatory contribution of Friends in this general field. Close working relations with a number of Quaker committees are implied and also with other outside bodies working in this field.

At the June 1960 meeting Sydney had in fact set out his intended work as falling within four main categories, which were summarised in the Trust minutes as follows:

(a) Research and writing on the procedural and institutional problems of the UN.

(b) The examination of international questions including disarmament.

(c) Contacts with diplomats, possibly with a view to developing the 'Quaker House' idea in London on a modified scale.

(d) Aspects of the peace testimony, with special emphasis on the relationship between religious principle and public action and the relationship between different kinds of public action.

Throughout the following 20 years Sydney has provided the Trust with regular written reports, and in addition to *ad hoc* meetings he and Brenda have joined the whole body of Trustees for a Friday evening in York once every three or four years. His general reports, of which the frequency has varied between three months and two years, and the minutes of those Friday evenings, form an illuminating summary of the development of his activity during this period. The four categories just cited form the framework for the earlier reports. Later, particular issues, names of particular organisations, and types of activity came to occupy the section headings. For example: the Middle East, Disarmament, Human Rights in Armed Conflicts, East-West Relations, China and South-East Asia, Prohibitions and Restraints in the Conduct of War, Arms Sales and Gifts, Voting in the Security Council; CCADD, ISIO, UNITAR, IISS, CCIA, BCC, FCO, CSIO, CIIR, WCC, RIIA; Books, Travel, Help to Official Bodies, Ecumenical Activities, Quaker Activities, Overseas Trips and Visitors, Speaking Engagements, Conferences, etc.

II

It is within this wide range that Sydney's contribution to 'Quaker international work' must be seen. At the outset, it is important not to fall into the trap of thinking that the only such work is that done by official Quaker bodies. One would wish to claim as Quaker work all that which is done not only corporately but also by individual Friends in working out the faith that is in them. Neither employment by a Quaker committee nor liberation by a Quaker Trust nor membership of a Quaker committee is necessary for this; membership of a Friends'

Meeting, as a continuing worshipping community, perhaps is.

Even Sydney's most 'technical' work, for example on the procedures of organs of the United Nations, I see as part and parcel of one whole, and 'Quaker' in at least two ways. First, in its motivation and purpose — and to say that it is motivated and purposeful is not to deny to it qualities of scholarship and objectivity, for even the scholar must select the areas and issues he tackles in accordance with some criteria of relevance and importance.

Secondly, I see Sydney's scholarly work as Quakerly precisely in its scrupulous regard for accuracy and realism regardless of the consequences. Quakers have no monopoly of objectivity but can claim from the outset to have been almost dogmatically undogmatic — accepting nothing on authority save that of the individual's own experience and finding no conflict or division between religious belief and the results of scientific investigation. At the same time it would be true as an empirical fact to say that Quakers show a high propensity to woolly-mindedness and wishful thinking particularly in their approach to peace; and Sydney's refusal to deny perplexity or to water down or de-emphasise the awkward fact draws on a basic Quaker emphasis to make his Quaker contemporaries healthily uncomfortable.

For Sydney has frequently returned from his work on international organisations and international issues, to use his great knowledge of these as a basis for reflection on some of the basic attitudes and testimonies which he shares with most Friends. A contribution of his to *New Christian* (16 June 1966) entitled 'Objections To Quaker Pacifism' is characteristic. It begins:

> I became a pacifist when I was fourteen years old as a result of hearing a sermon at school on the text 'Render unto Caesar the things that are Caesar's'. The preacher, who happened to be an Anglican, told us that the essence of what our Lord wanted to say was that we had an obligation to obey the commands of the State. We were then only little Christians, but one day we would become big Christians and could join the army and so preserve and even extend the British Empire.

> I was immature and simple-minded at fourteen, but I knew in a flash that the essence of Christ's reply was that it had two parts. Reacting against the naive militarism of the Venerable Archdeacon, I turned to an equally naive pacifism. I had not then come across the word 'pacifism', and for several years I thought I was the only person in the world who had ever derived a pacifist conclusion from

Christ's teaching. I thought I must be either a religious genius or a freak, and I had no desire to be either.

I am now more experienced and, I hope, wiser, and I find pacifism unsatisfactory in almost every respect.

He than briefly sets out six objections to the pacifist's position, each more cogent than the last and together quite overwhelming and simply ends: 'If I am asked why, in view of these objections, I remain a Quaker and a pacifist, I must reply that it is because I find the alternative even more unsatisfactory.'

Sydney's work in examining the dilemmas of the Christian in relation to war (and particularly in a nuclear age) has been principally carried out in ecumenical bodies and is thus considered elsewhere in this book. It is characteristic that the bodies he has worked with have included both pacifists and non-pacifists — CCADD and BCC rather than (say) FoR, PPU and CND. His attitude has been that if sincere and well-meaning and intelligent people can take a position different from his own it is important to try to understand why. It need only be stated here that his fellow Quaker pacifists appreciate and benefit from this work — even those who feel called primarily to campaigning work in support of what might be seen as an oversimplified message.

In 1978 Sydney introduced a Yearly Meeting session on 'Our Vocation of Reconciliation'. This made it plain that he sees Quaker international affairs work as only part of a larger whole. In an article he based on this address, he was to write:

I sometimes see our responsibilities in diagrammatic form as a triangle. In the centre is worship, with spokes going to the three apexes. One angle is marked 'service', another is marked 'peace', the third 'reconciliation'. The three activities all spring from the same source, worship, and they are closely inter-related.[1]

and again

My own work has been in the realm of international affairs and it is out of that background that I write. I hope that those who know about reconciliation in other spheres will contribute from their own experience, for we need to learn from one another.

And the character of Quaker international work is seen as distinctive:

We may facilitate reconciliation by creating the conditions in which adversaries may meet face-to-face, or by interpreting the fears and hopes of one side to the other, or simply by carrying messages.

> The faith in face-to-face contact is an essential component in the programme of international conferences and seminars, the belief that an important element in almost every conflict is a misperception, a misunderstanding, of the intentions of the other side. In recent years, Quaker staff have arranged a number of small private gatherings for Middle Easterners, including Jews and Arabs, in which a long accumulation of misunderstanding, fear and bitterness can be slowly dissolved because the atmosphere fosters simplicity, listening, mutual respect, and trust.

This in turn is based on a distinctive faith and insight:

> Reconciliation, in the biblical sense, is not about ideologies or beliefs but about people, their relationship and response to God, and their relationship and response to each other. God was in Christ, reconciling the world to himself, and he calls each of us to a ministry or vocation of reconciliation.

The same address included some moving examples of the effects of Quaker relief work in opening doors for Friends engaged in international affairs work. Elsewhere Sydney suggested that Friends' peace work might

> increasingly take the form of service rather than advocacy of solutions. And by service, I have two kinds in mind: first, work of a practical nature to remove the causes of conflict; and secondly, service which I can only describe as pastoral, a spirit of upholding and helping the men and women with political responsibilities. The first kind of service is traditional for Friends, but the second may require an adjustment in our attitude so that we come to think of those whose vocation it is to deal with political questions as 'we' rather than 'they'.
>
> The two most effective non-governmental peace efforts since the War of which I have personal knowledge have been the Pugwash conferences and the Quaker conferences for diplomats. Both have been conceived as disinterested service to a professional group, and it seems to me that one reason they have been successful has been that the sponsors have tried to cultivate attitudes rather than to promote solutions.

To quote from addresses or articles might suggest that Sydney has been an individual voice in the Society of Friends rather than a member of groups working together towards corporate conclusions and decisions. Though his principal responsibilities of office have lain outside rather than within the Society, this is far from being the case. He has been notably effective in working with officers and committees.

Yet he has (with many others) frequently chafed under the Society's committee structure. Addressing Trustees in 1965 he

took as his main theme the extent to which Quaker testimonies could be expressed through formal organisation as well as through individual concern. He felt that most Quaker institutions were under-provided in personnel, in finance and in creative ideas. Committees were frequently carrying the burden of old concerns, and lacked any criteria as to when and how to lay down existing work.

One outcome of this process is that the organisation concerned becomes programme-orientated, grappling with a vast field of activity, and no longer able to undertake fundamental thinking on specific problems.

The central element in Sydney's contribution to Friends' international work has lain in his contacts with diplomats. Partly this has been in a clearly Quaker organisational context — as a member of the Quaker UN Program, as host at Quaker House or William Penn House, as a member of a deputation to Ministers or officials expressing a particular concern of a particular Friend body, or in the Clarens conferences for diplomats or other conference or seminar programmes. His regular visits to the Middle East have been in the context of Quaker service in that region and in many of his discussions there he has been accompanied by Friends working on the spot.

But though often working in the closest collaboration with other Friends Sydney has also worked alone. His work in this mode has been none the less Quaker international work — whether he has sailed under the Quaker flag or been known and accepted as plain Sydney Bailey. It is Quaker if in its character it embodies principles and a tradition — a tradition from which he has taken strength and to which he has also contributed.

Much of this work is delicate and confidential, and this poses a problem if it has to be rooted in an understanding constituency. Sydney expressed this problem in his 1960 memorandum about a Quaker House in London. 'The informal, quiet and intangible nature of the work, the fact that Friends could not drop in without notice to see it in operation, the fact that it would be physically separate from Friends House and the International Centre would require constant and careful efforts at interpretation.'

III

Sydney's contribution to Quaker international affairs work cannot, then, in the last resort be disentangled from the totality of his work. That contribution cannot be summed up as a particular perspective on substantive international issues whether of disarmament, East-West relations, the Middle East or the principles and practice of mediation. It does not consist only in the extent to which his work has influenced the attitudes and actions of other Friends concerned with international relations in the United States, the United Kingdom and elsewhere. It must lie in some considerable measure in the extent to which opportunities have opened for concerned citizens of the world fulfilling certain conditions (such as the possession of patience and humility) to engage with the professionals because the professionals or their predecessors have earlier found such engagement fruitful.

It is perhaps more important to ask wherein has lain the Quaker ingredient in Sydney's contribution to the practice of intervention in international relations from a non-official base. That ingredient lies in some amalgam of concern for peace, commitment to non-violence, disinterestedness, recognition that one does not have the answers and finally a profound respect and warm compassion for those with whom one deals.

Sydney and Brenda's most recent Friday evening with the Trust in York was in November 1980. A minute relating to the following morning stated: 'In a subsequent discussion among Trustees a sense of privilege was expressed in being associated with SDB's work.'

Note

1. Sydney D. Bailey, 'Our Vocation of Reconciliation', *Friends' Quarterly*, vol. 22, no. 2 (April 1980).

2 SYDNEY BAILEY'S WORK IN ECUMENICAL PERSPECTIVE

Michael Rose

For close on 30 years Sydney Bailey has been near the centre of the work of the British churches in international affairs. He first joined the international department of the British Council of Churches (which has since become the Division of International Affairs — DIA) in 1952, was Chairman from 1971 to 1974 and is now Vice-Chairman and an influential member of its Standing Committee.

The second main focus of his ecumenical work has been the Council on Christian Approaches to Defence and Disarmament (CCADD), which was founded in 1963 as an offshoot of the Institute for Strategic Studies by an international group of clergymen and lay people to study and define Christian approaches to these complex subjects. He attended the founding conference in London, was a member of the first executive committee and has been Chairman of the British Group since 1978. There are also autonomous groups in the Federal Republic of Germany, France, the Netherlands and the United States and members in Denmark, Finland, Norway and Sweden; and all meet together at an international conference every year.

His contribution to the ecumenical work of the British churches has been primarily in three fields which over the years he has made very much his own: the United Nations, the Middle East and defence and disarmament.

United Nations

Since he returned from New York in 1960, he has provided the main source of expertise on the UN at the disposal of the BCC and has moreover through his contacts there enabled successive Secretaries of the DIA to visit New York to study at first hand the work of the organisation. Of all international institutions there are few which are nearer the heart of the churches than the UN and none perhaps whose labyrinthine ways are less easy for them to understand. Sydney has performed this work of interpretation for the churches as few others could have done; and I dare not think how often the DIA would have gone astray in its judgements if he had not been there to inform and guide it.

Middle East

The second area where Sydney has made a singular contribution is the Middle East, with a particular focus on the Arab-Israel dispute. He is acting chairman of the BCC Advisory Committee on the Middle East, which produced the booklet, *Some Reflections on the Arab-Israeli Conflict.* The British churches have benefited greatly from his deep knowledge of the area, derived from years of study, extended visits to the region and personal acquaintance with many of those directly involved on either side. They have benefited even more perhaps from his remarkable gift for understanding the assumptions from which other people proceed even if they are remote from his own, and so for seeing beyond the immediate crisis to the long-term significance of what is happening. Few of us will forget his sober assessment of the Camp David agreements between Egypt and Israel at a time when everybody else was carried away by the euphoria of the moment.

Defence and Disarmament

Sydney's ecumenical work on defence and disarmament has been largely in the context of CCADD. Over several years a division of labour has gradually grown up whereby CCADD provides the technical and ethical studies on the basis of which the DIA makes its judgements and formulates policy resolutions for the BCC Assembly. This is not the place to attempt even the most cursory review of his contribution to their joint work over the last 20 years — from *The British Nuclear Deterrent* (1963) through *Peace is Still the Prize* (1966), *The Search for Security* (1973) and *The Sale and Transfer of Conventional Arms, Arms Systems and Related Technology* (1977) to *The Future of the British Nuclear Deterrent,* which he largely inspired and presented in a masterly exposition to the BCC Assembly in 1979. During these years there has been no aspect of the defence and disarmament work of the BCC on which he has not left his personal imprint: his emphasis, for example, on the importance of peace-making as well as peace-keeping, his concern with the control of chemical weapons and the passionate regard for international morality which led him to wage a major campaign in the press as well as the churches to persuade the British government to reverse its unilateral decision to exclude CS gas from the prohibition of chemical weapons contained in the Geneva Protocol of 1925.

In CCADD Sydney built on the work of Bishop Stopford, Anthony Buzzard, Kenneth Johnstone, David Edwards and others; but in three ways at least he has made his own distinctive contribution. First, it is largely thanks to his relations of close personal confidence with Bishop Kunst, to his contacts in America and to his painstaking work in preparing the agenda for the annual conference that the international character of CCADD has been sustained and developed and indeed enlarged to include representatives from Eastern Europe and the Third World. Secondly, under his guidance the reconciling role of the Council has been reinforced. Himself a pacifist, the humility with which he nevertheless seeks to understand and the instinctive charity that he shows towards the position of those who cannot accept the pacifist view, has made CCADD a meeting place where the two groups can really listen to one another. Serving officers and senior government officials have felt able to take part in the Council's work not least because of SDB's expert knowledge and his ability to present critical views in terms that attract as well as compel their attention. The third contribution is the emphasis he has given to CCADD's role of making more widely available information about defence and disarmament issues with ethical implications. Within the last three years CCADD has produced three major reports for the BCC, and two more are in the pipeline.

In addition Sydney has always been deeply concerned for the protection of human rights and in particular its formulation in international treaties. In 1963 he was a member of the BCC Working Group which produced the report on *The Future of South Africa.* Under his chairmanship the DIA published further papers on South Africa and a major report on the churches in Eastern Europe – *Discretion and Valour* (London: Collins, 1974), by Trevor Beeson. During the same period he was also involved in issues as various as the EEC, Bangladesh, Taiwan and the admission of the People's Republic of China to the UN. As Chairman he presented the Division's work to the BCC Assembly where his clarity and conviction always commanded attention and respect. Over the years he has influenced more than most the corporate thinking of the churches and the views of countless individuals within them.

Two particular examples of his influence outside the BCC are worth mentioning – his relations with the Roman Catholic Church and with government. For some years he was a member of the Education Committee of the Catholic Institute for International Relations, where his work was deeply appreciated. He is a member of the Foreign and

Commonwealth Office advisory group on UN affairs and advisory panel
on Arms Control and Disarmament. A senior civil servant has written, 'I
count him one of the most remarkable people I have known.' The
respect that his knowledge and judgement have won has helped to
ensure that the opinion of the churches is taken seriously.

What first strikes anyone about Sydney is his encyclopedic knowledge
of international affairs, and then the phenomenal memory which keeps
it all in place, and the industry which ensures that it is up to date. He
will not speak on any subject until he has mastered it. This knowledge
is informed by a Christian vision of the world as it might be, and
ordered by a realistic understanding of the world as it is, so that it
becomes a source not merely of information but of wise and practical
advice. He does not deal in generalities. He knows that a solution is
most likely to be found at the end of a long and unspectacular step-by-
step process of negotiation. As a colleague has said, 'He is profoundly
Christian and at the same time deeply practical.' This blend of vision
and realism, of Quaker concern for peace and Quaker emphasis on
consensus and reconciliation, of expert knowledge and Christian
commitment is perhaps his unique contribution to ecumenical work
in international affairs.

It is not easy for an outsider to write of Sydney's Christian commitment; and yet the picture is incomplete without it. So I quote his own
words from an article in *Crucible* (July-September 1979) on 'The
Christian Vocation of Reconciliation':

> Christian practice is rooted in religious worship and spiritual experi-
> ence. Each of us is given a centre of inner tranquillity, so that we
> may live unflurried and unconquered amid the conflicts which
> surround us: conflicts in the family, among neighbours, at work, and
> in national and international politics.

Sydney never conceals that this is the spring from which all his thought
and action flow. I have a vivid recollection of a meeting on nuclear disarmament which was in danger of getting bogged down in technical and
political detail, when SDB recalled us to base by reminding us that we
were under orders to love our enemies. In this he is in the direct line of
the early ecumenical leaders who took as their slogan: 'Christ is Lord of
all, or he is not Lord at all.'

I cannot end this note without some mention, however inadequate,
of those personal qualities that have won Sydney the affection as well as
the respect of his colleagues: the fortitude which has learned to live with

suffering and to surmount it, the shy smile and flash of humour which suddenly light up his normally austere manner, the care and attention with which he is always ready to listen to others, the kindness that has often gone out of its way to help a colleague in need. All of us who have had the privilege of working with Sydney, in the BCC and CCADD, are deeply thankful for all that we have gained from knowing him.

BIBLIOGRAPHY

This bibliography, compiled and cross-checked from a number of publicly available sources, lists Sydney Bailey's books, including those he has edited (E), and publications in pamphlet format (P), up to 1980. They are arranged in date order of first publication, and alphabetically by title within each year. Subsequent editions are indicated simply by year, whether issued as revised or second editions, etc. Series reference numbers, where known, are added in parentheses. The main bibliography is followed by a separate list, in date order, of chapters he has contributed to other, multiple-author publications; and by a list of British Council of Churches Reports to which Sydney Bailey has been a signatory (subsequently published in the year shown). Any unintentional errors or omissions from these lists are regretted.

It should be added that the omission of Sydney Bailey's articles in learned journals and the press, amounting already to several hundreds, is not intended to suggest that they are an unimportant part of his *oeuvre* or to diminish their significance in any way: it arises, rather, from editorial reluctance to make a necessarily arbitrary selection or to risk the presentation of a seriously incomplete list.

Books and Pamphlets

(P)   *United Europe* (London: National News-Letter, 1948).

(P)   *The Palace of Westminster* (London: Hansard Society for Parliamentary Government, 1949).

(E)   *Aspects of American Govenment* (London: Hansard Society for Parliamentary Government, 1950).

(P)   *Constitutions of the British Colonies,* pamphlet no. 9 (London: Hansard Society for Parliamentary Government, 1950).

(P)   *The Korean Crisis,* Peace Aims Pamphlets, no. 9 (London: National Peace Council, 1950).

(P)   *Lords and Commons* (London: His Majesty's Stationery Office, 1951).

(E)   *Parliamentary Government in the Commonwealth* (London: Hansard Society for Parliamentary Government; New York: Philosophical Library, 1951).

(E)   *The British Party System* (London: Hansard Society for Parliamentary Government; New York: Praeger, 1952, 1953).

Ceylon (London: Hutchinson University Library 1952).

(P)   *Parliamentary Government* (London: Hansard Society for Parliamentary Government, 1952; British Council, 1958).

Naissance de nouvelles démocraties: introduction et développement des institutions parlementaires dans les pays de l'Asie du Sud et dans les territoires coloniaux, Fondation Nationale des Sciences Politiques, Cahiers, no. 50 (Paris: Armand Colin, 1953).

Parliamentary Government in Southern Asia, 1947-1952 (London: Hansard Society for Parliamentary Government; New York: Institute of Pacific Relations, 1953).

(E)   *Problems of Parliamentary Government in Colonies* (London: Hansard Society for Parliamentary Government, 1953).

(E)   *The Future of the House of Lords* (London: Hansard Society for Parliamentary Government; New York: Praeger, 1954).

British Parliamentary Democracy (Boston: Houghton Mifflin, 1958; London: Harrap, 1959, 1962, 1964, 1971). Also in Arabic.

The General Assembly of the United Nations, Carnegie Endowment for International Peace, United Nations Studies, no. 9 (London: Stevens; New York: Praeger, 1960; London: Pall Mall Press; New York: Praeger, 1964; Westport, Connecticut: Greenwood Press, 1978 reprint of 1964 rev. edn).

The Secretariat of the United Nations, Carnegie Endowment for International Peace, United Nations Studies, no. 11 (London: Pall Mall Press; New York: Praeger, 1962, 1964; Westport, Connecticut: Greenwood Press, 1978 reprint of 1964 rev. edn).

(P)   *The Troika and the Future of the United Nations* (New York: Carnegie Endowment for International Peace, 1962).

A Short Political Guide to the United Nations (London: Pall Mall Press; New York: Praeger, 1963). Also in Hindi, Japanese and Portuguese.

(P)   *Veto in the Security Council*, International Conciliation, no. 566 (New York: Carnegie Endowment for International Peace, 1968).

Voting in the Security Council (Bloomington, Indiana and London: Indiana University Press, 1969).

(P)   *Chinese Representation in the Security Council and the General Assembly of the United Nations*, ISIO Monographs, series 1 no. 1 (Brighton: University of Sussex, 1970; with supplement, 1971).

(P)   *Peaceful Settlement of International Disputes: Some Proposals for Research*, UNITAR Peaceful Settlement Series, no. PS 1 (New York: UNITAR, 1970, 1971, 1973, after mimeo 1969).

Prohibitions and Restraints in War (London: Oxford University Press for the Royal Institute of International Affairs, 1972).
The Procedure of the UN Security Council (Oxford: Clarendon Press, 1975).

Chapters Contributed to Other, Multiple-Author Publications

'Organizing World Peace' in Kenneth Johnstone *et al., Peace is Still the Prize* (London: SCM Press, for the Conference on Christian Approaches to Defence and Disarmament, 1966).
'The Troika and the Future of the United Nations: the Secretary-general' in Richard A. Falk and Saul H. Mendlovitz (eds.), *The Strategy of World Order,* vol. III: *The United Nations* (New York: World Law Fund, 1966).
'The United Nations Secretariat' in Evan Luard (ed.), *The Evolution of International Organizations* (London: Thames and Hudson, 1966).
'UN Voting: Tyranny of the Majority? in Robert W. Gregg and Michael Barkun (eds.), *The United Nations System and its Functions: Selected Readings* (Princeton, New Jersey and London: Van Nostrand, 1968).
'The United Nations and World Order' in George Cunningham (ed.), *Britain and the World in the Seventies: a Collection of Fabian Essays* (London: Weidenfeld and Nicolson, 1970).
'Peaceful Settlement of International Disputes: Some Proposals for Research' in K. Venkata Rahman (ed.), *Dispute Settlement through the United Nations* UNITAR Peaceful Settlement Series, no. PS 10 (Dobbs Ferry, NY: Oceana Publications for UNITAR, 1977).

Reports of Working Parties to the British Council of Churches Signed by Sydney Bailey

The British Nuclear Deterrent (London: SCM Press, 1963).
The Future of South Africa (London: SCM Press, 1965).
The Search for Security: a Christian Appraisal (London: SCM Press, 1973).
    Note: other reports of the International Department, its successor the Division of International Affairs and their working parties have remained unpublished, while reports commissioned by the British Council of Churches from CCADD (e.g. *The Future of the British Nuclear Deterrent,* 1979) have been published but without names of signatories. See also the Appreciation by Michael Rose, pp. 197-201.

NOTES ON CONTRIBUTORS

LORD CARADON was Minister of State at the Foreign and Commonwealth Office from 1964 to 1970 and concurrently the UK Permanent Representative to the United Nations at New York. Earlier, as Sir Hugh Foot, he had held senior posts in the Colonial Service, which he entered in 1929 and which took him to Palestine, Transjordan, Cyrenaica, Cyprus, Jamaica and Nigeria, culminating in his return to Jamaica as Captain-General and Governor-in-Chief 1951-7 and to Cyprus as Governor and Commander-in-Chief 1957-60. In 1961-2 he was Ambassador and UK Representative on the UN Trusteeship Council. He was a member of the UN Expert Group on South Africa in 1964, and since leaving New York in 1970 has carried out a number of assignments for the United Nations Development Programme.

G.R. DUNSTAN is F.D. Maurice Professor of Moral and Social Theology at King's College, and Dean of the Faculty of Theology, in the University of London. He was ordained priest in 1942 and held successive parochial responsibilities and collegiate appointments; he then worked as Secretary of the Church of England Council for Social Work 1955-63 and of the Church Assembly Joint Board of Studies 1963-6. He was Editor of *Crucible* (1962-6) and of *Theology* (1965-75). From 1970 to 1974 he served on the Foreign and Commonwealth Office Advisory Panel on Arms Control and Disarmament. He was appointed a Chaplain to The Queen in 1976. His books include *The Sacred Ministry* (1970), *The Artifice of Ethics* (1974) and, as editor, *Duty and Discernment* (1975).

JOHN HABGOOD has been Bishop of Durham since 1973. Educated at Eton and King's College, Cambridge, he took a Double First in Natural Sciences and a PhD in Physiology, worked at Cambridge from 1950 to 1953 as University Demonstrator in Pharmacology, then trained for ordination at Cuddesdon College, Oxford. After ordination in 1954 he had parochial experience in London and Scotland. From 1956 to 1973 he taught theology, as Vice-Principal of Westcott House, Cambridge; part-time at Coates Hall, Edinburgh; and as Principal of Queen's College, Birmingham. Author of *Religion and Science* (1964), *A Working Faith: Essays and Addresses on Science, Medicine and Ethics* (1980) and numerous articles and reviews, he is President of the Council on

Christian Approaches to Defence and Disarmament.

ROSALYN HIGGINS is Professor of International Law in the University of London, having in 1981 rejoined the London School of Economics where she was a Junior Fellow in International Studies (1961-3) and a Visiting Fellow (1974-8). She worked at Chatham House as Research Specialist in international law and UN affairs from 1963 to 1974 and was Professor of Law in the University of Kent at Canterbury from 1978 to 1981. Her books include *The Development of International Law through the Political Organs of the United Nations* (1963), *Conflict of Interests: International Law in a Divided World* (1965), *International Organization: Law in Movement* (edited, with J.E.S. Fawcett, 1974) and four volumes of *United Nations Peacekeeping: Documents and Commentary* (1969, 1971, 1980, 1981).

BISHOP HERMANN KUNST was Plenipotentiary of the Council of the Evangelical Church in Germany (EKD) at the seat of the Federal Republic from 1949 to 1977, and Protestant Bishop of the Armed Forces from 1956 to 1972. His first pastorship began in 1932 at Herford, where he became Superintendent in 1940. He was imprisoned during the War. Appointed Director of the EKD *Landeskirchenamt* for Westphalia in 1945, he became the EKD representative at Bonn in 1949. He was one of the founders of the Conference (now Council) on Christian Approaches to Defence and Disarmament and is regarded as its elder statesman. Chairman of the Social Academy at Friedewald and of the Foundation for New Testament Research, he has published several books including four on Martin Luther.

W. GRIGOR McCLELLAND has been a Trustee of the Joseph Rowntree Charitable Trust since 1956 and was its Chairman from 1965 to 1978. He served in the Friends Ambulance Unit from 1941 to 1946 and was subsequently active in Quaker work for East-West relations, visiting the USSR, China and the USA. In 1948 he entered the family business, Laws Stores Ltd, of which he is now Chairman. He was Senior Research Fellow in Management Studies at Balliol College, Oxford (1962-5) and Director of the Manchester Business School (1965-77). He has been a member of the National Economic Development Council and the Social Science Research Council. He is Chairman of Washington Development Corporation and holds a Visiting Chair at Durham University. He is the author of two books on retailing and of the 1976 Swarthmore Lecture, *And a New Earth.*

WOLF MENDL is Head of the Department of War Studies at King's College and Reader in War Studies in the University of London. From 1955 to 1961 he worked in Japan, organising international student seminars for the American Friends Service Committee, and in Paris as the Quaker International Affairs Representative there. Since 1965 he has been teaching at King's. He is the author of three books, *Deterrence and Persuasion: French Nuclear Armament in the Context of National Policy, 1945-1969* (1970), *Prophets and Reconcilers: Reflections on the Quaker Peace Testimony* (1974), *Issues in Japan's China Policy* (1978), and is currently writing a fourth, on the security of Western Europe and Japan.

BARRIE PASKINS is a moral philosopher and has been Lecturer in War Studies at King's College, London since 1971. He has played an active part in the Council on Christian Approaches to Defence and Disarmament, notably as convenor of the working groups which prepared its reports for the British Council of Churches on *The Sale and Transfer of Conventional Arms, Arms Systems, and Related Technology* (1977) and *The Future of the British Nuclear Deterrent* (1979). He is author of *The Ethics of War* (with Michael Dockrill, 1979) and of related essays which include 'Obligation and the Understanding of International Relations' in *The Reason of States: a Study in International Political Theory*, ed. Michael Donelan (1978).

EDWARD ROGERS was General Secretary of the Christian Citizenship Department, and later the Division of Social Responsibility, of the Methodist Church from 1950 to 1975. He was President of the Methodist Conference for 1960 and Moderator of the Free Church Federal Council (FCFC) for 1968; he is Chairman of the FCFC Executive and a Vice-President of the Council on Christian Approaches to Defence and Disarmament. He has served as Chairman of several British Council of Churches committees, including the 1969-72 Working Party on Defence and Disarmament which produced *The Search for Security: A Christian Appraisal* (1973). Among his many other publications have been *A Commentary on Communism* (1951), *Living Standards* (1964), *Plundered Planet* (1973) and *Thinking About Human Rights* (1978).

MICHAEL ROSE has been Chairman of the British Council of Churches Division of International Affairs since 1974 and is Treasurer of the Council on Christian Approaches to Defence and Disarmament. He entered the Diplomatic Service in 1937 and his overseas postings included

Oslo, Algiers, Copenhagen, Berlin and Bonn before taking him to Léopoldville as HM Ambassador to the Congo (1963-5). He was a Fellow of the Centre for International Affairs at Harvard (1958-9), Assistant Under-Secretary of State at the Foreign Office (1965-7) and Deputy Secretary at the Cabinet Office (1967-8). From 1969 to 1980 he was Director and Secretary of the East Africa and Mauritius Association, a trade association based in London, and travelled extensively.

NICHOLAS A. SIMS is a Lecturer in International Relations at the London School of Economics and Political Science. His main research areas are disarmament diplomacy within the UN system, with special reference to verification and negotiations on biological and chemical weapons, and the disarmament policy process. His publications include *Approaches to Disarmament* (1974, 1979), a bibliography, *British Writing on Disarmament from 1914 to 1978* (with Lorna Lloyd, 1979) and a chapter in the *SIPRI Yearbook 1981*. Rapporteur to the British Council of Churches' Working Party on Defence and Disarmament (1969-72), he is a founder member of its Advisory Forum on Human Rights. He was a member (1966-80) and Chairman (1974-80) of successive British Quaker committees on the UN and disarmament.

J. DUNCAN WOOD was Quaker Representative to the United Nations and Director of the Quaker Centre from 1952 to 1977 at Geneva, where he was also Chairman of the Special NGO Committee on Disarmament from its establishment in 1969 until his retirement. His earlier career as a schoolmaster was interrupted by wartime service with the Friends Ambulance Unit which included three years in China. His Swarthmore Lecture, *Building the Institutions of Peace*, was published in 1962, and he has contributed to the *Year Book of World Affairs* and other publications. He is currently Chairman of the Quaker Peace and Service United Nations Committee and Clerk of Lancaster Monthly Meeting of the Religious Society of Friends.